THE INTERNATIONAL
ECONOMY UNDER STRESS

THE INTERNATIONAL ECONOMY UNDER STRESS

NORMAN S. FIELEKE

Ballinger Publishing Company
A Subsidiary of Harper & Row, Publishers, Inc.

International Standard Book Number: 0-88730-224-6

Library of Congress Catalog Card Number: 88-19248

Printed in the United States of America

Library of Congress Cataloging-in-Publication Data

Fieleke, Norman S.
  The international economy under stress.

  Includes index.
  1. International economic relations. 2. Free trade and protection—
Protection. 3. Balance of payments. 4. International finance.
5. Petroleum products—Prices. I. Title.
HF1359.F54   1988   337   88-19248
ISBN 0-88730-224-6

89 90 91 92 HC 10 9 8 7 6

To my mother and the memory of my father

CONTENTS

List of Figures   xi

List of Tables   xiii

Preface   xix

Introduction   xxi

Chapter 1
Oil Shocks   1

The Two Price Increases   2
Forebodings   6
Adjustment to the Adverse Shocks   8
Consequences of the 1986 Price Decline   13
OPEC: Shadow or Substance?   17
Some Policy Considerations   20
Summary   25

Chapter 2
Protectionism: A Hardy Virus   29

The "New" Protectionism: Nontariff Barriers   30
The Scope of Nontariff Barriers   31
The Effects of Protection: Some Quantitative Estimates   35
The Growth of State-Directed Trading   44
Countertrade   47
Is Bilateralism Growing?   52
Justifications and Explanations for Protection   56
Negotiating Reductions in Trade Barriers   58
Summary   61
Appendix: The Case for Free Trade   63

Chapter 3
Less Developed Countries in Arrears   67

The Nature of the Problem   67
Changes in the World Economy   72
Imprudence in Borrowing and Lending   75
Faulty Policies in Developing Countries   79
Curtailment of Bank Lending   85
Dealing with the Problem: Some General Considerations   86
Debt Relief Accompanied by Adjustment Programs   88
Growing Debtor Resistance: The Baker Plan   91
The Balance-of-Payments Adjustment Process   92
Some Indexes of Progress   98
Remedies   103
Summary   107

Chapter 4
The United States in Debt   113

The Magnitude of U.S. Indebtedness   113
Supply-Side Explanations: Price Competitiveness   119
Supply-Side Explanations: Nonprice Factors   124
Competitiveness, Comparative Advantage, and
    Aggregate Supply   126
Aggregate Supply and Demand   130

Unfair Foreign Trading Practices 130
Probable Causes of the U.S. Trade and Current
  Account Deficits 135
Deindustrialization? 142
A Moderating Influence 150
The Coming Adjustment 151
The Nature of the Adjustment 156
Summary 159
Appendix: Data Used in Table 4–14 and Figure 4–5 160

Chapter 5
The International Monetary System:
Out of Order?

The International Monetary System:
Out of Order? 165

The Par Value System 166
The Problems of Liquidity, Confidence,
  and Adjustment 167
A Composite System 170
Exchange-Rate Volatility and Risk 174
The Role of Speculation 178
Exchange-Rate Misalignment 182
The Issue of Discipline 186
Target Zones 187
Regulation of International Liquidity 188
A Brief Apology for the Composite System 189
Summary 190

Chapter 6
Economic Interdependence and
Policy Coordination

Economic Interdependence and
Policy Coordination 195

Measures of Integration or Interdependence 196
Movements of Goods, Labor, and Capital 197
Price Movements: Labor and Capital 201
Price Movements: Goods 207
International Transmission of Economic
  Disturbances 212
The Case for Coordination 219
Some Arguments Against Coordination 222

An Illustration: International Debate Over Macroeconomic
  Policy   224
Mechanisms for Coordination   230
Summary   234

Index   239

About the Author   253

LIST OF FIGURES

1–1   The Real Price of Crude Petroleum, 1973–86   3
1–2   Percentage Changes in Real Gross Domestic
       Product and in Consumer Prices in the
       United States and in the OECD Area,
       1972–86   4
1–3   Production of Crude Oil, 1973–87   10
1–4   OECD Oil Stockdraw Capabilities Compared
       with Previous Supply Disruptions   24

3–1   Average Loan Rate Spreads (Over London
       Interbank–Offered Rate) Charged to Selected
       Borrowing Countries, First-Quarter 1979
       Through Second-Quarter 1982   79

4–1   Net External Assets of Selected Major Industrial
       Countries at Year-End, 1983 and 1985   118
4–2   Weighted Average Foreign Exchange Value
       of U.S. Dollar, 1980–87   122
4–3   The Current Account and Federal Budget Deficits
       of the United States   139
4–4   The Real Exchange Rate and the Federal Budget
       Deficit of the United States, 1973–87   140

4–5   Exports Less Competing Imports and Insured
       Employment for Seventy-three Manufacturing
       Industries, 1980–86   148

6–1   Three-Month Interest Rates in the United States
       and Abroad, and Foreign Currency Value of U.S.
       Dollar, 1976–87   202
6–2   Interest Arbitrage: Three-Month Funds, 1984–87   205
6–3   U.S. and Average Foreign Real Long-term
       Government Bond Yields, Quarterly,
       1976–87   206
6–4   Indexes of Prices for Magnesium, Pig Iron,
       and Steel Wire Rods in West Germany
       and the United States   211

LIST OF TABLES

I–1   Summary Measures of the World Economy's
       Performance   xxiv

1–1   Measures of Energy Efficiency for Selected
       Countries, 1973–85   8
1–2   Components of World Primary Energy Production,
       1973 and 1985   11
1–3   U.S. Net Imports of Petroleum from OPEC and
       Other Sources as a Percentage of U.S. Petroleum
       Consumption, 1973–86   12
1–4   Investment Position of Oil-Exporting Countries
       in the United States, December, 1982   13
1–5   Portfolio Composition of Investments by OPEC   14
1–6   Coefficients of Correlation Between Annual Crude
       Oil Production Levels in Selected Country
       Groupings, 1973–87   19
1–7   Net Imports of Petroleum and Products Per Billion
       Dollars of Gross Domestic Product in Seven Major
       Industrial Countries, 1973 and 1985   21

2–1   Receipts from Customs and Import Duties
       Accruing to OECD Countries as a Percentage of
       the Value of Their Imports: 1965–80   30

2–2   Measures of Nontariff Import Restrictions for
       Manufactured Goods in Developed Countries   32
2–3   Frequency of Application of Various Nontariff
       Barriers Against Agricultural Imports in
       Industrial Countries, 1984   34
2–4   Estimated Nominal Protection Coefficients
       for Selected Commodities in Industrial
       Countries, 1980–82   39
2–5   Distribution of Annual Costs and Benefits from
       Special Protection in Effect in the United States
       in 1986   42
2–6   Distribution of Annual Domestic Costs and Benefits
       of Agricultural Protection in the EEC, Japan, and
       the United States   43
2–7   Estimated Efficiency Gains from Liberalization
       of Selected Commodities, by Country Group, 1985   44
2–8   Estimated (Maximum) Countertrade Among
       Various Categories of Countries, 1983   48
2–9   Sum of Individual Country Trade Balances as a
       Ratio of Those Countries' Aggregate Exports Plus
       Imports, 1965–85   53
2–10   Average Ratio of Country Trade Balance to Total
       Exports Plus Imports for the Country, 1965–85   54
2–11   Average Ratio of Bilateral Balance to Bilateral
       Trade, 1965–85   55

3–1   External Debt of Developing Countries, by Class
       of Creditor, End of Year, 1979–86   69
3–2   U.S. Bank Claims on Developing Countries,
       1978–86   70
3–3   Trading Prices for Selected Sovereign Debt,
       10 December 1987   72
3–4   Impact of External Shocks on the Balance of
       Payments in Selected Developing Countries,
       1981–82   74
3–5   Total Liabilities of Banks in the United States and
       Liabilities to Oil-Exporting Countries,
       1977–81   75
3–6   Debt Indicators for Non-oil Developing Countries
       Published by International Monetary Fund,
       1973–82   78

3-7   Consumption, Gross Domestic Investment, and
        Gross Domestic Saving as a Percentage of Gross
        Domestic Product, for Selected Country
        Groupings and Years   80
3-8   External Debt Relative to Exports of Goods and
        Services, for Developing Countries   82
3-9   Capital Flight and Gross Capital Inflows
        in Selected Countries, 1979–82   83
3-10   Real Effective Exchange Rates for Argentina,
        Mexico, and South Korea, 1978–83   85
3-11   Changes in Outstanding Bank Claims on
        Developing Countries, 1981–86   86
3-12   Aggregate Debt Relief Provided for Developing
        Countries, 1983–86   88
3-13   Current Account Transactions of Developing
        Countries with Recent Debt-Servicing Problems,
        1979–86   93
3-14   Annual Percentage Changes in Real GDP and
        Real GDP Per Capita in Developing Countries
        with Recent Debt-Servicing Problems, 1969–86   95
3-15   Change in Net Exports of Argentina, Brazil,
        and Mexico, in Constant Prices, by Major
        Component, 1981–86   96
3-16   Change in Net Exports of Argentina, Brazil, and
        Mexico, in Constant Prices, by Output and
        Absorption, 1981–86   97
3-17   Debt Indicators and Balance-of-Payments Errors
        and Omissions, for Countries with Recent Debt-
        Servicing Problems, 1979–86   99
3-18   Revision in IMF Projection of 1987 Debt Ratio
        for Non-oil Developing Countries   102

4-1   International Investment Position of the United
        States at Year-end, 1970–86   114
4-2   The U.S. Net International Investment Position:
        Summary of Changes During 1986   115
4-3   Net International Investment Position of the United
        States at Year-end, by Area, 1981 and 1986   117
4-4   U.S. Balances on Selected Components of
        International Current Account Transactions,
        1970–86   120

4–5   Output Per Labor-Hour in Manufacturing
       in Selected Industrial Countries, 1970–86   123
4–6   Shares (Percentage) in Value of World
       Manufactures Exports   126
4–7   Industry Share in Total U.S. Manufactured
       Exports as a Percentage of the Industry Share
       in World Manufactured Exports, 1982   127
4–8   U.S. and OECD Gross Domestic Product and
       U.S. Trade Balance, 1981–86   128
4–9   Real GNP and Real Domestic Demand in the
       United States and Other OECD Countries,
       1981–86   129
4–10   U.S. Merchandise Trade, by Major Trading
       Partners or Areas, 1980 and 1986   132
4–11   U.S. Merchandise Trade, by Major End-Use
       Category, 1980 and 1986   133
4–12   Major Categories of Saving and Investment
       as a Percentage of GNP for the United States,
       1970–87   137
4–13   Capital Transactions in the U.S. Balance of
       Payments, 1980–86   141
4–14   U.S. Manufactured Exports, Imports, and
       Exports Less Imports, by Industry, 1986 and
       1980   144
4–15   Percentage Changes in U.S. Real Output During
       Recessions and the Succeeding Expansions   149
4–16   Selected Debt Burden Indicators for the United
       States and Other Areas, 1986   152
4–17   Net U.S. Interest Burden from External Debt
       Under Differing Assumptions   155

5–1   Month-to-Month and Quarter-to-Quarter Average
       Absolute Percentage Changes in Effective
       Exchange Rates for Seven Major Industrial
       Countries, for Selected Periods   176
5–2   Net Positions Taken by U.S. Banking and Non-
       banking Firms, for Selected Currencies and Dates   180

6–1   International Commerce as a Percentage of Gross
       Domestic Output, for Selected Countries and
       Years   198

6-2   Selected Statistics on Current Account Balances
       for Fourteen Industrial OECD Countries,
       1952–85   200
6-3   Correlation Coefficients Between Weekly
       Measures of the Three-Month U.S. CD Rate and
       the Weighted Average Foreign Three-Month
       Interest Rate, 1976–87   203
6-4   Percentage Excess of Market Average Foreign
       Exchange Rates Over Purchasing-Power Parities
       for Gross Domestic Product, for Seventeen
       Countries, 1970–84   208
6-5   Simulated Effects in Home Country of a One-
       Percentage-Point Decrease in a Policy-Controlled
       Domestic Interest Rate   214
6-6   Simulated Effects on Real GNP in Other Countries
       of a One-Percentage-Point Decrease in a Policy-
       Controlled Domestic Interest Rate   215
6-7   Simulated Domestic Effects of a Sustained
       Decline in Real Government Expenditure Equal
       to One Percent of GNP   217
6-8   Simulated Effects on Real GNP in Other Countries
       of a Sustained Decline in Real Government
       Expenditure Equal to One Percent of GNP   218
6-9   International Current Account Balances of Major
       OECD Countries, 1982–86   225
6-10   Growth in Real Domestic Demand and Real GNP
       in Major Industrial Countries, 1970–86   226

PREFACE

Upon completing a work of this sort, the author customarily offers a justification for contributing still another book to the multitude already in print. My first defense is that this volume is not large. My second is that the time seemed ripe to gain perspective on the remarkable international economic phenomena of the past fifteen to twenty years, including the oil shocks, the developing country debt crisis, the growth of a new protectionism, the breakdown of an international monetary system, and the soaring indebtedness of the United States.

What the book offers, then, is an analytical survey of the major disruptions and challenges facing the international economy, primarily during the period 1970–87. The discussion will be intelligible to the sophisticated layperson and the advanced undergraduate and may constitute a useful reference for the expert.

The approach taken is not chronological but functional; the focus is on major problems rather than on periods of time. While these problems are treated in separate chapters, interrelationships are noted. In particular, oil shocks contributed to stagflation and recession, which contributed to the developing country debt crisis, which contributed to the U.S. current account deficit. On the other hand, not too much is made of this sequence, because it is not nearly the whole story.

Important assistance in the preparation of this work came from a number of sources. Helpful comments on earlier drafts were supplied by Benjamin J. Cohen, Henry S. Terrell, and anonymous reviewers. The World Bank, and David A. Cieslikowski in particular, provided some much-needed data. Competent research assistance was rendered by Deanna Young and Valerie Hausman, and secretarial assistance by Jean Zafiris. Finally, I am indebted to my employer, the Federal Reserve Bank of Boston, for allowing me time and supporting facilities to carry through with the project. None of these parties should be held responsible for the views expressed in this volume or for any errors.

INTRODUCTION

For the world economy, the 1970s and 1980s have been extraordinarily stressful. These years have witnessed soaring inflations, severe recessions, oil shortages, growing protectionism, rising unemployment rates, an international debt crisis, and the breakdown of an international monetary system. If the world can learn from its mistakes, much is to be learned from this period.

An early sign of the times appeared on 15 August 1971, when the U.S. government announced that it would no longer convert foreign official holdings of dollars into gold or other reserve assets. By the spring of 1973, the Bretton Woods system of fixed exchange rates between national currencies had given way to much greater exchange-rate flexibility. The new, more flexible system has eased the problems that undermined the Bretton Woods system, but has functioned much less smoothly than its advocates had expected. Sharp, short-term fluctuations and wide, long-term swings in exchange rates suggest that the system has lacked stabilizing speculation, with adverse consequences for international trade and investment.

Hard on the heels of the international monetary upheaval came the first oil shock. In an unprecedented exercise of monopolistic power, the Organization of Petroleum Exporting Countries (OPEC) raised the relative price of crude oil by nearly 170 percent between 1973 and 1974, fostering high inflation and recessions in the industrial countries. OPEC's repeat performance in 1979–80 had similarly severe consequences. More than any other event in living memory, these two oil price increases brought home to the residents of industrial societies that the world economy had become a highly interdependent system. Fears of future oil shocks have been sustained by the continuing turmoil in the Middle East.

The perils of interdependence were further manifested in the developing-country debt crisis that erupted in August 1982. Having borrowed heavily, many developing countries experienced growing difficulty in servicing their debts as interest rates soared in the early 1980s and as their export sales decreased in response to recessions in the industrial countries. As a result, it seemed that major creditor banks in the industrial countries might be forced into insolvency by their inability to collect payments coming due. This concern gradually diminished as the banks reduced the share of their capital at risk in the developing countries. On the other hand, the problem debtor countries had made no progress by 1987 in restoring their creditworthiness—as customarily appraised—and were failing to receive the infusions of new capital deemed necessary to raise their growth rates to historically more normal levels.

As the developing countries were struggling with their indebtedness—much of which was to U.S. banks—the United States itself suddenly went deeply into debt. Having attained a peak net creditor position of $141 billion in 1981, the nation became a net international debtor in the amount of $264 billion by the end of 1986, with much deeper indebtedness in the offing. The nation's huge international trade deficits aroused anxiety about its ability to compete in world markets and provoked allegations that other countries were engaging in unfair trading practices. Concern was also voiced that the great depreciation of the dollar in the foreign exchange markets would be accompanied by markedly higher U.S. inflation and interest rates, especially if little progress was made in reducing the massive federal budget deficit.

Less dramatic than these problems, but of similar gravity, has been a fairly steady increase in protectionist barriers. Although tariffs in the industrial countries were at historic lows in the mid-1980s, nontariff restrictions against imports had intensified considerably; virtually every product in international trade encountered such a restriction in at least one country. The import barriers have preserved some jobs in the protected industries, but the cost to consumers has often been painfully high—amounting, for example, to about $105,000 per year for every job saved in the U.S. automobile industry. Moreover, governmental readiness to flout the established international rules against both quantitative restrictions and discrimination in trade has discouraged businesses from investing in more efficient facilities oriented toward export markets.

In light of these developments, it should not be surprising that the world economy has been performing rather poorly during the 1980s. As shown by Table I–1, gross national product (GNP) per capita grew significantly faster, on average, during the 1960s and the 1970s, both for the world and for each category of countries. Similarly, inflation rates in the 1980s have been high for developing countries and for the world, especially by comparison with the 1960s. Data on unemployment rates, available only for the industrial countries, reveal a much higher incidence of unemployment in the 1980s than during the 1960s and 1970s.

The problems besetting the international economy have stimulated calls for coordinated assaults upon them. But thorny obstacles impede the successful coordination of macroeconomic policies among nations. More needs to be known about how the world economy functions, and even with full knowledge, countries would differ on their economic goals.

In what follows these matters are explored in much greater detail. We discover no panacea, and we shun placebos. Partial remedies sometimes come to light; they should not be spurned.

Table I-1. Summary Measures of the World Economy's Performance.

Year	Percent Change in Real GNP Per Capita				Percent Change in Consumer Prices			Rate of Unemployment (percent) in OECD Countries[d]
	Industrial Countries	Developing Countries[a]	High Income Oil Exporters	World[c]	Industrial Countries	Developing Countries[b]	World[c]	
1962	3.8	0.8	N.A.	N.A.	2.5	9.0	3.5	N.A.
1963	3.6	3.4	N.A.	N.A.	2.6	11.0	4.0	N.A.
1964	5.1	4.9	11.5	4.3	2.4	15.9	4.5	N.A.
1965	4.0	2.7	10.7	3.0	2.9	14.7	4.8	N.A.
1966	4.1	2.9	10.5	3.0	3.4	13.3	5.0	N.A.
1967	2.9	-0.1	6.4	1.5	3.0	10.6	4.2	3.0
1968	4.7	2.3	5.6	3.2	3.9	6.9	4.4	3.0
1969	4.3	6.5	6.5	3.8	4.7	6.9	5.1	2.9
1970	2.5	7.3	5.6	2.4	5.6	8.2	6.0	3.3
1971	2.5	3.7	1.2	1.9	5.2	9.5	5.9	3.7
1972	4.4	1.7	2.3	3.0	4.6	11.4	5.7	3.8
1973	5.5	5.7	-5.3	4.4	7.6	19.7	9.5	3.5
1974	-0.3	3.1	6.7	-0.3	13.1	23.6	15.2	3.9
1975	-1.3	2.5	2.6	-1.4	13.1	22.3	14.8	5.1
1976	4.1	2.6	13.6	3.0	8.3	22.7	11.0	5.3
1977	3.1	3.7	5.1	2.5	8.4	23.3	11.3	5.4
1978	3.3	3.7	1.2	2.5	7.2	20.2	9.7	5.3
1979	2.8	2.7	5.8	2.1	9.1	23.3	12.5	5.3

1980	0.4	2.8	2.9	0.3	11.8	28.4	15.8	6.2
1981	1.2	1.1	2.7	0.4	9.9	27.8	14.1	7.0
1982	-1.3	-0.6	-10.2	-2.2	7.5	29.3	12.5	8.4
1983	1.6	0.4	-12.0	0.3	5.1	39.3	12.7	8.9
1984	4.1	3.3	-7.2	2.9	4.8	46.0	13.7	8.5
1985	2.4	3.1	-8.3	1.5	4.2	46.9	13.5	8.4
1986	2.1	3.2	-11.0	1.2	2.4	30.6	8.7	8.3

N.A.: Not available.

aExcluding high-income oil-exporting countries.

bIncluding high-income oil-exporting countries.

cExcluding some countries, among them sizable nonmarket economies.

dOrganization for Economic Cooperation and Development.

Source: GNP per capita data from World Bank staff; consumer price data from International Financial Statistics 41 (January 1988): 71, and International Financial Statistics Supplement on Price Statistics, Supplement Series No. 12 (Washington, D.C.: International Monetary Fund, 1986), pp. 4–5; unemployment data from OECD Economic Outlook 42 (December 1987): 191.

1 OIL SHOCKS

More than any other recent event, the steep oil price increases of 1973–74 and 1979–80 forcefully brought home to John Q. Public that the world economy is a highly interdependent system. Everyday living was keenly affected. In the United States, for example, homeowners added insulation to their houses, and automobile purchasers switched to smaller cars to obtain better gasoline mileage.

These "oil shocks" posed a severe test of the resiliency of the world economy, especially the industrial, oil-consuming sector. Fears were aroused that rapid exhaustion of the world's oil reserves would cause continuing stagflation and that the massive flows of funds to and from the oil-exporting countries would generate a major financial crisis. For economics, the appellation, "dismal science," seemed more appropriate than ever.

With the passage of time and the sharp 1986 drop in oil prices, the worst fears subsided. But to some analysts the 1986 price decline was merely a brief reprieve, and indeed, prices moved upward again in 1987. The specter of future scarcity had not been dispelled.

This chapter analyzes the impact of the abrupt oil price changes experienced since 1973 and considers some policies for coping with similar shocks in the future. In the course of the analysis, attention is given to the continuing price-fixing efforts of the Organization of Petroleum Exporting Countries (OPEC), whose members are Algeria, Ecuador,

Gabon, Indonesia, Iran, Iraq, Kuwait, Libya, Nigeria, Qatar, Saudi Arabia, the United Arab Emirates, and Venezuela.

THE TWO PRICE INCREASES

The first oil crisis was an event without parallel in the annals of international commerce. Never before had the world witnessed an exercise of monopoly power on such a scale and with such success.

The drama began in mid-October 1973. In an attempt to enlist support for the Arab cause in the ongoing Arab-Israeli conflict, nine Arab oil-producing states announced on October 17 that they would reduce their production and their exports to nations considered friendly or neutral toward Israel. Although this action was not the work of OPEC, its thirteen members were not taken by surprise. On the contrary, in anticipation of the production cuts, six Persian Gulf members of OPEC had agreed on October 16 to raise the posted price for their crude oil by 70 percent; late in December the price was raised again, this time by 130 percent. Other oil-producing states followed with comparable price increases. Then, as Arab-Israeli hostilities subsided, the production and export cutbacks were relaxed; on 11 July 1974 the last of the export embargoes was lifted.[1] The price hikes were maintained, however, and OPEC production in August remained below the level of September 1973.

Crude oil sales prices remained relatively stable from 1974 until 1979, when the oil-exporting countries again raised prices. (See Figure 1–1.) Between 1978 and 1981, nominal oil prices soared by 167 percent. Prices then declined from 1981 to 1986, especially in 1986.

If all prices had changed to the same degree as the price of oil, the huge oil price increases would not have been newsworthy. It was the rise in the price of oil relative to other prices generally that constituted the shock to the international economy. This "real" price of oil—measured relative to the price of industrial country exports—soared by 168 percent between 1973 and 1974, and by 112 percent between 1978 and 1981.

These price increases not only boosted rates of inflation, but also retarded economic growth in the countries that import oil. Consumer prices rose extraordinarily rapidly and gross domestic product grew very slowly—a combination that was christened "stagflation"—in the twenty-four relatively advanced and mostly oil-importing countries of the OECD

Figure 1-1. The Real Price of Crude Petroleum, 1973–86.

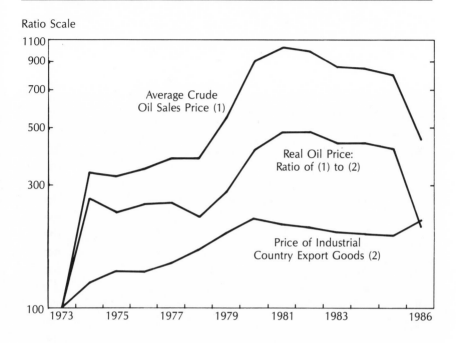

Note: Underlying prices are measured in U.S. dollars.

Source: U.S. Central Intelligence Agency, *Economic and Energy Indicators*, 19 June 1987, chart entitled "Average Crude Oil Sales Price"; *International Financial Statistics Yearbook*, 1987, p. 129.

(Organization for Economic Cooperation and Development) during or immediately following the years when oil prices skyrocketed. (See Figure 1–2.) Although the rise in oil prices was not the sole cause of the stagflation, it was an important contributor.

It might seem that an economy should be able to adjust to a large oil price rise with little or no increase in inflation. When the price of oil rises more rapidly, other unrelated prices could rise more slowly, so that the overall rate of inflation need not increase. Some analysts would say that if the overall rate of inflation did go up, the money supply was being allowed to increase too rapidly, so that too much money was chasing the available supply of goods.

This view is not without merit, if only because it serves as a reminder that the money supply is an important variable to be considered in any

Figure 1-2.   Percentage Changes in Real Gross Domestic Product and in Consumer Prices in the United States and in the OECD Area, 1972–86.

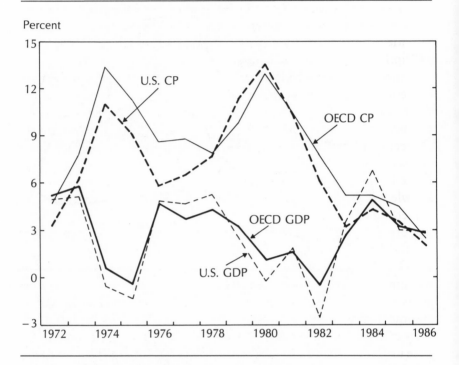

Source: *OECD Economic Outlook* 42 (December 1987): 174, 184.

analysis of inflation. The real world, however, is more complex than this view admits. One complication is that few people readily accept a reduction in real income; not only do they resist cuts in pay that would allow the prices of what they produce to fall—so as to offset a jump in the price of oil—but they want their incomes to rise just as rapidly as prices generally. Labor unions are no exception; and they can threaten to strike in order to obtain wage increases that match price increases, including oil price increases. If employers grant such wage increases, unemployment will grow in the short run unless the monetary authorities allow the money supply to increase so as to finance the wage increases. Since monetary authorities are concerned about unemployment, the inflation can become generalized, rather than remain limited to oil and related products. By the mid-1980s labor had become less militant in pressing wage claims, at least in the United States, so that the threat of generalized inflation from oil price increases had probably diminished somewhat.

In countries that relied heavily on imported oil, the price increases also depressed economic growth. One reason was that certain industrial activities—such as the production of "gas-guzzling" automobiles—promptly suffered a decrease in sales; employees were laid off and were not immediately absorbed by other industries. Another reason was that the residents of oil-importing countries were obliged to spend a larger share of their income on foreign oil rather than on goods and services produced at home, since nothing could readily take the place of foreign oil.

Precise quantification of even the short-term effects of such oil price increases is very difficult, requiring—among other things—knowledge of the importance of oil in production as well as in consumption and knowledge of the possibilities of substituting other factors for it. Nonetheless, a consensus seems to have emerged regarding the effects on output and inflation in the industrial countries. For the typical industrial country, a 10 percent rise in world oil prices is thought to lower real GNP by between 0.5 and 1 percent in the second year and to raise consumer prices by somewhat more.[2] This combination of effects poses a severe dilemma for economic policymakers seeking both high economic growth and low inflation.

By contrast, the oil-exporting countries reaped huge gains from the price increases, since the price increases dramatically improved the terms on which they traded with the oil importers. Between 1973 and 1981, OPEC's crude oil sales price went up by 918 percent, while the average price of what the industrial countries exported rose by 112 percent (Figure 1–1). In other words, the quantity of goods that industrial countries had to give up in return for a barrel of imported oil was nearly five times as great in 1981 as in 1973.

One result was that the oil-exporting countries succeeded in multiplying their oil revenues without selling more oil. In 1980 the members of the OECD imported (net) a smaller quantity of oil than in 1978, but paid $135 billion more for it. This *increase* of $135 billion was greater than the 1980 gross national product of Sweden and amounted to about 1.75 percent of the collective gross national product of the twenty-four OECD countries.[3]

Had the oil-exporting countries immediately spent their increased revenues on goods produced by the oil importers, the contractionary impact suffered by the latter would have been substantially reduced. Such was not the case, however. For the period 1974–81, the merchandise trade balance of the oil-exporting countries was a surplus totaling nearly $708 billion, and their current account balance (which includes transactions in services and unilateral transfers, as well as transactions in merchandise) was a surplus of nearly $360 billion.[4]

FOREBODINGS

These unprecedented developments led to dire predictions. Among the prevailing anxieties, the most basic was that the world's petroleum reserves were being exhausted at an alarming rate. A 1977 analysis by one U.S. government agency reached the following conclusions:

> In the absence of greatly increased energy conservation, projected world demand for oil will approach productive capacity by the early 1980s and substantially exceed capacity by 1985. In these circumstances, prices will rise sharply to ration available supplies. . . . Between 1979 and 1985, increasing world demand and stagnating oil production in the major consuming countries will result in increased reliance on OPEC oil. By 1985 . . . demand for OPEC oil will reach 47 to 51 million [barrels per day]. . . . This is well above . . . projected 1985 capacity. . . . Non-oil energy supplies cannot be counted on to appreciably relieve the problem between now and 1985.[5]

The forebodings were not confined to the matter of energy supply and demand. Much concern was also voiced that the huge surpluses accruing to OPEC would disrupt the international financial system and the world economy. At the aggregate, or macroeconomic, level, doubts were expressed that all of the countries thrown into deficit by higher oil imports bills would be able to borrow readily from OPEC, either directly or indirectly, the funds that they required to finance their deficits. At the detailed, or microeconomic, level, apprehension was voiced about the ability of private financial institutions to handle the flows of OPEC funds. These were the two chief aspects, macroeconomic and microeconomic, of the so-called "recycling problem"—the problem of redistributing the surplus revenues of the oil-exporting countries.

One example of the anxiety generated by this problem is a January 1975 *Foreign Affairs* article by several prestigious authors, who sounded the following alarm:

> In all likelihood, unless further approaches to cooperative action are made within the next few months, some oil-importing countries will have run

out of goods to sell, or markets to reach, or capacity to borrow to cover their deficits, and a number may become unable to meet the servicing on the enlarged debts. Whether that would result in currency devaluations, in defaults by banking and business firms in those countries, in national debt moratoria, or in political revolution and debt repudiation, the entire structure of world payments, and of trade and financial relationships, would certainly be fractured.

Thus there is the immediate danger of progressive collapse, triggered by defaults both by individual industrialized countries and by developing countries lacking natural resources.[6]

A few months earlier, David Rockefeller, then chairman of Chase Manhattan Bank, had asserted, "It has become abundantly clear that the private banking system, which thus far has borne the brunt in the process, cannot continue to recycle such massive sums of money without seriously eroding its own stability and liquidity."[7] That this viewpoint was appropriate for the large international banks was argued as follows by another leading banker:

> They simply do not choose to continue taking on sizable amounts of very short-maturity deposits [from OPEC] and lending them out for comparatively long periods, as borrowers typically desire. To do so would rapidly weaken ratios of risk assets to capital and unbalance the maturity structure of their liabilities relative to their assets. . . . The capital positions of banks would not justify the incredible ballooning of balance sheets that would be involved if the borrowing needs of oil-deficit countries were met predominantly by extensions of bank credit.[8]

Moreover, in 1980, at the height of the second oil shock, this problem of "recycling" OPEC's surplus funds was perceived by some analysts to be even more severe than during the first oil shock. The chief international economist at a major New York bank put it as follows:

> The situation is considerably graver than in 1974. This year's OPEC current-account surplus will be close to $120 billion . . . almost twice as large as in 1974. In addition, banks are much less aggressive and more selective in international lending than in 1974. . . . Accordingly, unless alternative channels of financing are expanded or created, borrowing countries may face the prospect of having to reduce their economic growth substantially.[9]

A related concern was that OPEC, by investing its surpluses, would come to control entire industries, some of them strategic. Indeed, before

Table 1–1. Measures of Energy Efficiency for Selected Countries, 1973–85 (1973 = 100).

Year	OECD Energy-to-GDP Ratio	OECD Oil-to-GDP Ratio	United States Energy-to-GDP Ratio	United States Oil-to-GDP Ratio	Japan Energy-to-GDP Ratio	Japan Oil-to-GDP Ratio	West Germany Energy-to-GDP Ratio	West Germany Oil-to-GDP Ratio
1974	98	93	99	97	102	100	97	90
1975	96	90	96	97	95	90	92	86
1976	96	93	97	100	98	94	95	90
1977	96	93	96	103	93	90	92	86
1978	94	90	95	100	90	87	92	86
1979	94	90	93	94	90	84	95	86
1980	91	79	89	85	83	74	89	76
1981	87	72	86	79	78	65	84	67
1982	83	69	84	76	76	61	82	67
1983	81	69	82	74	73	58	82	62
1984	81	66	79	71	76	58	82	62
1985	81	62	78	71	71	52	82	62

Note: Gross domestic product (GDP) is valued at 1980 prices and 1980 exchange rates.

long Iran did acquire 25 percent of Krupp, the large German conglomerate; Kuwait bought Santa Fe International, a U.S. oil field service business, as well as 25 percent of Daimler-Benz, the manufacturer of Mercedes cars and trucks; and Libya bought a chunk of Fiat, the Italian automobile maker.[10] Also, it seemed that OPEC might at any time disrupt some major financial market—not only the banking system—by suddenly withdrawing huge investments.

In the event, neither the recycling problem nor the energy scarcity problem proved to be insurmountable. The requisite adjustments were neither easy nor immediate, but they were forthcoming.

ADJUSTMENT TO THE ADVERSE SHOCKS

Part of the adjustment to the energy scarcity, or to the higher relative price of energy, was to improve the efficiency with which energy was used. Dramatic testimony to this improvement is offered by the data in Table 1-1, which indicate that for the entire OECD area a unit of

France		United Kingdom		Italy		Canada	
Energy-to-GDP Ratio	Oil-to-GDP Ratio	Energy-to-GDP Ratio	Oil-to-GDP Ratio	Energy-to-GDP Ratio	Oil-to-GDP Ratio	Energy-to-GDP Ratio	Oil-to-GDP Ratio
97	91	98	95	95	93	99	97
91	83	93	86	95	90	98	100
91	83	91	82	98	90	98	97
88	78	93	82	95	87	98	95
91	78	89	82	93	87	95	90
91	78	91	77	93	87	97	90
91	74	86	68	88	80	97	85
88	65	84	64	85	77	92	79
82	61	82	64	83	73	92	74
85	57	80	59	83	73	89	67
85	52	77	73	83	67	89	64
85	52	80	59	83	67	89	62

Source: Organization for Economic Cooperation and Development, International Energy Agency, *Energy Balances of OECD Countries, 1970–1985* (Paris: OECD, 1987).

gross domestic product could be produced in 1985 with only about four-fifths of the total energy and three-fifths of the oil that had been required in 1973. Among the "Big Seven" OECD countries, none exceeded the efficiency gains made by Japan, either in oil or in total energy.

A second phase of the adjustment was to expand the production of substitutes for OPEC oil. The most direct substitute, of course, was non-OPEC oil, the output of which grew steadily as OPEC production fluctuated and then declined. (See Figure 1–3.) Most of the expansion in non-OPEC production came from the Soviet Union, the North Sea, and Mexico. From 1973 to 1987, OPEC's share of world crude oil production fell from 56 percent to 32 percent. In addition, the world substituted other forms of primary energy for crude oil. As shown in Table 1–2, the share of crude oil in total primary energy output fell from 48 percent in 1973 to 38 percent in 1985, while the share of every other primary energy source went up.

Because the United States imports more petroleum than any other country and is far and away the leading petroleum consumer, the U.S. adjustment to the oil scarcity is of special interest. For a number of years,

Figure 1-3.   Production of Crude Oil, 1973–87.

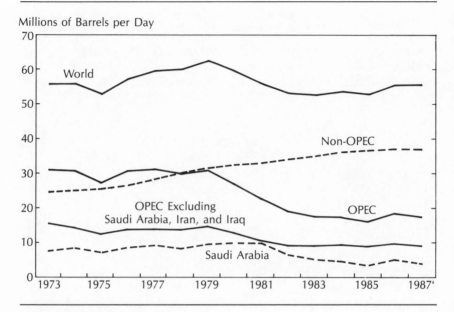

Millions of Barrels per Day

Note: Data do not include natural gas liquids.

aPreliminary.

Source: Department of Energy, Energy Information Administration, *Annual Energy Review 1986* (Washington, D.C.: U.S. Government Printing Office, 1987), p. 237; U.S. Central Intelligence Agency, *International Energy Statistical Review*, 29 March 1988, pp. 1, 2.

U.S. policy was especially inept in one important respect. During most of the 1970s, the U.S. government employed price controls that artificially suppressed the price of domestically produced petroleum. The perverse result was to discourage production and to encourage consumption of a scarce resource. Fortunately, the controls were phased out between 1979 and 1981, when world oil prices were rapidly escalating; U.S. dependence on imported oil, especially OPEC oil, then declined sharply to levels well below the 1977 peak. (See Table 1–3.)

Petroleum and related materials comprised more than four-fifths of U.S. imports from OPEC in 1986. Although the composition of U.S. exports to OPEC was more varied, half of the total consisted of machinery and transport equipment, of which nearly two-fifths went to Saudi Arabia.[11] Of course, on those occasions when oil prices shot upward, U.S. imports from OPEC increased much faster in value than U.S. exports to OPEC; and the U.S. trade deficit with OPEC reached

Table 1-2. Components of World Primary Energy Production, 1973 and 1985.

	Percent of Total	
Component	1973	1985
Natural gas liquids	1.7	2.2
Nuclear	.9	4.9
Hydroelectric	5.5	6.9
Dry natural gas	17.6	20.0
Coal	26.4	28.4
Crude Oil	47.9	37.6
Total	100.0	100.0

Source: Department of Energy, Energy Information Administration, *International Energy Annual* (Washington, D.C.: U.S. Government Printing Office): 1980, pp. 6–12; and 1985, p. xi.

a peak of $38 billion in 1980, more than offsetting the slim U.S. surplus with the rest of the world. By 1986, however, the U.S. deficit with OPEC had shrunk and U.S. trade with the rest of the world had fallen into substantial deficit, so that the deficit with OPEC had become a small fraction of the total.

If the energy scarcity problem was not catastrophic, neither was the recycling problem. OPEC's current account surplus did not remain very large for many years. Following the first oil shock, OPEC's current account fell into deficit by 1978, rose to a sizable surplus in 1979–81, and then fell back into persistent deficit.[12] One reason is that the rest of the world economized on oil, especially OPEC oil. Another reason is that the members of OPEC increased their imports rapidly when their oil revenues soared. Most embarked in 1974 on large-scale development plans that required more capital equipment imports, and some spent more on armaments. Some, such as Saudi Arabia, also employed more laborers from abroad. Thus, OPEC's current account surplus was not very long-lived.

Moreover, OPEC's investments never came close to dominating the financial markets in which they were made. In the abstract, these investments seemed formidable, as illustrated in Table 1–4, which presents data on OPEC's investment holdings in the United States at or near their likely peak at the end of 1982. Viewed in relation to similar investments by all parties, however, OPEC's holdings seem less portentous. For example, OPEC's $41.4 billion of U.S. Treasury securities at the end of 1982

Table 1–3.   U.S. Net Imports of Petroleum from OPEC and Other Sources as a Percentage of U.S. Petroleum Consumption, 1973–86.

Year	OPEC	Non-OPEC	Total
1973	17.3	17.5	34.8
1974	19.7	15.7	35.4
1975	22.0	13.8	35.8
1976	29.0	11.6	40.6
1977	33.6	12.9	46.5
1978	30.5	12.0	42.5
1979	30.4	12.7	43.1
1980	25.2	12.1	37.3
1981	20.6	13.0	33.6
1982	14.0	14.1	28.1
1983	12.1	16.2	28.3
1984	13.0	17.0	30.0
1985	11.6	15.7	27.3
1986	17.1	15.7	32.8

Source: Department of Energy, Energy Information Administration, *Annual Energy Review 1986* (Washington, D.C.: U.S. Government Printing Office, 1987), p. 113.

constituted less than 3.5 percent of all Treasury securities then outstanding, while OPEC's holdings of U.S. corporate bonds were only one percent of all such bonds outstanding. OPEC's U.S. direct investment, together with its portfolio holdings of corporate equities, amounted to less than one percent of the total value of U.S. corporate equities. OPEC's deposits in U.S. banks, generally placed with the larger ones, made up only 2.1 percent of the deposits of the large U.S. banks.[13] While such percentages are not insignificant, they were hardly cause for alarm.

As indicated by the bankers' comments quoted above, the recycling problem involved not just the volume of OPEC's investments but also the maturity distribution that OPEC seemed to desire. Bankers in particular were apprehensive that the OPEC members, which were investing heavily in short-term deposits, might someday want to withdraw their deposits suddenly—after the banks had reinvested them longer term—thus threatening a liquidity crisis for any banks suffering heavy withdrawals. To be sure, surges in OPEC's cash surplus were largely invested at first in bank deposits. (See Table 1–5.) But as time passed, the preponderance of OPEC investments was channeled into longer term, presumably higher yielding, instruments. Thus, at the end of 1979—a

Table 1-4. Investment Position of Oil-Exporting Countries in the United States, December 1982[a].

Type of Investment	Amount (billions of dollars)
U.S. Treasury securities	41.4
Federal agency securities	6.0
Corporate bonds	5.9
Corporate equities	9.6
Bank liabilities	16.9
Other nonbank liabilities	5.4
Other U.S. government liabilities[b]	4.6
Direct investment[b]	4.4
Total	94.3

Note: Detail does not add to total shown because of rounding. Data do not include any OPEC investments in the United States held under the name of non-OPEC residents.

[a]Oil-exporting countries are OPEC plus Bahrain and Oman, unless otherwise indicated.
[b]OPEC alone.

Source: Richard P. Mattione, *OPEC's Investments and the International Financial System* (Washington, D.C.: The Brookings Institution, 1985), p. 39.

year in which OPEC's surplus rose sharply—more than half of OPEC's outstanding investments were in bank deposits, but by 1983 the share of bank deposits had declined to 37 percent. In the event no "OPEC runs" on banks came about, but even if runs had developed, the banks losing deposits should have been able to borrow offsetting funds readily from the banks gaining those deposits or from the central banks—provided, of course, that the assets of the banks experiencing the runs were basically sound.

In spite of these considerations, the developing-country debt crisis that broke out in 1982 is sometimes attributed in part to the earlier flow of funds from oil-exporting countries into commercial banks, which loaned heavily to the developing countries. Our skepticism that this phenomenon should be viewed as a major cause of the debt crisis is explained in Chapter 3.

CONSEQUENCES OF THE 1986 PRICE DECLINE

As can be seen in Figure 1-3, OPEC crude oil production was reduced fairly steadily between 1979 and 1985, while non-OPEC production

Table 1-5. Portfolio Composition of Investments by OPEC (in billions of dollars).[a]

Description	Bank Deposits	U.S. and U.K. Treasury Bills	Medium- and Long-Term Obligations of U.S., U.K., and West German Governments	International Reserves (excluding foreign exchange)	Equities, Property, and Other Investments	Placements with Less Developed Countries	Total Identified Net Cash Surplus (flows) or Investment Position (levels)
Flows:							
1974	28.6	8.0	1.2	2.4	7.0	4.9	52.1
1975	9.9	-.5	3.0	5.0	13.7	6.5	37.6
1976	12.0	-2.1	4.8	1.7	14.4	6.4	37.2
1977	17.9	-1.2	4.9	.4	11.0	7.0	40.0
1978	7.3	-.8	-2.4	-.3	7.8	6.2	17.8
1979	40.6	3.3	-1.0	-.8	3.7	8.7	54.5
1980	44.3	1.3	17.1	1.7	20.1	6.3	90.8
1981	2.5	-.5	18.1	2.1	25.0	7.2	54.4
1982	-12.3	.4	8.4	2.1	5.6	3.9	8.1
1983	-11.3	-1.2	-5.6	4.3	-2.7	1.2	-15.3
Levels (end of year):[b]							
1979	131.3	7.0	10.7	10.5	58.0	39.7	257.2
1983	140.5	6.9	42.9	20.8	110.6	58.3	380.0

[a]Includes Bahrain, Brunei, Oman, and Trinidad and Tobago, as well as OPEC members.
[b]Some stock, or level, data were not available and were estimated by accumulating flow data.
Source: *Bank of England Quarterly Bulletin* 25 (March 1985): 71.

continuously increased. During the latter part of 1985, OPEC, especially Saudi Arabia, stepped up its production in an attempt to enlarge its receipts and/or its market share. The increased output, along with relatively weak demand, brought about a steep price decline in 1986, amounting to 43 percent in nominal dollar terms and 50 percent in real terms. (See Figure 1–1.)

At the time, this sharp fall in the oil price was widely expected to provide a marked stimulus to the economies of the oil-importing countries. To be sure, it was recognized that the stimulus would not be undiluted. For example, some industries in the oil-importing countries, especially industries related to oil exploration and production, would be adversely affected. Also, the oil-exporting countries would have less to spend on goods produced in the oil-importing countries. But these contractionary influences were expected to be outweighed within the oil-importing countries by an increase in domestic spending (out of the savings from reduced oil import bills) and by the positive effects of lower inflation and improved business and consumer confidence. Thus, both the International Monetary Fund's *World Economic Outlook* of April 1986 and the *OECD Economic Outlook* of the following month projected that the oil price decline would add about 0.75 of a percentage point to the economic growth rate of the industrial countries over the eighteen-month period beginning in mid-1986.[14]

In the event, it was hard to discern this overall favorable impact. Rather than growing at the generally projected rate of 3.25 percent, real GNP in the industrial countries went up at only a 2.5 percent rate between mid-1986 and mid-1987. At least for the near term, the positive effect of the oil price decline on industrial-country GNP had been overestimated.

On the other hand, consumer price inflation turned out to be even lower than had been expected. As shown in Figure 1–2, consumer prices in OECD countries rose only 2.5 percent in 1986, nearly two percentage points less than in 1985. This inflation rate was the lowest since the early 1960s; the drop in oil prices, while not solely responsible, was a major contributing factor.

The oil-importing countries also realized an improvement in their international trade and current account balances in 1986, when the decline in the price they paid for oil more than offset an increase in the volume of their oil imports. By contrast, OPEC experienced a marked deterioration in its current account balance—from a surplus of $4 billion in 1985 to a deficit of $32 billion in 1986.[15]

Whatever short-run benefits may have accrued to the oil-importing countries from the price decline, the long-run consequences were more problematical. Over time, a sharply reduced price would enlarge consumption, eliminate marginal producers, and probably render consumers more dependent on OPEC, which, according to some analysts, might then restrict its output to drive up the price. Indeed, in March 1986, Sheik Ahmed Zaki Yamani, the Saudi Arabian oil minister, issued a warning of future energy shortages even in the absence of restrictive action by OPEC:

> You are putting the whole world into a situation where you will have an energy crisis not invoked by a political crisis, like 1973 and 1979, but by a serious shortage in the supply of energy. . . . What disturbs me is that some cuts will be forever. Once you shut down stripper wells, you are not going to reopen them again unless the price of oil goes to $50 [per barrel] or more.[16]

In fact, the U.S. Interstate Oil Compact Commission estimated that a sustained price of $15 per barrel—the average price in 1986—would result in the abandonment of more than 20 percent of the 450,000 American stripper wells and in a corresponding loss of 3 percent of the nation's production.[17] Stripper wells are highly vulnerable to price declines, being high-cost, low-volume facilities that yield ten barrels or less a day; if permanently abandoned, they must be sealed with concrete for safety and environmental reasons.

It is not only the sealing of stripper wells that would render the world more dependent on OPEC oil. Prices as low as those in 1986 also discourage exploration and development of oil reserves. Worldwide exploration and development expenditures by large oil companies dropped by about 30 percent between 1985 and 1986, and the number of oil-drilling rigs in active service throughout the world fell from 3,500 at the end of 1985 to 2,200 at the end of 1986. Further smaller declines in exploration and development were expected for 1987.[18] In the United States, employment in oil and gas exploration and oil field services declined by about 30 percent during 1986, and drilling activity was the lowest it had been in forty-six years.[19]

Unless sizable new reserves are discovered elsewhere, oil consumers will have to rely increasingly on OPEC, especially the historically unstable Persian Gulf region. At the beginning of 1986, 68 percent of the world's oil reserves were within OPEC, and 56 percent were within just five Persian Gulf members of OPEC: Saudi Arabia, Kuwait, Iran,

Iraq, and the United Arab Emirates.[20] Moreover, aside from oil reserves, only OPEC had the idle production capacity in 1987 to satisfy any sudden surge in world oil demand.[21]

In these circumstances, it might seem that the oil-importing countries should take steps to shield their own oil production industries from the effects of price declines such as that in 1986, with the goal of lessening their future dependence on OPEC. But significant protection of domestic crude oil production would be far from costless. Whether such a course should be adopted depends on a number of factors, and especially on the likely behavior of OPEC. Because past behavior may be a guide to the future, it is worth considering whether OPEC has in fact behaved as an effective cartel in suppressing competition and in maintaining prices above competitive levels.

OPEC: SHADOW OR SUBSTANCE?

At the time OPEC was founded, oil export prices were set by the international oil companies, which paid taxes to the countries from which they withdrew oil. During 1959 and 1960, the companies reduced oil prices substantially in response to weakening market conditions. United in their opposition to these price reductions, representatives from Iraq, Iran, Kuwait, Saudi Arabia, and Venezuela met in Baghdad in September 1960. There they founded the Organization of Petroleum Exporting Countries, whose stated principle purpose was to coordinate their petroleum policies and to determine the best means for safeguarding their interests.

OPEC is not a business entity and does not engage in commercial transactions; it is an intergovernmental organization registered with the United Nations Secretariat. By November 1973, the membership had expanded from the founding five to the current thirteen. To gain membership, a country had to be a net exporter of crude petroleum and had to be accepted by three-fourths of the full members, including all of the founding five. All decisions at OPEC conferences require a unanimous vote.[22]

Although OPEC is not a business entity, its members have attempted to coordinate their sales of crude oil so as to influence the price. Indeed, OPEC is surely a cartel in the sense that it is a combination of producers that is designed to limit competition. How successful it has been is another matter. That OPEC will triumph was recently asserted by Sheik Yamani, who allowed that "market forces" would set prices until the end of 1987 but that thereafter, "OPEC will come again and fix the price of oil," and "nothing . . . oil consumers can do" will prevail against OPEC's commanding share of the world's oil reserves.[23] Unpersuaded by such polemics, some analysts believe that OPEC never has succeeded—and never will—in keeping oil prices very far from their competitive levels for very long.[24]

That OPEC is a failure is suggested by its widely reported internal disputes over economic issues and also by marked political differences among the members. Economic disputes have revolved around such matters as prices and production levels; political differences between Iran and Iraq, two of the founding members, have led to outright warfare. Public disagreements, however, are not necessarily proof of failure. History offers an illustration of close economic association even among nations at war with each other—in the war of 1866 involving the member states of the Germanic customs union known as the *Zollverein*.[25]

In trying to assess the impact of OPEC, one is handicapped by the unavailability of an empirically verified and generally accepted economic model to explain either cartel behavior or changes in the market price of petroleum.[26] What does seem clear is that OPEC has tried to manipulate the price of oil. (See Figures 1–1 and 1–3.) In particular, OPEC's total crude oil output was reduced slightly from 1973 to 1974, when the price of oil was soaring and non-OPEC production was growing; and OPEC production diminished further in 1975. Similarly, during the major price rise from 1979 to 1981, OPEC's output again began to shrink, leveling off only after the real oil price reached its peak in 1982. Non-OPEC production steadily increased throughout this period.

Moreover, developments in the latter part of 1986 and during 1987 offered some support for Yamani's prediction that OPEC would "come again and fix the price of oil." In August 1986, the members of OPEC agreed to restore the individual-country production quotas that they had openly abandoned late in 1985, and in December 1986 these quotas were revised downward by about 5 percent. With the reduction in OPEC output, world crude oil prices recovered smartly from their August 1986 low of about $9.25 per barrel and were averaging more than $17.50 per barrel by mid-1987.[27] (While the higher price meant bigger bills for the oil-importing countries, it also meant new life for marginal oil production facilities and new incentive for exploration and development.)

Not only has OPEC's output decreased during periods when prices were sharply rising and non-OPEC output was growing, but OPEC's output as a percentage of its productive capacity has declined when prices were soaring.[28] These relationships suggest that OPEC was restricting its output at least in part to raise the price.

Moreover, these production shifts by OPEC are not attributable solely to Saudi Arabia, the major producer, or to the Iraqi-Iranian conflict that began in the fall of 1980. (See Figure 1–3.) In fact, production by Saudi Arabia has been much more closely correlated with production by the rest of OPEC (whether or not Iran and Iraq are included) than with non-OPEC production. (See Table 1–6.) This finding also is consistent with the view that OPEC displays cartel behavior, however successful or unsuccessful it may have been in dictating the price of oil.[29]

In light of such behavior, one analyst has labelled OPEC a "partial market sharing cartel."[30] In this kind of cartel, the members generally raise and lower production jointly, although some may make larger percentage changes than others. OPEC is not, by this interpretation, a "dominant-firm cartel," in which Saudi Arabia (perhaps with a few other members) acts as the residual or swing producer while other members behave competitively. Although the financial press often seems to subscribe to the dominant-firm–cartel model, OPEC's behavior more nearly resembles that of a partial market-sharing cartel.

Because market-sharing behavior is the weakest kind of cartel arrangement, the conduct of such a cartel is difficult to predict. In the case of OPEC, prediction may be especially hazardous. For one thing,

Table 1–6. Coefficients of Correlation Between Annual Crude Oil Production Levels in Selected Country Groupings, 1973–87.

Country Groupings	Saudi Arabia	Non-OPEC
OPEC		− 0.88
Non-OPEC	− 0.63	
OPEC excluding Saudi Arabia	0.64	
OPEC excluding Saudi Arabia, Iran, and Iraq	0.75	− 0.86

Source: Department of Energy, Energy Information Administration, *Annual Energy Review, 1985* (Washington, D.C.: U.S. Government Printing Office, 1986), p. 235; U.S. Central Intelligence Agency, *International Energy Statistical Review,* 29 March 1988, pp. 1, 2.

settlement of the Iran-Iraq war would probably lead to expanded output by those two countries and to disputes among OPEC members as to how production quotas should then be allocated. For another thing, abiding differences exist among OPEC members as to the most profitable, long-term pricing strategy. Some with vast reserves, such as Saudi Arabia, seem to prefer a price low enough to discourage consuming countries from switching over the long term to non-oil energy sources. Others with smaller reserves show less concern about ensuring a future market.

In view of these centrifugal forces within OPEC, the safest prediction about its output and pricing policy may be the famous prediction about the stock market: it will fluctuate. And fluctuations in OPEC's output will generate marked fluctuations in oil prices because neither market demand nor non-OPEC supply reacts very much to price change in the short run. Forecasts of the trend around which prices will fluctuate are much more problematic.

SOME POLICY CONSIDERATIONS

The sharp fluctuations in oil market conditions, due largely to OPEC's machinations, have aroused understandable anxiety within the oil-importing countries. Oil, after all, is not a luxury good, but the world's leading primary energy source. Countries with the most cause for concern are those that rely most heavily on oil imports, all other things being equal. Dependence on foreign oil—as measured by net oil imports per billion dollars of gross domestic product—underwent a sizable decline in every major, noncommunist, industrial, oil-importing country between 1973 and 1985. Among these countries, Italy and Japan were the most dependent on imported oil in 1985, as can be seen in Table 1-7.

Although the United States is not the most reliant on foreign oil, proposals to impose a tariff on imported petroleum received significant support during the 1986 price decline. Proponents argued that a protective tariff would preserve marginal U.S. producers—such as stripper wells, which might otherwise be lost forever—and would also encourage exploration and development within the United States. With its own supply thus enhanced, the United States would be less vulnerable to future disruptions or manipulations of the foreign supply. Opponents of the tariff were quick to point out that it would raise the price of oil

Table 1-7. Net Imports of Petroleum and Products Per Billion Dollars of Gross Domestic Product in Seven Major Industrial Countries, 1973 and 1985.

| | Thousands of Barrels Per Billion Dollars of GDP[a] | |
	1973	1985
Italy	2,337	1,422
Japan	2,470	1,199
France	1,763	881
West Germany	1,473	872
United States	944	516
Canada	−607	−494
United Kingdom	1,717	−557

Note: Minus sign signifies net exports.

[a]GDP valued at 1980 prices and 1980 exchange rates.

Source: U.S. Central Intelligence Agency, *International Energy Statistical Review*, 26 May 1987, pp. 5–7; Organization for Economic Cooperation and Development, International Energy Agency, *Energy Balances of OECD Countries, 1970–1985* (Paris: OECD, 1987), pp. 165, 219, 237, 309, 327, 507, 525.

for U.S. purchasers and, among other things, would also weaken the international competitiveness of energy-intensive U.S. industries.

In 1987, at the request of President Reagan, the Energy Department completed a review of U.S. energy security, including an analysis of the effects of oil import fees.[31] The fee analysis was comprehensive, embracing a number of alternative assumptions and scenarios. Most relevant to the concern over the health of U.S. oil producers was one analysis based on the assumption that crude oil prices would remain low, amounting to about $15.50 per barrel in 1990 and $21.50 per barrel in 1995 if no fees were imposed.

In this analysis, a $5 fee on U.S. imports of crude oil and refined petroleum products was estimated to yield the following "benefits" for the United States:

1. By raising oil prices in the United States, the fee would expand U.S. crude oil production by 240,000 barrels a day by 1990, but would yield no additional expansion by 1995.
2. In both 1990 and 1995, U.S. oil imports subject to the fee would be 800,000–850,000 barrels a day lower than in the absence of

the fee; oil import payments would be about $3.5 billion lower in 1990 and $6.5 billion lower in 1995.

3. Savings of $14 billion might be realized from the nation's improved ability to cope with a foreign supply disruption assumed to occur in, say, 1995, and assumed to drive up prices to $70 a barrel.
4. The U.S. government would collect about $12 billion from the import fee in 1990 and $17 billion a year by 1995.

On the other side of the ledger, the "costs" to the United States from a $5 import fee were estimated as follows:

1. The prices of gasoline, heating oil, and other petroleum products would go up by 8–10¢ per gallon, boosting the consumer price index by 1–2 percentage points and increasing consumer payments to domestic energy producers by more than $20 billion per year.
2. The higher cost of oil to businesses would impair their international competitiveness, and the higher cost to consumers would reduce their real income; such factors would reduce U.S. GNP below the levels that would be attained without the fee, the reductions amounting to $20 billion in 1990 and $15 billion in 1995.
3. Total employment would be 230,000 lower in 1990 and 170,000 lower in 1995 than it would be in the absence of the fee.
4. The lower GNP would tend to reduce federal tax receipts, and the higher level of prices would tend to raise those federal expenditures indexed to inflation, so that the federal budget deficit might increase in spite of the oil import fees collected by the government.

Adding up the present value of all such costs and benefits for the period 1988–95—based on the $5 fee and relatively low crude oil prices assumed above—one finds that total costs would exceed total benefits by more than $70 billion (measured in 1985 dollars). Although these estimates are far from precise, the conclusion that costs would greatly exceed benefits holds true even with substantial changes in the underlying assumptions, including an assumption of appreciably higher oil prices and a $10 import fee. Thus, an oil import fee would seem to be a mistaken response to U.S. oil concerns. The country would be better off suffering the costs of occasional sharp supply disruptions than bearing the costs associated with an oil tariff.

If tariffs are an inappropriate response, what measures, if any, should be taken by oil-importing countries to mitigate the impact of future oil shocks? One significant program of action has already been adopted by a number of industrial countries. Recognizing that energy security is a matter of collective security, sixteen member countries of the OECD signed an agreement on an International Energy Program (IEP) on 18 November 1974—thirteen months after the outbreak of the first oil crisis. In the same month, the OECD created the International Energy Agency (IEA) to oversee the program. At this writing, twenty-one OECD countries belong to the IEA and participate in the IEP.[32]

The chief goals of the IEA and the IEP are:

i) co-operation among IEA Participating Countries to reduce excessive dependence on oil through energy conservation, development of alternative energy sources and energy research and development;

ii) an information system on the international oil market as well as consultation with oil companies;

iii) co-operation with oil-producing and other oil consuming countries with a view to developing a stable international energy trade as well as the rational management and use of world energy resources in the interest of all countries;

iv) a plan to prepare Participating Countries against the risk of a major disruption of oil supplies and to share available oil in the event of an emergency.[33]

To attain the last of these goals, each IEA member is to maintain an emergency stock of oil equal to ninety days' worth of net imports and is to be prepared to reduce oil consumption in the event of a supply disruption. Provision is also made for the sharing of available oil supplies under crisis conditions. At the end of 1986, most IEA members held stocks well in excess of the stated goal, with OECD total emergency stocks amounting to about 1.5 billion barrels. More to the point, IEA accessible stocks came to more than four months' worth of net imports.[34] The OECD seems to be well prepared to cope with supply disruptions on the scale of those in 1973–74 or 1978–79. (See Figure 1–4.) Emergency stocks thus constitute the first line of defense against future oil shocks. If drawn upon quickly, these stocks could buffer the countries holding them from sudden interruptions of customary sources of supply.

The United States has actively participated in the stock-building program; some 515 million barrels of oil were stored in the U.S. Strategic Petroleum Reserve at the end of 1986. This federally owned oil is stored mainly in underground caverns in Texas and Louisiana. While the reserve does entail maintenance costs and interest on the funds borrowed to acquire the oil, these charges have been estimated to be much lower

Figure 1-4. OECD Oil Stockdraw Capabilities Compared with Previous Supply Disruptions.

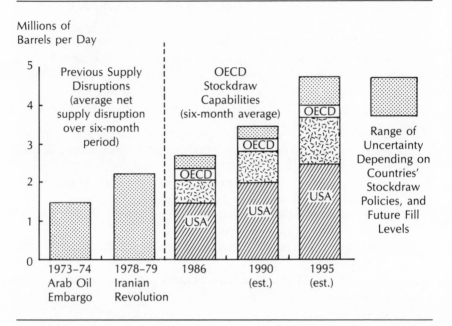

Source: U.S. Department of Energy, *Energy Security: A Report to the President of the United States* (Washington, D.C.: 1987), p. 35.

then the costs associated with an oil import tariff that would provide somewhat comparable protection from a foreign supply interruption.[35]

Oil stocks make a better investment if acquired when oil prices are low. As already noted, however, the forecasting of oil prices is no simple matter and is complicated even in the short run by the unpredictability of OPEC behavior and of Middle Eastern politics.

For the long run, it seems that the price (net of marginal extraction costs) of a presumably limited natural resource such as oil should rise at a rate not greatly different from the rate of interest. If oil reserves were expected to rise in price more rapidly than money compounds at interest, oil reserve owners would have an incentive to hold onto their oil, causing the price to jump to a level from which only a slower subsequent rate of price appreciation could be expected. On the other hand, if oil prices were expected to rise much more slowly than the rate of interest, oil owners presumably would sell more oil and invest the proceeds at interest, until the price of oil dropped to a level from which it could be expected to rise roughly at the rate of interest. One problem with this line of analysis is that expectations about oil prices and long-term interest rates can be in appreciable error for long periods. Moreover, some analysts, pointing to continuing new discoveries and very low extraction costs in some countries, argue that oil should not be analyzed as an exhaustible resource.[36]

In sum, the magnitudes of the underlying determinants of oil supply and demand are very difficult to quantify with much precision. Thus, it is often hard to say whether the price of oil is deviating significantly from levels that would be set by a well-functioning competitive market. With such uncertainty, extreme oil policy measures would be hard to justify. More cautious approaches, such as the buildup of emergency oil stocks, seem more likely to yield net benefits.

SUMMARY

The huge oil price increases launched in 1973 and 1979 sent shock waves through the world economy, reducing economic growth and employment and raising prices in oil-importing countries, while ballooning the receipts of the oil exporters. Anxiety was widespread that the world was rapidly running out of oil and that deficit countries would be hard-pressed to finance their oil imports without exposing the banking system to undue risk.

But life did go on. Energy, especially oil, was used more efficiently, and oil production outside of OPEC grew steadily, as did the production of energy sources other than oil. Oil-importing countries thrown into deficit by the oil price hikes regained external balance as they economized on oil and sold more of their own goods to OPEC.

In 1986 the oil-importing countries were granted a *favorable* shock: oil prices plummeted when OPEC suddenly expanded its output in order to enlarge its share of the oil market. Rates of inflation in industrial countries were lowered by the oil price decline. On the other hand, it was hard to discern any near-term favorable effects on output and employment, partly because marginal oil producers in industrial countries suffered from the price decline and partly because oil-exporting countries had less to spend on industrial-country goods.

As was true of the two abrupt increases, the 1986 oil price decline was largely the work of OPEC. Because the behavior of partial market-sharing cartels such as OPEC is difficult to predict, the safest forecast about OPEC's pricing and production policy is that it will fluctuate.

Concerned by OPEC's unpredictability and by possible future disruptions of oil supply, some observers have urged that oil-importing countries take steps to bolster their own oil-producing industries. Within the United States, for example, a tariff on imported oil was proposed for the purpose of shielding domestic producers from sharp price declines such as those of 1986. Analysis indicates that the benefits to the nation from such a tariff would be heavily outweighed by the costs, including the higher domestic oil prices and the lower GNP and employment that the tariff would bring about. A more economical precaution against future foreign supply disruptions is to hold reserve stocks of oil. By the end of 1986, twenty-one OECD countries had accumulated emergency stocks equivalent to more than four months of net imports.

NOTES

1. For a discussion of these 1973–74 developments, see George Lenczowski, "The Oil Producing Countries," in Raymond Vernon, ed., *The Oil Crisis* (New York: W.W. Norton, 1976), pp. 59–72.
2. James M. Boughton, et al., "Effects of Exchange Rate Changes in Industrial Countries," in International Monetary Fund, *Staff Studies for the World Economic Outlook*, World Economic and Financial Surveys (Washington, D.C.: IMF, 1986), p. 139.
3. *OECD Economic Outlook* 30 (December 1981): 122; *OECD Economic Outlook* 38 (December 1985): 160; *Main Economic Indicators*, March 1986: 172.
4. International Monetary Fund, *International Financial Statistics Yearbook, 1986* (Washington, D.C.: IMF, 1986), pp. 133, 135.
5. Central Intelligence Agency, *The International Energy Situation: Outlook to 1985* (Washington, D.C.: U.S. Central Intelligence Agency, 1977), pp. 1–2. For another pessimistic forecast published in the same year, see Workshop on Alternative Energy Strategies, *Energy: Global Prospects 1985–2000* (New York: McGraw-Hill, 1977).
6. Khodadad Farmanfarmaian, Armin Gutowski, Saburo Okita, Robert V. Roosa, and Carroll L. Wilson, "How Can the World Afford OPEC Oil," *Foreign Affairs* 53 (January 1975): 204.
7. As quoted in *Boston Globe*, 23 October 1974, p. 35.
8. Lewis Preston (Executive Vice President, Morgan Guaranty Trust Company), "Oil-Using Nations Must Accept High Costs of OPEC Aspirations," *American Banker*, 4 November 1974.
9. Rimmer de Vries, "Economic Scene," *New York Times*, 6 and 8 August 1980.

10.   Robert Z. Aliber, *The International Money Game,* 5th ed. (New York: Basic Books, 1987), pp. 137, 145.

11.   National Institutes of Health, Division of Computer Research and Technology, *Command Procedures.*

12.   *OECD Economic Outlook* 39 (December 1986): 141; *OECD Economic Outlook* 38 (December 1985): 153; and *OECD Economic Outlook* 26 (December 1979): 125.

13.   Richard P. Mattione, *OPEC's Investments and the International Financial System* (Washington, D.C.: The Brookings Institution, 1985), pp. 39–40; and *Federal Reserve Bulletin* 69 (March 1983): A20.

14.   *OECD Economic Outlook* 39 (May 1986): 1; and International Monetary Fund, *World Economic Outlook,* April 1986 World Economic and Financial Surveys (Washington, D.C.: IMF, 1986), pp. 25–26.

15.   *OECD Economic Outlook* 41 (June 1987): 138.

16.   As quoted in John Taglialrie, "Yamani Issues Warning as Oil Session Adjourns," *New York Times,* 25 March 1986.

17.   Robert D. Hershey, Jr., "Drop in Oil Prices Is Raising Fears of New U.S. Reliance on Imports," *New York Times,* 13 March 1986.

18.   Department of Energy, *Energy Security: A Report to the President of the United States* (Washington, D.C.: DOE, 1987), pp. 5–6.

19.   Ibid., pp. 59–60.

20.   Department of Energy, Energy Information Administration, *International Energy Annual 1985* (Washington, D.C.: U.S. Government Printing Office, 1986), p. 72; and Energy Information Administration staff.

21.   DOE, *Energy Security,* p. 18.

22.   For accounts of the origin, purposes, and early functioning of OPEC, see Abdul Amir Q. Kubbah, *OPEC: Past and Present* (Vienna: Petro-Economic Research Centre, 1974); Zuhayr Mikdashi, "The OPEC Process," in Vernon, *The Oil Crisis;* and Nazli Choucri, *International Politics of Energy Interdependence* (Lexington, Mass.: D.C. Heath, 1976).

23.   As quoted in Felix Dearden, "Yamani Optimistic on OPEC," *Journal of Commerce,* 25 April 1986.

24.   For example, see Paul W. MacAvoy, *Crude Oil Prices as Determined by OPEC and Market Fundamentals* (Cambridge, Mass.: Ballinger, 1982); and Paul W. MacAvoy, "The Punishing Costs of Fixing Oil Prices," *New York Times,* 29 December 1985.

25.   W.O. Henderson, *The Zollverein* (Cambridge, U.K.: Cambridge University Press, 1939), p. 307.

26.   Dermot Gately, "A Ten-Year Retrospective: OPEC and the World Oil Market," *Journal of Economic Literature* 22 (September 1984): 1100–14.

27.   Department of Energy, Energy Information Administration, *Weekly Petroleum Status Report,* 5 June 1987: 19.

28. *International Energy Statistical Review,* various issues; and Department of Energy, Energy Information Administration, *Annual Energy Review* (Washington, D.C.: U.S. Government Printing Office), various issues.

29. For a similar conclusion, see James M. Griffin, "OPEC Behavior: A Test of Alternative Hypotheses," *American Economic Review* 75 (December 1985): 954–63.

30. James M. Griffin, " 'Comments and Discussion' on Dermot Gately, 'Lessons from the 1986 Oil Price Collapse,' " in *Brookings Papers on Economic Activity,* 1986: 2, p. 279.

31. DOE, *Energy Security,* Appendix D.

32. Ulf Lantzke, "The OECD and Its International Energy Agency," in Vernon, *The Oil Crisis,* pp. 223–27; M.A.G. Van Meerhaeghe, *International Economic Institutions,* 4th ed. (Dordrecht, The Netherlands: Martinus Nijhoff Publishers, 1985), pp. 205–07; and Organization for Economic Cooperation and Development, International Energy Agency, *Energy Policies and Programmes of IEA Countries: 1985 Review* (Paris: OECD, 1986), pp. 2, 89.

33. OECD, *Energy Policies and Programmes,* p. 2.

34. DOE, *Energy Security,* pp. 34–35, 232.

35. Keith B. Anderson and Michael Metzger, *A Critical Evaluation of Petroleum Import Tariffs: Analytical and Historical Perspectives* (Washington, D.C.: Federal Trade Commission, 1987), pp. 42–50.

36. On these matters, see Shantayanan Devarajan and Anthony C. Fisher, "Hotelling's 'Economics of Exhaustible Resources': Fifty Years Later," *Journal of Economic Literature* 19 (March 1981): 65–73; Gately, "Ten-Year Retrospective"; and M.A. Adelman, " 'Comments and Discussion' on Dermot Gately, 'Lessons from the 1986 Oil Price Collapse,' " in *Brookings Papers on Economic Activity,* 1986: 2, pp. 272–76.

2 PROTECTIONISM
A Hardy Virus

Of all the problems confronting the international economy, none has been more tenacious than protectionism. The scope has been widespread, and the costs have been high. For example, about 35 percent (by value) of the manufactured goods consumed in the United States in 1983 fell into categories whose importation was subject to some kind of nontariff restriction. For the European Economic Community (EEC), the comparable figure was 28 percent, and for Japan 16 percent. For several basic agricultural commodity groupings, including grains, sugar, meat, and dairy products, the average price paid by the Japanese consumer in 1980–82 was roughly twice the world price as a result of protection that Japan provided its farmers. For the EEC, the domestic price of these goods was more than one and one-half times the world price, and for the United States nearly one and one-fifth times the world price.[1] Clearly, protectionism was far from extinct in the 1980s, although it had changed in form from earlier years.

Protectionism persists despite the well-established principle of "comparative advantage": a nation benefits from importing the goods that it cannot produce with as much relative efficiency as other nations can. (An illustration of this important principle is given in the appendix to this chapter.) What protectionist devices have become most prominent, and what costs have they imposed? Can such practices be justified? If not, can nations be persuaded to curtail them?

THE "NEW" PROTECTIONISM: NONTARIFF BARRIERS

Judging merely by the height of tariffs, one would conclude that protectionism in the mid-1980s was in remission, if not defeated. At least among the industrial countries, tariff levels declined fairly steadily after the mid-1930s, and as suggested by the data in Table 2–1, marked and widespread declines continued as the 1980s approached.[2] Further

Table 2-1. Receipts from Customs and Import Duties Accruing to OECD Countries as a Percentage of the Value of Their Imports: 1965–1980.

	1965	1970	1975	1980	Percentage Change 1965–1980
Australia	9.62	12.30	12.21	10.13	+5.3
Austria	8.57	6.42	4.04	1.70	−80.2
Belgium/ Luxembourg	3.79	2.70	1.49	1.38	−63.6
Canada	7.95	5.66	5.46	4.62	−41.9
Denmark	2.84	2.19	1.46	1.02	−64.1
Finland	9.97	4.21	2.81	1.37	−86.3
France	6.05	2.33	1.43	1.07	−82.3
West Germany	4.64	3.04	2.36	1.81	−61.0
Greece	11.73	9.81	5.55	5.51	−53.0
Ireland	15.75	14.02	10.43	0.90	−94.3
Italy	5.94	4.66	0.57	0.78	−86.9
Japan	7.55	7.03	2.96	2.46	−67.4
Netherlands	5.72	2.98	1.68	1.40	−75.5
Norway	4.03	1.05	1.32	0.86	−78.7
Portugal	11.72	10.28	6.63	3.41	−70.9
Spain	16.56	14.51	12.66	9.46	−42.9
Sweden	6.26	6.62	2.37	1.72	−72.5
Switzerland	6.93	4.15	2.95	1.57	−77.3
Turkey	53.55	52.71	29.80	15.20	−71.6
United Kingdom	5.97	2.76	2.25	2.17	−63.7
United States	6.75	6.08	3.79	3.08	−54.4
OECD weighted average	6.77	5.05	3.32	2.43	−64.1

Source: Organization for Economic Cooperation and Development, *Costs and Benefits of Protection* (Paris: OECD, 1985), p. 27.

reductions beyond those shown in the table were made after 1980, and nominal tariffs fell to a record low, amounting to less than half the levels prevailing during the renowned "free-trade" era of the nineteenth century.[3]

These low tariffs are the fruit of a long sequence of international trade negotiations, during which the participating countries perceived a mutual gain from reductions in trade barriers. The most recently concluded negotiation, the "Tokyo Round," involved ninety-nine countries and six years of bargaining. Carrying on the tradition, a new round of trade negotiations, the "Uruguay Round," was launched in Punta del Este, Uruguay, by more than seventy nations in September 1986.

So, why worry? There are several reasons. For one thing, even though industrial-country tariffs are generally low, these countries do impose high tariffs on some important categories of goods. For example, on textiles, clothing, and footwear the average industrial-country tariff is about 13 percent.[4] In addition, many less developed countries maintain high average tariff levels. But the real worry—as the agenda for the Uruguay Round makes clear—is that *non*tariff obstacles to international trade are substantial and have been growing in importance.

Nontariff barriers take a number of forms. Most prominent are quantitative restrictions that place limits on the volume of goods flowing from one country to another. Other nontariff barriers are less explicit and less easily identified: for example, in their purchasing policies governments may grant preferential treatment to domestic suppliers.

THE SCOPE OF NONTARIFF BARRIERS

The use of nontariff barriers is widespread, if not ubiquitous. A 1983 report by the United Nations Conference on Trade and Development showed that 98 percent of the products in international trade enountered restrictions in at least one country.[5] Moreover, countries have expanded their use of such barriers, as illustrated by the two general measures in Table 2–2 relating to imports of manufactured goods.

The measures in this table require a few words of explanation. To begin with, the underlying definition of *nontariff barriers* is fairly narrow; it mostly includes various quantitative restrictions. In measuring "restricted manufactured imports" as a percentage of "total manufactured imports," one discovers that restrictions on import categories are often applied against some but not all exporting countries; the measure

Table 2-2. Measures of Nontariff Import Restrictions for Manfactured Goods in Developed Countries.

Measure	Period		United States	European Economic Community[a]	Japan
I. Restricted manufactured imports as a percent of total manufactured imports	1980:	year-end	6.20	10.80	7.20
	1981:	change	5.53	1.38	
	1982:	change	0.69	0.18	
	1983:	change	0.30	2.50	
	1983:	year-end	12.72	14.86	7.20
II. Consumption of restricted manufactured goods as a percent of total consumption of manufactured goods	1980:	year-end	20.3	23.7	15.7
	1981:	change	12.4	2.3	
	1982:	change	2.1	0.3	
	1983:	change	0.2	2.1	
	1983:	year-end	35.0	28.4	15.7

aTrade *among* EEC countries is not included.

Source: Bela Balassa and Carol Balassa, "Industrial Protection in the Developed Countries," *World Economy* 7 (June 1984): 187.

in Table 2–2 counts as restricted manufactured imports only those supplied by the restricted countries, rather than all imports in the category.

While suggestive, the data in this table will not permit profound conclusions. In particular, a low percentage for restricted imports in 1980 would not necessarily imply a low level of restriction, because restrictions themselves reduce the level of imports. For example, a country that prohibited all imports of cars would report a zero value of restricted imports in this category. To reduce this bias, the import percentages for restrictions added in years following 1980 are based on 1980 import values so that restrictions added later could not affect those values.

Another measurement problem stems from the difference between countries in the endowment of natural resources. Simple intermediate products with a high natural-resource content, such as gasoline, are seldom subjected to severe import restrictions; these products constitute a large share of imports for countries poor in natural resources, like Japan. Such countries would therefore exhibit a relatively low percentage of restricted imports even if they imposed rather severe restrictions on finished manufactures. To mitigate any such distortion, the second measure in the table relates *consumption* of the kinds of goods restricted to total *consumption*. This consumption-based measure also alleviates the bias arising from the fact that restrictions reduce the level of imports (the bias present for the year 1980 under the first measure). On the other hand, this second measure counts an entire group of goods as restricted if any products within the group are restricted; the first measure can be applied with more precision, counting as restricted only those imports that actually are.

Under either of these measures, the scope of nontariff barriers was significant in 1983 and had been increasing in both the United States and the EEC. The share of restricted products in total manufactured imports rose over the period 1980–83 from 6.2 percent to 12.7 percent for the United States and from 10.8 percent to 14.9 percent for the EEC. By year-end 1983, 35 percent of manufactured goods consumed in the United States consisted of restricted product groups; for the EEC, the comparable figure was 28.4 percent. The substantial rise in U.S. restrictions is attributable to the limitations on automobile imports from Japan under "voluntary" export restraints accepted by the government of that country in 1981. Although this formal export control program expired in 1985—allowing a sizable increase in Japanese auto exports to the United States—the Japanese government continued to exercise a measure of restraint.

Table 2-3. Frequency of Application of Various Nontariff Barriers Against Agricultural Imports in Industrial Countries, 1984 (Percent).

Commodity	Tariff Quotas and Seasonal Tariffs (1)	Quantitative Restrictions (2)	Minimum Price Policies		Total[a] (5)
			All (3)	Variable Levies (4)	
Meat and live animals	12.3	41.0	26.0	23.8	52.2
Dairy products	6.9	29.6	28.6	25.6	54.6
Fruits and vegetables	15.7	18.8	4.9	0.8	33.1
Sugar and confectionary	0.0	21.7	58.0	58.0	70.0
Cereals	1.7	10.9	21.7	21.7	29.0
Other food	0.8	16.3	13.5	13.2	27.0
Tea, coffee, cocoa	0.4	4.0	2.5	2.5	6.6
Other beverages	18.5	22.9	18.4	0.6	42.3
Raw materials	0.0	7.5	0.3	0.3	7.8
All agriculture	8.2	17.2	11.5	8.2	29.7
Manufactures	2.2	6.7	0.6	0.0	9.4

Note: Data are the number of import items subject to the nontariff barriers shown as a percentage of the total number of import items. The industrial-country markets considered are Australia, Austria, the EEC, Finland, Japan, Norway, Switzerland, and the United States.

aThis column will be less than the sum of columns 1, 2, and 3 if some imports are subject to more than one barrier.

Source: World Bank, *World Development Report 1986* (New York: Oxford University Press, 1986), p. 117.

In recent years nontariff protection has been extended to some industries that customarily have received relatively little protection from foreign competition, such as automobiles, machine tools, and consumer electronics. Moreover, this kind of protection has been increased for the traditionally protected industries, including textiles, clothing, footwear, and steel. Similarly, additional countries have had their exports restricted, while the traditionally restricted exporters, including Japan and the Asian newly industrializing countries, have been confronted with even more barriers.

According to the data in Table 2–2, Japan made relatively little use of nontariff barriers against manufactured goods in 1983. However, the table does not include "invisible" nontariff barriers, and these are often said to be much more important in Japan than in most other nations. In general, invisible barriers are systems and regulations that apply to both domestic and foreign producers but operate, intentionally or unintentionally, to reduce the share of imports in domestic consumption. Most criticism of Japan has focused on its setting of standards that products must meet and the testing of those products, on its wholesale and retail distribution systems, and on government procurement policies. Without doubt, Japanese imports have been significantly affected by the practices followed in each of these areas. One study asks what would be the increase in Japan's manufactured imports if Japan's invisible barriers were reduced to levels corresponding to those in the United States and the EEC. The conclusion is that Japan's manufactured imports might rise by 27 percent, equivalent to a 7 percent rise in the nation's total imports.[6]

As revealed in Table 2–3, nontariff barriers have been at least as prominent in agriculture as in manufactured goods. Within a large group of industrial countries, nontariff restrictions were applied to 29.7 percent of all agricultural import items and to 9.4 percent of manufactured import items in 1984. As might be expected, raw materials and tropical beverages could be imported into the industrial countries with few restrictions. On the other hand, 70 percent of their sugar and confectionary imports and more than half of their meat and dairy product imports encountered at least one obstacle.

THE EFFECTS OF PROTECTION: SOME QUANTITATIVE ESTIMATES

The fundamental motivation underlying most nontariff barriers is, of course, the same as that underlying most tariffs: the protection of domestic producers from import competition. Has this goal been achieved, and if so, at what cost? The answer is: in part, and at appreciable cost.

An import barrier is most effective if it is applied against all foreign goods—whatever the source—that compete closely with the domestic production to be protected. During the 1970s, however, new import restrictions were often applied only to those supplying countries deemed most threatening to domestic producers. Moreover, the degree of restriction and the products to be covered within an industry were usually negotiated between the importing and the exporting country. Consequently, product categories in which import competition had been relatively light were subjected to only slight restriction.

The holes in such protective barriers were fairly readily exploited. Export supply expanded from some countries that had been exempted from restrictions; in countries that were covered, export supply shifted into products that had been exempted. Such circumvention of import barriers was most prominent in the so-called "footloose," or mobile, industries in which relatively little investment was required either in plant and equipment or in the training of skilled labor. Prime examples are clothing, footwear, and other light manufactures. Moreover, in these footloose activities many less developed countries enjoyed a clear comparative advantage over the industrial countries imposing the restrictions.

The penetration of import barriers was no doubt facilitated by structural changes that tended to link national economies more closely. In particular, a growing number of less developed countries were developing the ability to compete in industries that the more advanced countries sought to protect. This phenomenon was assisted by the expansion of multinational enterprises eager to tap the cheapest productive sources and by the increasing internationalization of capital markets, which made it easier for less developed countries to borrow for the establishment and expansion of new industries.

For all these reasons, the import barriers erected during most of the 1970s had seemingly little impact on the aggregate import competition confronting the sectors that the industrial countries sought to protect. Two examples will illustrate. In 1977, when the United States negotiated an orderly marketing agreement (OMA) limiting nonrubber footwear imports from Korea, 70 percent of Korea's footwear exports were nonrubber and 30 percent were rubber. Within one year, Korea had reversed these percentages and had increased the value of its overall footwear exports. Second, under the Multi-Fiber Arrangement (MFA), the EEC (along with other industrial countries) has restricted the import of textiles and clothing from selected exporting countries. Between 1976 and 1980, the volume of EEC imports of MFA products from the Asian newly industrializing countries grew by only 2.2 percent per year—but grew by 9.5 percent per year from other less developed countries enjoying preferential access to the EEC market.[7]

The reaction of the restricting countries was predictable. The protective barriers were extended to cover more products and more exporting countries, apparently slowing the expansion of trade in the restricted categories during the early 1980s. During the first Multi-Fiber Agreement (MFA I), for example, the United States had bilateral agreements with nineteen exporting countries, and none of the agreements placed individual limits on the importation of so-called "sensitive items." By contrast, such individual limits were incorporated into U.S. bilateral agreements with seven countries under MFA II and with fourteen countries during MFA III. Similarly, the number of countries covered under the EEC's bilateral agreements rose from thirty-three under MFA I to forty-three under MFA III, and the number of product categories specified rose from twenty-three to forty-eight.

It was not merely the wider scope of the restrictions that enhanced their effectiveness. Their extension also served as a deterrent to potential exporters not already restricted. For instance, the 1977 OMA limiting the shipment of color television receivers from Japan to the United States was followed by a fourfold increase in U.S. imports of such receivers from Taiwan and Korea in 1977–78, an outcome that led the United States to negotiate OMAs with those two countries in December 1978. This prompt extension of the restrictions discouraged other potential suppliers—including Mexico, Singapore, and Thailand—from exercising their newly acquired ability to enter the U.S. market.[8]

The efficacy of restrictions has also been increased by the general application of these more recent measures to less footloose industries, which cannot readily migrate from one supplying country to another. By the early 1980s, barriers had been erected against imports of automobiles, video-recorder equipment, and machine tools—items that require relatively large inputs of capital or skilled labor and that are less likely to be produced quickly in volume by new suppliers.

As restrictions became more effective in limiting import volumes, they became more effective in raising the prices of imported goods in protected markets. Correspondingly, domestic producers competing with such imports found it easier to maintain or raise their prices and profit margins. Quantitative restrictions are likely to result in higher foreign supply prices if the foreign exporters have the opportunity to ship higher quality, higher valued items under the quantitative limitations, or if they can organize, perhaps tacitly, to raise the price of the smaller volume they are constrained to ship. In the unlikely event that foreign suppliers fail to raise the price, importing firms in the protected market surely will do so. In this respect, a tariff is clearly preferable to a quantitative restriction from the standpoint of the importing country, because the increase in price on the imported units is captured in the form of tariff revenue by the importing country's government rather than by foreign suppliers or by domestic importers.

The forgone tariff revenues are not small. According to one estimate, the imposition of quantitative restraints increased the profit margin on Japanese sales of steel to the United States by at least 10 percent, or some $200 million a year—roughly equivalent to half of Japan's yearly expenditures on steel research and development. Similarly, restrictions under the MFA on the United Kingdom's imports of clothing and textiles have been estimated to transfer twice as much income to foreign suppliers as to U.K. producers, with U.K. consumers, of course, footing the bill.[9]

Costs to consumers are indeed high, in both the manufacturing and the agricultural sectors. Many clothing items made in the United States under a protective umbrella could be purchased abroad for about half the cost. Steel provides another example: early in 1984, U.S. transaction prices for cold rolled-sheet steel were some 40 percent above those prevailing in world markets.[10] With respect to agriculture, a recent analysis reports:

> In Japan, rice farmers receive three times the world price for their crop. . . .
> In 1985, farmers in the EEC received 18¢ a pound for sugar that was then sold on the world markets for 5¢ a pound. . . . Milk prices are kept high in nearly every industrial country, and surpluses are the result: Canadian farmers will pay up to eight times the price of a cow for the right to sell that cow's milk at the government's support price.[11]

Table 2–4 conveys some idea of the extent to which domestic prices in the industrial countries have been raised above world prices for selected agricultural commodities. The "nominal protection coefficients" are estimates of the ratio of internal prices to world market, or border, prices. By this measure, dairy products, sugar, and rice received widespread high protection in the early 1980s. Not surprisingly, higher protection

Table 2-4. Estimated Nominal Protection Coefficients for Selected Commodities in Industrial Countries, 1980–82.

Country or Region	Wheat	Coarse Grains	Rice	Beef and Lamb	Pork and Poultry	Dairy Products	Sugar	Weighted Average[a]
Australia	1.08	1.00	1.75	1.00	1.00	1.40	1.40	1.09
Canada	1.12	1.00	1.00	1.00	1.10	1.95	1.30	1.16
EEC[b]	1.30	1.40	1.40	1.90	1.25	1.80	1.70	1.56
Other Europe[c]	1.70	1.45	1.00	2.10	1.35	2.40	1.80	1.81
Japan	1.25	1.30	2.90	4.00	1.50	2.90	2.60	2.08
New Zealand	1.00	1.00	1.00	1.00	1.00	1.00	1.00	1.00
United States	1.00	1.00	1.00	1.00	1.00	2.00	1.40	1.17
Weighted average	1.20	1.16	2.42	1.51	1.17	1.93	1.68	1.43

Note: Nominal protection coefficients shown are domestic prices divided by border prices.

[a] Averages are weighted by the values of consumption at border prices.

[b] Excludes Greece, Portugal, and Spain.

[c] Austria, Finland, Norway, Sweden, and Switzerland.

Source: World Bank, *World Development Report 1986* (New York: Oxford University Press, 1986), pp. 112–13.

was accorded to farmers in Japan and Europe than to farmers in countries with sizable agricultural export surpluses. In Japan, which has the greatest agricultural protection, consumers paid four times the world price for beef and lamb and nearly three times the world price for rice, dairy products, and sugar.

While nontariff barriers have raised domestic prices, they have had little success in preserving jobs in import-competing industries. One reason already noted is that at least until recently, the selective, noncomprehensive nature of the restrictions allowed them to be penetrated by foreign exports not initially covered. Even where protection succeeds in preserving domestic output, however, domestic employment usually does not fare so well as output. In slowly growing, import-competing industries, any long-term improvements in cash position resulting from reduced import competition are likely to be invested in new equipment that allows higher output per worker—and the replacement of workers—rather than in duplicating old equipment and adding additional workers. In the textile industry, for example, capital-labor ratios have risen from well below the average for all manufacturing in the 1950s to 20 percent above the average; this capital deepening, with the associated productivity gains, has contributed materially to the industry's long-run employment decline in the advanced industrial nations.[12] Import restrictions are likely to be most effective in preserving employment in industries that have little opportunity for such productivity-raising investment.

In any event, the raw data suggest that protection has not preserved many jobs. In the industrial countries, employment has declined faster in the highly protected sectors than in manufacturing as a whole. For example, the OECD reports, "Over the past ten years manufacturing employment in the EEC fell by 11 percent, but in textiles and clothing the drop was about 40 percent . . . and in steel over 40 percent."[13]

Insofar as import restrictions do bolster employment, the jobs saved often do not go to those who have the most difficulty in finding work, but to more mobile, better educated workers. For instance, between 1968 and 1977 employment in the highly protected U.S. textile industry was virtually constant, but 60,000 white-color jobs replaced an approximately equal number of manual jobs requiring less formal education.[14] Moreover, the cost to consumers of saving a job can be very high. To take but one fairly representative case, the restrictions on U.S. imports of color television receivers raised the price of such equipment so that the cost to U.S. consumers per job saved in that industry was about $60,000 per year in the late 1970s, and much more by 1982.[15]

Some more comprehensive estimates of the costs and benefits of special protection in the United States are provided in Table 2–5. In 1986 each of the industries listed was sheltered by some nontariff barrier, and all but book manufacturing received tariff protection as well. Even allowing for a substantial margin of error, these estimates indicate that the cost to consumers from the higher prices generated by import restrictions can be very high, ranging as high as $27 billion per year for the textile and apparel industries.

Where a tariff is involved, a part of the cost to consumers takes the form of tariff revenue collected by the government on imports. Where a quantitative restriction is involved, part of the cost paid by consumers goes to foreign exporters, who charge more for the reduced supply of their goods to U.S. consumers. Typically, however, the bulk of the cost paid by consumers is pocketed by U.S. producers, who can both produce and charge more because of the rise in price for the reduced supply of competing imports.

In addition to these income transfers, trade restrictions entail "efficiency losses." With their purchases constrained by higher prices, consumers wind up with a smaller total quantity of the restricted goods, even though domestic production expands. The expansion in domestic production at artificially high prices utilizes resources that, if the economy is functioning well, could and should have been employed at market prices in unprotected industries. As is true of consumer costs, efficiency losses have been highest in textiles and apparel.

Because restrictions are often motivated largely by a desire to preserve employment, the estimates in Table 2–5 of the cost to consumers per job saved are especially interesting. Ranging from $21,000 in the fishing industry to an astronomical $1 million per job per year in specialty steel manufacturing, these estimates imply that other methods of assisting the unemployed—even a pure dole—would be far less costly to the consumer-taxpayer.

The agricultural sector enjoys special protection in many industrial countries, even in countries, like the United States, that traditionally have been net exporters of agricultural products. Table 2–6 reports the costs of such protection, including not only direct protection against imports but various other major financial transfers to agriculture through programs such as price supports. According to these estimates, the costs to the EEC of its "common agricultural policy," after deducting producer benefits, were $15.4 billion in 1980, or 0.6 percent of the EEC's gross domestic product. For each of the three areas listed, producers gain

Table 2-5. Distribution of Annual Costs and Benefits from Special Protection in Effect in the United States in 1986.

Case	Cost of Restraints to Consumers		Gain from Restraints to Producers (million dollars)	Welfare Costs of Restraints		
	Totals (million dollars)	Per Job Saved (dollars)		Gain to Foreigners (million dollars)	Tariff Revenue (million dollars)	Efficiency Loss (million dollars)
Manufacturing						
Book manufacturing	500	100,000	305	Neg.	0	29
Textiles and apparel	27,000	42,000	22,000	1,800	2,535	4,850
Carbon steel	6,800	750,000	3,800	2,000	560	330
Specialty steel	520	1,000,000	420	50	32	30
Automobiles	5,800	105,000	2,600	2,200	790	200
Motorcycles	104	150,000	67	Neg.	21	17
Services						
Maritime industries	3,000	270,000	2,000	Neg.	10[a]	1,000
Agriculture and fisheries						
Sugar	930	60,000	550	410	5	130
Dairy products	5,500	220,000	5,000	250	34	1,370
Peanuts	170	1,000/acre	170	Neg.	9	14
Meat	1,800	160,000	1,600	135	44	145
Fish	560	21,000	200	170	177	15

Neg.: Negligible.

[a] Estimated duties collected on ship repairs performed abroad.

Source: Gary Clyde Hufbauer, et al., *Trade Protection in the United States* (Washington, D.C.: Institute for International Economics, 1986), pp. 14–15.

Table 2-6. Distribution of Annual Domestic Costs and Benefits of Agricultural Protection in the EEC, Japan, and the United States (in billions of dollars, unless otherwise noted).

Area and Year	Consumer Costs +	Taxpayer Costs −	Producer Benefits =	Total Domestic Costs	Transfer Ratio[a]
EEC (1980)[b]	34.6	11.5	30.7	15.4	1.50
Japan (1976)	7.1	−0.4	2.6	4.1	2.58
United States (1985)	5.7	10.3	11.6	4.4	1.38

[a]The ratio of consumer plus taxpayer costs to producer benefits.

[b]Excludes Greece, Portugal, and Spain.

Source: World Bank, *World Development Report 1986* (New York: Oxford University Press, 1986), p. 121.

less than the total cost to consumers and taxpayers, suggesting the efficiency losses involved. Thus, in Japan agricultural protection in 1976 cost $2.58 for every dollar transferred to producers, as shown by the transfer ratio (the ratio of total consumer and taxpayer costs to producer benefits). This high transfer ratio for Japan reflects higher import barriers than those in the EEC and the United States, both of which provide more of the total agricultural support through subsidies to exports and domestic consumption and through payments to farmers, all financed from taxes.

The losses imposed by the agricultural support policies of the industrial countries are not limited to those countries alone. By expanding their agricultural output while reducing demand in their home markets, industrial countries depress the prices that can be earned by producers in other countries, which then devote fewer resources to agriculture—and more to manufacturing—than they would if free market prices prevailed. For example, some Asian less developed countries produce less rice than they would if Japan lowered its import barriers against that commodity. This kind of inefficiency is compounded by the fact that many less developed countries pursue policies favoring manufacturing in spite of their natural comparative advantage in agriculture.

What gains would the world realize if both the developing and the industrial-market economies were to abandon their trade barriers and domestic interventions in the agricultural sector? The question is extraordinarily complex; an answer is available, however, although it is partial

Table 2–7.   Estimated Efficiency Gains from Liberalization
of Selected Commodities, by Country Group, 1985.

Country Group	Efficiency Gains (billions of 1980 dollars)
Developing countries	18.3
Industrial-market economies	45.9
East European nonmarket economies	– 23.1
Worldwide	41.1

Note: Data are based on the removal of the rates of protection in effect in 1980–82 for wheat, coarse grains, rice, beef and lamb, pork and poultry, dairy products, and sugar.

Source: World Bank, *World Development Report 1986* (New York: Oxford University Press, 1986), p. 131.

and imprecise. Table 2–7 presents estimated gains from such liberalization for seven major commodity groups: wheat, coarse grains, rice, beef and lamb, pork and poultry, dairy products, and sugar. Both the developing- and the industrial-market economies would have benefited substantially, realizing total gains of about $64 billion (1980 dollars) per year—more than double the annual level of official development assistance from the industrial to the developing countries during 1980–84. By contrast, the East European nonmarket economies would have lost from this liberalization, partly because their export response would have been less favorable than that of the developing countries.[16]

Although these various estimated costs of protection are substantial, they almost certainly understate the true costs. The estimates fail to take into account the gains that liberalization would allow in the form of greater economies of scale from increased specialization, as well as other longer run, dynamic benefits accruing from more efficient patterns of research and investment. Especially for the developing countries, much evidence shows that the countries with the more market-oriented trade and exchange-rate policies have generally enjoyed faster growth than the countries with more restrictive policies.[17] The manner in which many nontariff barriers are being implemented makes them especially costly in these respects, as the next section indicates.

THE GROWTH OF STATE-DIRECTED TRADING

The growing use of quantitative restrictions is a reversal of the trend toward liberalization initiated after World War II. The Great Depression, the war, and the ensuing economic dislocation were accompanied by widespread direct government control over international trade; the architects of the postwar economic order sought to reduce that control. Thus, the General Agreement on Tariffs and Trade (GATT), which became effective in January 1948 after signature by twenty-three countries, contains language that generally prohibits the introduction of quantitative restrictions. Moreover, with few exceptions the agreement calls for trade to be nondiscriminatory: no country is to bestow special trading advantages (or to impose special disadvantages) on another, but each is to treat all other countries equally. Progress was slow, but conviction lay behind these principles. In particular, quantitative restrictions on industrial products had been largely dismantled by the early 1960s.[18]

By the end of the 1960s, a new direction had become apparent. Although tariffs generally continued to decline, a reversion to quantitative restrictions was in evidence. During the early part of the decade, the GATT rules against discrimination and quantitative restrictions had been formally suspended through multilateral arrangements providing for bilateral (individual, country-by-country) quota limitations on trade in cotton textiles. The purpose of the suspension was to avoid "market disruption" in importing countries. The United States and other industrial countries then prevailed on Japan and individual developing countries to restrain their textile exports, first of cotton, then of wool and synthetic fibers.

The example was not lost on other industries seeking protection. Steel restraints were negotiated by the United States in 1968, and by the EEC a few years later. Soon color television sets and receivers from Asia, and then automobiles, were subjected to similar restraints.

The "voluntary" export restraints employed in these agreements were an innovation designed to circumvent the strictures of the GATT against discrimination and quantitative restrictions. Although contrary to the spirit of the GATT, a voluntary export restraint does not violate the letter of its rules. Exporting countries impose such self-restraints after being threatened with more severe measures if they fail to cooperate. But if the exporters can combine to raise their prices on the reduced volume they will supply, their restraint pill is considerably sweetened, making cooperation even more likely.

This method of protection is "the core of the new protectionism."[19] The new protectionism differs markedly from the 1930s' rampant protectionism, which was largely a panic response to the depression and to the provocative escalation of U.S. tariffs under the Hawley-Smoot

Tariff Act. By contrast, the new protectionism is more carefully planned, is internationally negotiated, and grows more slowly. In the words of the former director of research for the GATT:

> Industries have used intelligent, long-term planning in creating an expanded system of protection. The expansion proceeds sectorally; instead of an effort to reduce all imports as much as possible, we are witnessing the construction of industrial protection systems, each tailored to the special needs of the industry in question, each administered by a highly specialized bureaucracy, often co-opted into public service from the respective industry association. . . . The protectionism of the 1930s was openly adversary; the new one, however, builds on negotiation, indeed, is in a perverse way the result of international cooperation. As a result, the new protectionism is politically stronger because it accommodates a broader range of interests. Where earlier forms of protection created vested interests in the importing country only, the new protectionism has built up almost equally strong vested interest on the export side as well.[20]

To be sure, measures to liberalize trade have been adopted in recent years. Increasingly, however, they have assumed the form of selective, or discriminatory, reductions of tariffs—which have become less important—while the more important nontariff barriers have been selectively increased. The net result, then, is a shift toward protection.[21]

New costs are associated with the new protectionism. Not least is the cost of documentation. In particular, where a trade restriction is discriminatory, the importing country must ascertain whether it is receiving the targeted country's goods via transshipment through other countries. Partly because of such concerns, the average transaction in international trade was said in 1985 to require 35 documents and 360 copies, a state of affairs likely to please few besides the paper industry.[22]

Besides all the red tape, the new protectionism not merely diminishes the role of prices in allocating resources, it vitiates that role. Once a quantitative restriction is in place, no amount of price reduction for imports will allow them to exceed the limit. Moreover, discriminatory restrictions prevent the most efficient supplying countries—which the restrictions are aimed at—from supplanting the less efficient. In addition, for reasons already set forth, quantitative restrictions encourage cartelization among exporters.

Perhaps most disturbing, however, is the displacement of a system of rules designed for the general interest by a nonsystem of case-by-case negotiations designed to serve much narrower interests. The frequent transgressions of the basic prohibitions against discrimination and quantitative restrictions generate uncertainty that new investment to develop more competitive industry would be worthwhile. It is not only international economic order that suffers from the exercise of such arbitrary discretion, but domestic order as well, since quantitative restrictions are commonly negotiated behind closed doors. They are not subjected to the kind of public debate that would disclose the full social costs in advance. Such processes are inimical to the openness required for effectively functioning democracy.

In view of these practices, it is somewhat ironic that the Soviet Union's 1986 initiative toward membership in GATT was discouraged on the grounds that the Soviet economy was not a market economy in which prices reflect underlying cost conditions and preferences. While it is true that trade based on noncompetitive prices could make the world worse off (especially the market-oriented sector, if the nonmarket sector behaved monopolistically), the trade practices of nations already in GATT were increasingly compromising the competitive ideal. In some respects, the market economies were becoming more like the nonmarket economies in their international trade practices. Nowhere is this convergence more apparent than in the practice of countertrade.

COUNTERTRADE

In a countertrade transaction, the exporter of goods to a country assumes responsibility for generating a counterpurchase of that country's merchandise.[23] For example, a few years ago Hawker Siddeley Canada, Inc. reportedly sold 379 railway cars to Indonesia, but was obliged in return to purchase, or find a buyer for, $17 million worth of Indonesian natural rubber. This swap of Indonesian rubber for Canadian railways cars is paralleled by swaps of Iranian oil for New Zealand frozen lamb, of Chrysler automobiles for Jamaican bauxite, and of British aircraft for Ecuadorian bananas.

In the financial press, these barterlike transactions are commonly estimated to constitute between 20 and 30 percent of all international trade. Although the available data suggest that this estimate is too high, there is no dispute over the assertion that countertrade has been growing rapidly.

A rough estimate of the geographic distribution of countertrade transactions is given in Table 2–8. According to this OECD estimate, countertrade may have accounted for nearly 5 percent of world trade in 1983

Table 2-8. Estimated (Maximum) Countertrade among
Various Categories of Countries, 1983

| | Countertrade | |
Country	In Billions of Dollars	As Percent of Total Trade
Industrial countries with:		
Eastern Europe	15.6	15
Oil-exporting developing countries	4.3	2
Other developing countries	16.6	5
Among each other	15.7	2
Developing countries with:		
Eastern Europe	14.2	30
Among each other	12.5	10
Total	79.0	· 4.8

Note: Excludes trade among East European countries and trade under clearing arrangements. Detail may not add to totals shown because of rounding.

Source: Organization for Economic Cooperation and Development, *Countertrade: Developing Country Practices* (Paris: OECD, 1985), pp. 11–12. For arrangement of data, see Robert Pringle, ed., *Countertrade in the World Economy* (New York: Group of Thirty, 1985), pp. 4–5.

(excluding trade among East European countries and trade under clearing arrangements) and for significantly higher percentages of trade among developing countries or trade involving Eastern Europe. A more recent estimate by the International Monetary Fund (IMF) is that countertrade amounted to as much as 10 percent of world trade in 1986, compared to one percent in 1980.[24]

The philosophy underlying countertrade is, "I will take your goods only if you will take mine." Countertrade is motivated by a government's desire to promote domestic employment or to improve the balance of trade. Thus, it has expanded in times of economic adversity, particularly with the decline in basic commodity prices and the sharp cutback in international lending accompanying the international debt crisis. In a number of less developed countries, lagging receipts from exports and from foreign loans, combined with rising unemployment, led governments to require that certain purchases from abroad must be offset by foreign counterpurchases of domestic goods.

Countertrade also flourishes where there is detailed government control over the economy—as in most communist countries—because the authorities can use countertrade as one means of carrying out the central economic plan. Similarly, countertrade can be employed—as some oil-exporting countries reportedly have done—in an effort to support an administered price for exports, or at least to avoid a general and explicit price reduction while granting a selective, implicit reduction. In addition, countertrade is invoked as a means of enlisting superior foreign marketing skills in order to sell abroad the domestic goods made available under a counterpurchase agreement.

Countertrading comes in several major variants: barter, counterpurchase, and compensation. Barter, the rarest and most primitive, is the direct exchange of goods without any transfer of funds. In a barter contract, two parties, usually governments, undertake to deliver specified quantities of certain goods to each other by fixed dates. It is not surprising that pure barter is the least used form of countertrading. Because barter forgoes the use of money as a medium of exchange, it is extremely inefficient. One has only to imagine the difficulty, in a world without money, of continually arranging swaps (of goods and services) that people would find mutually satisfying. Other forms of countertrade do not rule out cash payments, so they provide more flexibility than pure barter does in striking an agreement.

In a counterpurchase, an exporter to a country contracts to make, or to arrange for, a (counter) purchase of goods that the importing country's government desires to have sold abroad. The value of the goods supplied by the exporter is usually greater than the value of the goods to be counterpurchased; the counterpurchase must be accomplished by a certain date; and all deliveries are paid for in cash.

Where the exporter aims to sell an entire production plant or substantial equipment, he may be required to accept payment largely or wholly in the form of goods to be produced by his equipment, or in similar goods. If the exporter accedes, he is said to "buy back" the output of the equipment he has supplied. These buy-back arrangements are known as "industrial compensation," or as simply, "compensation." The value of the transactions involved is usually much larger than in a barter or counterpurchase arrangement, and the period over which the transactions occur is usually much longer, sometimes extending for many years. For the country demanding it, industrial compensation offers a way of securing long-term financing for a productive facility from the foreign supplier, and a way of shifting risk for the success of the facility to him as well. Thus, compensation appeals to governments that eschew market uncertainty, and especially to governments with economic plans to be enforced.

In all types of countertrade transactions the possibility exists that the exporter will be unable to use or market profitably the foreign goods that he has agreed to accept or purchase. Thus, the exporter may sell the goods at a discount to a trading firm that specializes in marketing them. These "switch traders" are located primarily in Western Europe and handle mainly East European goods.

A key feature of countertrade is that it is under the direct control of the government demanding it; and a deal offered by a countertrading government often embodies an implicit tax or subsidy, or both. For example, if a countertrading government buys enough of an item to affect its price in world markets, the government can depress the price it pays by restricting its purchases, just as they would be restricted by a duty on imports into the country. Whether countertrading governments generally succeed at influencing, or even attempt to influence, the terms on which they trade through such implicit taxation is an open question. For authoritarian governments with central economic plans, the acquisition of high-priority imports for fulfilling a plan is more important than shaving the price by restricting purchases; for crucial imports, those governments will not even insist upon countertrade.

Indeed, recent studies and interviews with countertrade specialists indicate that governments frequently pay more, not less, than the going market price for the imports that the foreign exporter is required to offset with a counterpurchase. This premium compensates the foreign exporter for the risk and expense involved in disposing of the goods he must counterpurchase and takes the place of a reduction in the price he pays for those goods. Experience suggests that such a premium is warranted. Not infrequently, goods counterpurchased by an exporter are delivered to him tardily and are poor in quality. Also, the countertrading government may demand that they be sold outside their accustomed markets, the goal being to avoid displacement of the government's ordinary sales and balance-of-payments earnings. Thus, the exporter may use some or all the premium he has received to reduce his selling price on the counterpurchased goods in order to attract a buyer; or the premium may be used to pay the commission of a countertrade specialist hired to market the goods.

It is revealing to note that a government could achieve much the same effect through a tax and subsidy program as through a counterpurchase program. In a counterpurchase operation, it is as if the government had imposed a duty on an import—raising the price paid within its territory for that import—and had then transferred the proceeds of the duty to the foreign supplier in order to subsidize his purchase of specified goods for export. Such a system of differential taxes on imports and subsidies on exports is analogous to a system of multiple exchange rates—that is, of differing rates of exchange between the home currency and foreign currency for differing products, with rates for some products providing a high incentive for foreign purchase.

If taxes and subsidies could achieve much the same economic results as countertrade, why do some governments engage in countertrade? One possible explanation is that countertrade is more certain in its effects and more flexible than a set of taxes and subsidies. Also, countertrade may encounter less political resistance—both domestically and internationally—than taxes and subsidies, largely because the impact of countertrade on the distribution of income is not so readily perceived, making protests less likely. In the international sphere, such protests against new import duties or export subsidies would often be in order under international conventions, and economic retaliation would commonly be forthcoming if the protests went unheeded. Therefore, some governments may be drawn to the hidden nature of the taxes and subsidies implicit in countertrade.

If free trade is taken as a standard or ideal, the greatest economic defect of countertrade is its thrust toward bilateralism, that is, toward the enforced balancing of trade flows between individual countries. If a firm in Country A exports to the countertrading government of Country B, the firm must make a counterpurchase in B, thereby striking an approximate balance in trade between the two countries for this transaction—unless the firm is fortunate enough to resell the counterpurchased items more profitably in a third country. Country B's countertrade requirement, however, will surely discourage some foreign firms from trading with it, so that any improvements that B engineers in its bilateral trade balances may well be purchased at the cost of a reduced total volume of trade.

The adoption of bilateralism by many countries could severely reduce the volume of world trade. Suppose that under free trade, Country A would export to Country B, Country B would export to Country C, and Country C would export to Country A—so that each country was in balance on its multilateral (overall) trade even though it was out of balance with every other country individually. Now, if no bilateral imbalances (or transshipments) were allowed, there would be no trade whatsoever if A had no demand for the goods of B, B no demand for the goods of C, and C no demand for the goods of A.

Not only does bilateralism reduce the volume of world trade by comparison with free trade, but it reduces the volume of international lending. One country lends real resources to another only if it exports more to that country than it imports from it. With bilateral balancing, such lending is impossible.

Countertrade, then, has little to commend it. A world of countertrade would be better than a world of no trade, but that is faint praise.

IS BILATERALISM GROWING?

Countertrade is only one of a number of government controls that tend to produce bilateral balancing of international trade flows. The most formal and formidable of these control mechanisms is the "bilateral payments arrangement," under which part or all of one country's receipts from a second country may be used only for payments to the latter. According to the IMF, the importance of bilateral payments arrangements in 1985 seems to have been both slight and diminishing. Between the end of 1975 and the end of 1985, the total number of bilateral payments arrangements maintained by IMF member countries declined from 220 to 134, in spite of an increase in IMF membership over that period. Moroever, the IMF estimates that no more than 0.14 percent of the value of world trade of IMF members was covered by these arrangements during 1985. On the other hand, the trade covered by other, less visible bilateral devices, including countertrade, may well have been increasing.[25] In fact, the IMF has voiced concern over a "proliferation" of countertrade arrangements.[26] Data examined in this section, however, suggest that bilateralism has shown no overall growth, in spite of the increase in countertrade.

Although no firm data are available on the share of world trade covered by bilateral arrangements, it is enlightening to examine the sizes of bilateral balances. To provide initial perspective, some summary data on the ratio of cumulated trade balances to total trade are offered in Table 2–9. If generally practiced, bilateral balancing would reduce the size of overall trade balances in relation to total trade. The ratios in the table fail to show any such downward trend. In this table, the overall trade balances of individual countries were summed (without regard to algebraic sign) year by year, and each yearly sum is expressed in the table as a ratio of the corresponding year's total trade, that is, as a ratio of the total exports and imports of the countries represented. For each of the two periods covered, all countries for which data were available

Table 2-9. Sum of Individual Country Trade Balances as a Ratio of Those Countries' Aggregate Exports Plus Imports, 1965-85.

Year	For 65 Countries with Data through 1984	For 47 Countries with Data through 1985
1965	0.080	0.080
1966	0.076	0.074
1967	0.085	0.084
1968	0.069	0.067
1969	0.065	0.063
1970	0.068	0.066
1971	0.075	0.073
1972	0.077	0.076
1973	0.076	0.075
1974	0.109	0.105
1975	0.079	0.075
1976	0.084	0.079
1977	0.094	0.088
1978	0.089	0.085
1979	0.079	0.074
1980	0.078	0.071
1981	0.073	0.067
1982	0.080	0.076
1983	0.095	0.091
1984	0.113	0.109
1985		0.117

Note: Country trade balances were summed without regard to sign. The forty-seven countries represented in the second column are among the sixty-five represented in the first column.

Source: Underlying data are from International Monetary Fund, *Direction of Trade Statistics* (magnetic tape).

for that entire period are included. The forty-seven countries with data through 1985 account for nearly 79 percent of world trade, and the sixty-five countries with data available only through 1984 account for nearly 81 percent.

The figures in Table 2-9 shed light on the question of what has happened to total trade balances in relation to total trade, but tell us nothing about the experience of the average country. The data in the table are influenced most heavily by the experience of the countries with the largest trade volumes, and their experience might not be representative of most countries. By contrast, in Table 2–10 countries are weighted equally, regardless of the magnitudes of their trade. For each year, each country's trade balance (without regard to sign) was expressed as a ratio of the country's total trade (exports plus imports), and the table shows the average of these country ratios for every year. Spreading bilateralism would tend to shrink the size of the average country's trade balance in relation to the country's total trade. Again, since the average ratios shown do not follow a downward trend, they do not support the view that bilateralism was intensifying.

Table 2–10.   Average Ratio of Country Trade Balance to Total Exports Plus Imports for the Country, 1965–85.

Year	For 65 Countries with Data through 1984	For 47 Countries with Data through 1985
1965	0.171	0.179
1966	0.169	0.169
1967	0.170	0.173
1968	0.168	0.171
1969	0.168	0.166
1970	0.168	0.168
1971	0.181	0.173
1972	0.160	0.153
1973	0.166	0.164
1974	0.188	0.176
1975	0.194	0.185
1976	0.174	0.163
1977	0.174	0.158
1978	0.195	0.171
1979	0.190	0.166
1980	0.192	0.163
1981	0.198	0.169
1982	0.194	0.170
1983	0.201	0.178
1984	0.191	0.168
1985		0.174

Note: Country trade balances were taken without regard to sign. The forty-seven countries represented in the second column are among the sixty-five represented in the first column.

Source: Underlying data are from International Monetary Fund, *Direction of Trade Statistics* (magnetic tape).

Rather than focus on the average country, Table 2–11 concentrates on the average *pair* of countries. For each year, the trade imbalance between every two countries that traded with each other was expressed as a ratio of their total trade, with total trade defined as the sum of each country's exports to the other; the average of these ratios for every year is also presented in the table. Once again, the absence of any marked decline in the ratios over time suggests that bilateralism did not increase, in spite of the growth of countertrade.

Table 2–11. Average Ratio of Bilateral Balance to Bilateral Trade, 1965–85.

Year	For 65 Countries with Data through 1984	For 47 Countries with Data through 1985
1965	0.473	0.473
1966	0.525	0.518
1967	0.518	0.509
1968	0.507	0.498
1969	0.543	0.534
1970	0.564	0.550
1971	0.571	0.558
1972	0.576	0.560
1973	0.574	0.558
1974	0.594	0.575
1975	0.610	0.594
1976	0.596	0.581
1977	0.611	0.600
1978	0.606	0.589
1979	0.609	0.592
1980	0.614	0.598
1981	0.617	0.603
1982	0.615	0.599
1983	0.613	0.597
1984	0.606	0.592
1985		0.586

Note: The forty-seven countries represented in the second column are among the sixty-five represented in the first column.

Source: Underlying data are from International Monetary Fund, *Direction of Trade Statistics* (magnetic tape).

JUSTIFICATIONS AND EXPLANATIONS
FOR PROTECTION

As noted at the beginning of this chapter, free trade maximizes world economic welfare, provided that we are satisfied with the resulting income distribution and that markets are competitive and functioning efficiently. These provisos are substantial. Many would object to the current apportionment of the world's income, and elements of monopoly and inefficiency are obvious in many markets. No doubt, import restrictions could contribute to more desirable outcomes in some cases. In general, however, import restrictions are inferior cures for our economic ailments. Better remedies are available.

The reason for this conclusion is that import restrictions usually are an unnecessarily roundabout and costly means of effecting a desired change.[27] An import barrier raises the domestic price of the restricted good, leading domestic consumers to cut back on their consumption and domestic producers to expand their output (which consumers buy in place of imports) with resources that could be used to produce other goods instead. The import barrier thus modifies both consumption and production and may be overkill; perhaps only one or the other really needs to be modified.

Suppose that we want to preserve employment or output in a particular domestic industry at a higher level than free international competition will permit. Perhaps the industry provides jobs that are well suited to its employees and not readily available in other industries at an "acceptable" wage, or perhaps the industry is important to our national defense. In such circumstances, a subsidy to the industry's production should be considered. Subsidizing production would attain our objective, and unlike an import restriction, a subsidy would not raise the price of the industry's output to consumers but would simply enable the industry to produce more at world prices. Thus, a subsidy provided directly to support production would be preferable to an import barrier that only indirectly supported production while obliging consumers to cut consumption of the protected good.

To take another example, we might want to discourage domestic consumption of a particular item—say, because it poses a health hazard—but we might not care whether the quantity consumed is produced at home or abroad. A tax on the sale of the item would serve the purpose. The sales tax would discourage domestic consumption; unlike an import restriction, however, it would not encourage domestic production by raising the domestic price above the world price, since it would be levied on all domestic sales whether the item was produced domestically or abroad. Thus, the tax levied directly on consumption purchases of the item would be preferable to an import restriction that only indirectly reduced consumption while diverting resources from other industries into the protected one.

In general, then, if welfare can be enhanced by changing domestic production or domestic consumption of a good, taxes or subsidies aimed directly at its production or consumption will be more efficient instruments than foreign trade interventions. Devices such as import restrictions entail unnecessary and costly side effects.

Even the hallowed "infant industry" argument will not withstand close scrutiny. According to this argument, some nascent industries cannot weather foreign competition immediately, but with protection they could gain experience and reduce their costs of operation so that they could eventually flourish without protection. But if an industry clearly falls into this category, then the question arises, why are *private* investors unwilling to take the short-term losses associated with the industry's development in order to reap the long-term gains? (Unless the long-term gains offset the short-term losses, the industry would be a bad investment from any standpoint.) The answer might be that private entrepreneurs fear they would fail to recover their investment in training employees, whom other employers, not having invested in such training, could afford to hire away at higher wages. In such a case, however, the remedy would be for the employees to share the cost of their own training, or perhaps for the government to subsidize it. An import restriction that raised prices to consumers would, again, be a clumsy and imprecise attack on the problem.

One argument for trade restrictions is recognized by economic theory as logically sound, but the argument is narrow and nationalistic. If a country looms large in the international economy, that country can turn international prices (the terms of trade) in its favor by restricting its purchases of foreign goods so as to drive down their price. But serious problems exist in implementing such a strategy. If imports are restricted too much, the restricting country suffers more from the reduced volume of trade than it gains from the lower purchase price, and it is extremely difficult to calculate the optimum degree of restriction. Moreover, other countries may retaliate with their own restrictions, reducing the first country's gain, or even converting it to a loss.

Since the economic justification for protectionism is next to nonexistent, and since protectionist barriers entail significant costs, why is protectionism so widely practiced? Some insight is provided by those studies showing that the most highly protected U.S. industries usually employ relatively high proportions of unskilled, low-paid, and older workers. Protection thus seems intended, at least in part, to preserve the jobs and income of this relatively poor and vulnerable class. Research also confirms that political pressure can be effective in securing protection for an industry. For example, in the last round of international trade negotiations, tariffs typically were cut less on the products of industries whose spokesmen had testified against further liberalization.[28]

More generally, protectionism is practiced because it is the most feasible, most politically acceptable—even if economically inferior—means of seeking certain objectives. The political feasibility of protectionism stems partly from popular underestimation of its total costs and partly from the wide dispersion of those costs among many consumers and unprotected industries, few of whom sense a sizable direct burden. Moreover, many are prepared to pay a premium for home-produced goods under the nationalistic and generally mistaken impression that such a sacrifice will help to ensure a stronger domestic economy in the international arena. Nowhere is this misconception more obvious than in the case of quantitative restrictions—especially voluntary export restraints—to which foreign countries may agree (rather than retaliating with their own restrictions) precisely because they may benefit at the importing country's expense from the higher prices generated by the restrictions.

NEGOTIATING REDUCTIONS IN TRADE BARRIERS

Even though trade barriers often harm the countries that impose them, countries rarely reduce them substantially without some incentive from other countries. The incentive may take the form of a carrot, such as the promise of one liberalization in return for another, or a stick, such as the threat of a new restriction in retaliation for another's restriction. The positive incentive of mutual liberalization has worked well in lowering tariffs, but nontariff barriers to trade have been mounting. Thus, it is encouraging that the current Uruguay Round of international trade negotiations, launched in 1986, is focusing more than previous negotiations did on the regulation and reduction of nontariff barriers.

Indeed, the Uruguay Round offers the promise of being broader in scope than any of the preceding seven rounds of multilateral trade negotiations staged under the GATT since its founding in 1947. For one thing, more countries than ever before are to participate, as the GATT now boasts ninety-three members, compared with only twenty-three at its inception. For another, more sectors of economic activity and more forms of protection are to be covered.

One noteworthy extension in coverage is the inclusion of all measures affecting agricultural trade, especially export subsidies. The agenda for the Uruguay Round calls for greater liberalization of agricultural trade by, among other things, reducing the negative effects of agricultural subsidies. By contrast, previous negotiations gave relatively little attention to such distortions of trade in farm commodities.

In addition, barriers to trade in services are the subject of negotiations for the first time. Among these barriers are government obstacles to international sales of banking services, insurance, telecommunications, construction services, transportation, computer services, consulting, tourism, and so on. Other first-time topics of negotiation include restrictive national conditions imposed on foreign investors, as well as proposals to curb the infringement of intellectual property rights such as patents, copyrights, and trademarks. Along with these new issues, the negotiations are considering improvements in existing codes that deal with nontariff barriers, improvements in the now ineffectual procedures for settling trade disputes, and improvements in the provisions allowing for temporary protection to forestall serious injury from import competition.

Several years will be required to complete the Uruguay Round negotiations. Even if the round fails to yield significant liberalization, it may well succeed in barring major new protectionist actions for the time being, since governments generally demonstrate their good faith by refraining from provocative trade measures during multilateral negotiations. Thus, the initiators of this latest round have taken the customary formal pledge not only to eschew new measures inconsistent with the GATT but to phase out those now in effect.

Some experienced observers are skeptical that Uruguay Round participants will be willing to relax their most important protectionist barriers—such as the discriminatory quantitative restrictions on imports of steel, textiles, and apparel—because of powerful opposition from threatened industries and their sympathizers. Thus, proponents of liberalization have suggested some new negotiating approaches designed to make liberalization more palatable, or at least to forestall intensified protection.

One such suggestion is that discriminatory quantitative restrictions be converted into nondiscriminatory tariffs and that the revenues from the tariffs be used to ease and promote the transfer of resources out of the protected industries. As these industries adapted, tariffs could eventually be lowered.[29] Even if the tariffs were not soon reduced, they would clearly be preferable to the quantitative restrictions now in force, for reasons already set forth.

Another suggestion is to introduce even more government discrimination into international trade, but with a view to expanding rather than restricting trade. At a modest level, this approach would follow the precedent of the Tokyo Round in limiting the direct benefits from newly adopted codes of government behavior to the countries that subscribe to the code, rather than extending the benefits to all countries on a nondiscriminatory basis. For example, governments might agree in their role as purchasers to acquire goods and services from foreign suppliers as readily as from domestic suppliers, but only from those foreign suppliers whose governments subscribed to the agreement. Advocates of this approach argue that countries are more likely to relax a nontariff barrier if the benefits are denied to those countries that refuse to pledge the same relaxation. Although initial nonsubscribers to an agreement should be allowed to join at any time, thereupon receiving all the benefits, there should be no "free riders."[30]

A more aggressive use of discrimination would extend it well beyond the negotiation of selected codes of behavior. For example, should it become clear that the Uruguay Round was failing due to the reluctance of the EEC to liberalize in such major sectors as agriculture, some would urge the United States to conclude a separate agreement with the Pacific Basin countries, as it did with Canada in 1987.[31] The hope, again, would be that other countries would eventually join such agreements.

An aggressively discriminatory strategy would run a serious risk, even though its avowed goal was eventual worldwide liberalization. Should the strategy fail, the globe might become divided into competing trading blocs, each with its own preferential, restrictive arrangements to which influential beneficiaries might become deeply attached. Be that as it may, the United States, for one, is unlikely to extend significant trade concessions to countries that do not reciprocate, given the widespread preception within the United States that the "playing field" of international competition is tilted against it.

SUMMARY

By the mid-1980s, protection against import competition was impos- ing costs too high to ignore. Although tariffs in the industrial countries were at historic lows, nontariff restrictions against imports had inten- sified markedly. According to a 1983 report of the U.N. Conference on Trade and Development, 98 percent of the products in international trade encountered such restriction in at least one country. Another study indicates that from 1980 to 1983, the share of restricted products in total manufactured imports rose from about 6 percent to nearly 13 per- cent in the United States, and from about 11 percent to almost 15 per- cent in the EEC. For agricultural products, the coverage was even more extensive: within a large group of industrial countries, nontariff restric- tions were applied to nearly 30 percent of all agricultural import items in 1984.

In both the manufacturing and the agricultural sectors, the costs to consumers of import restrictions have been appreciable. In the United States, many clothing items manufactured under a protective umbrella could be purchased abroad for half the cost. In Japan, consumers paid four times the world price for beef and lamb and almost three times the world price for rice, dairy products, and sugar because of barriers against agricultural imports.

While import restrictions have raised prices paid by consumers, they have had little success in preserving jobs in import-competing industries. Protection from import competition may improve the cash positions of these industries, but the improvement usually is invested in labor-saving equipment. In the industrial countries, the highly protected sectors, in- cluding textiles, clothing, and steel, have reported greater percentage employment declines than the rest of manufacturing. Moreover, the jobs that are saved by import restrictions may not be the intended blue-collar jobs, which often are replaced by white-collar positions.

Because the cost of import restraints is substantial and few jobs are preserved, the cost to consumers per job saved is excruciatingly high. For the United States in 1986, the annual consumer-cost-per-job-saved was estimated to be $42,000 in textiles and apparel, $105,000 in automobiles, and $1,000,000 in specialty steel. Other methods of aiding the unemployed would be far less costly to the consumer-taxpayer.

The inefficiencies associated with such protection imply that its aban- donment would yield sizable net gains. To illustrate, estimates have been made of the benefits to be realized from liberalizing trade in seven major agricultural commodity groups. By relinquishing their trade barriers and domestic interventions for these commodities, the developing- and industrial-market economies could have reaped total gains of about $64 billion (1980 dollars) per year, more than double the annual level of official development assistance from the industrial to the developing countries during 1980–84. Sizable as they are, all such estimates surely underestimate the true gains from liberalization, for the estimates do not include benefits from increased specialization leading to greater economies of scale, and for more efficient patterns of research and investment.

Concern is warranted not only over the intensification of protection but over its form. The new protectionism makes use of discriminatory quantitative restrictions rather than tariffs, in clear violation of the spirit, if not the letter, of the General Agreement on Tariffs and Trade—the multilateral treaty that laid the basis for the historic liberalization of trade following World War II. Because exporters may capture the rise in price generated by quantitative restrictions on their sales, and because the costs to consumers are not so obvious as with tariffs, quantitative restrictions have encountered relatively little opposition from exporters or consumers, while marshaling the usual support from protected industries. Thus, the new protectionism has become politically entrenched.

By flouting the established rules against discrimination and quantitative restrictions, governments have generated uncertainty that discourages investors from developing more competitive industry. The trend toward more arbitrary government intervention in international trade is also manifested in the growth of countertrade, under which a government requires that a foreign exporter who sells into its territory must arrange for a counterpurchase of goods made there. Even more than quantitative restrictions, countertrade conceals the cost of protection.

The goals sought through protection could be obtained by less costly methods, but those methods may not be politically feasible. The political feasibility of protectionism stems partly from popular underestimation of its total costs, partly from the wide dispersion of those costs, and partly from sheer chauvinism.

The strength of the new protectionism is being formally tested by a new round of international trade negotiations launched in Uruguay in 1986. More than previous negotiations, the Uruguay Round aims to reduce nontariff barriers to trade, including barriers in the agricultural and service sectors.

SUGGESTIONS FOR FURTHER READING

For analysis of the effects of international trade barriers, as well as brief discussions of trade policy, see Richard E. Caves and Ronald W. Jones, *World Trade and Payments: An Introduction,* 4th ed. (Boston: Little, Brown, 1985), chs. 11–14; and Peter B. Kenen, *The International Economy* (Englewood Cliffs, N.J.: Prentice-Hall, 1985), chs. 8–10.

Broad coverage of trade-policy issues can be found in the following: C. Michael Aho and Jonathan David Aronson, *Trade Talks: America Better Listen!* (New York: Council on Foreign Relations, 1985); Robert E. Baldwin and Anne O. Krueger, eds., *The Structure and Evolution of Recent U.S. Trade Policy* (Chicago: University of Chicago Press, 1984); Robert E. Baldwin and J. David Richardson, *International Trade and Finance: Readings,* 3d. ed. (Boston: Little, Brown, 1986); and William R. Cline, ed., *Trade Policy in the 1980s* (Cambridge, Mass.: MIT Press, 1983).

Also see the references cited in the notes to this chapter.

APPENDIX: THE CASE FOR FREE TRADE

The essence of the argument for free trade can be expressed in a simple illustration. Suppose that a certain physician can clean her house in half the time taken by her maid, but prefers to spend that time seeing patients in her office. Is this choice financially wise? It would seem so, since the typical doctor earns at least twice as much per hour as the typical maid. Thus, the arrangement between the doctor and the maid is beneficial to both, even though the doctor is more efficient in both medicine and housekeeping.

Similarly, even if one nation is more efficient than another across the broad spectrum of industrial activity, both nations can benefit from commerce between them. For example, suppose that in "Moreland" each "unit" of resources can produce either twenty tons of rice or two tons of aluminum, while in "Lessland" each comparable unit can produce only fifteen tons of rice or one tone of aluminum. Without trade between the two nations, one ton of aluminum will be worth ten tons of rice in Moreland, but will command fifteen tons of rice in Lessland. Thus, Moreland would have an incentive to ship aluminum to Lessland in exchange for rice, even though Moreland can produce more rice with a unit of resources than Lessland can. Correspondingly, Lessland would have an incentive to ship rice to Moreland, where fifteen tons exchange for one and one-half tons of aluminum, instead of the one ton it buys in Lessland.

Once commerce is allowed between the two countries, the price ratio between rice and aluminum will settle somewhere between the prices that had prevailed in the two countries without trade, so that both can benefit from the exchange of goods. (A qualification: if total supply and demand are such that the price ratio settles at a level that had prevailed in one of the countries before trade, then only the other country can benefit from the opportunity to deal at a price ratio new to it.)

This simple example illustrates the well-established principle of comparative advantage—the principle that a nation can find a market, to its benefit, for the goods that it produces most efficiently (or least inefficiently) by comparison with the rest of the world, even though that nation exhibits a lower absolute level of efficiency in every good. This principle, enunciated by David Ricardo in 1817, is the cornerstone of the case for free trade as opposed to autarky. More generally, it is possible to show that for any given income distribution, free trade maximizes world economic welfare, provided competition is unfettered and markets are working well.

NOTES

1. See Tables 2–2 and 2–4.
2. There is more than one way to measure an average tariff level. Table 2–1 essentially weighs each tariff rate by the percentage of imports to which the tariff applies, while a simple average would weigh each tariff rate equally.
3. Organization for Economic Cooperation and Development, *Costs and Benefits of Protection* (Paris: OECD, 1985), p. 28.
4. Ibid., p. 29.
5. Shaileudra J. Anjaria, Naheed Kirmani, and Arne B. Petersen, *Trade Policy Issues and Developments,* Occasional Paper No. 38 (Washington, D.C.: International Monetary Fund, 1985), pp. 22, 89.
6. This estimate excludes macroeconomic repercussions. See Dorothy Christelow, "Japan's Intangible Barriers to Trade in Manufactures," *Federal Reserve Bank of New York Quarterly Review,* Winter 1985–86: 17.
7. OECD, *Costs and Benefits,* pp. 13, 46.
8. Ibid., pp. 18–19.

9. Ibid., p. 14.
10. Ibid., p. 48.
11. World Bank, *World Development Report 1986* (New York: Oxford University Press, 1986), p. 110.
12. OECD, *Costs and Benefits,* pp. 15, 57.
13. Ibid., p. 14.
14. Ibid., p. 60.
15. Ibid., p. 15. For an estimate that the cost had risen to $420,000 per job in 1982, see Gary Clyde Hufbauer, Diane T. Berliner, and Kimberly Ann Elliott, *Trade Protection in the United States: 31 Case Studies* (Washington, D.C.: Institute for International Economics, 1986), p. 224.
16. World Bank, *Development Report 1986,* p. 131.
17. See, for example, Anne O. Krueger, *Trade and Employment in Developing Countries,* vol. 3, *Synthesis and Conclusions* (Chicago: University of Chicago Press, 1983). For a somewhat contrary view, see Jeffrey Sachs, "Trade and Exchange Rate Policies in Growth-Oriented Adjustment Programs," in Vittoria Corbo, Morris Goldstein, and Mohsin Kahn, eds., *Growth-Oriented Adjustment Programs* (Washington, D.C.: International Monetary Fund and the World Bank, 1987), pp. 291–325.
18. John W. Evans, *The Kennedy Round in American Trade Policy* (Cambridge, Mass.: Harvard University Press, 1971), pp. 48, 85–86.
19. Jan Tumlir, *Protectionism: Trade Policy in Democratic Societies* (Washington, D.C.: American Enterprise Institute for Public Policy Research, 1985), p. 39.
20. Ibid., pp. 38–39.
21. Sidney Weintraub, "Selective Trade Liberalization and Restriction," in Ernest H. Preeg, ed., *Hard Bargaining Ahead: U.S. Trade Policy and Developing Countries* (Washington, D.C.: Overseas Development Council, 1985), p. 177.
22. OECD, *Costs and Benefits,* p. 35.
23. This section draws heavily upon the following two publications of the Organization for Economic Cooperation and Development: *East-West Trade: Recent Developments in Countertrade* (Paris: OECD, 1981) and *Countertrade: Developing Country Practices* (Paris: OECD, 1985).
24. International Monetary Fund, *Annual Report on Exchange Arrangements and Exchange Restrictions, 1986* (Washington, D.C.: IMF, 1986), p. 33.
25. Another important bilateral device is the practice of "offset." Under this device, government purchasing agencies choose among competing foreign suppliers partly on the basis of supplier willingness to either (1) produce some of the desired goods within the purchasing country, or (2) "offset" in some other way the budgetary, employment, or foreign

exchange "losses" presumed to occur when the country buys from a foreign rather than a domestic supplier. Offsets are most commonly employed in connection with major government purchases of capital goods, such as military aircraft, and often serve to transfer technology from the foreign supplier to the purchasing country.

26. The data in this paragraph are from International Monetary Fund, *Annual Report on Exchange Arrangements and Exchange Restrictions, 1983* (Washington, D.C.: IMF, 1983), pp. 44–46, and IMF, *Annual Report on Exchange . . . 1986*, pp. 32–33.

27. See Harry G. Johnson, "Optimal Trade Intervention in the Presence of Domestic Distortions," in R.E. Baldwin, et al., *Trade, Growth, and the Balance of Payments* (Chicago: Rand-McNally, 1965), pp. 3–34.

28. Robert E. Baldwin, *The Political Economy of U.S. Import Policy* (Cambridge, Mass.: MIT Press, 1985), pp. 175–80; Robert E. Baldwin, "Trade Policies in Developed Countries," in R.W. Jones and P.B. Kenen, eds., *Handbook of International Economics*, vol. 1 (New York: Elsevier, 1984), pp. 572–82; Real P. Lavergne, *The Political Economy of U.S. Tariffs: An Empirical Analysis* (New York: Academic Press, 1983); and Norman S. Fieleke, "The Tariff Structure for Manufacturing Industries in the United States: A Test of Some Traditional Explanations," *Columbia Journal of World Business* 11 (Winter 1976): 98–104.

29. Gary Clyde Hufbauer and Jeffrey J. Schott, *Trading for Growth: The Next Round of Trade Negotiations* (Washington, D.C.: Institute for International Economics, 1985), pp. 16–17.

30. Ibid., pp. 19–22.

31. Lawrence B. Krause, "Agenda for a New GATT Round," in Robert E. Baldwin and J. David Richardson, eds., *Current U.S. Trade Policy: Analysis, Agenda, and Administration* (Cambridge, Mass.: National Bureau of Economic Research, 1986), pp. 41–42.

3 LESS DEVELOPED COUNTRIES IN ARREARS

Of all the problems surveyed in this book, none has been both so ominous and so unrelenting as the developing-country debt problem. At the end of 1986, fifty-seven of the poorer, or "developing," countries were in arrears on their international obligations, more than double the number at the end of 1980. Over the same six years, the total amount of such arrears sextupled, increasing to $43.9 billion.[1] Not only are many developing countries behind in their international payments, but some of their governments have issued statements tantamount to declarations of default, although none has formally repudiated its debt.

What is the precise nature of this debt problem, and how did it develop? Is the world economy in peril? What remedies are available?

THE NATURE OF THE PROBLEM

Simply put, the problem is a widespread failure of debtors in developing countries to pay their foreign debts on schedule. This failure was first dramatized in August 1982 by the extension of billions of dollars in emergency credit to Mexico to enable that nation to avoid outright default. But the waters had been troubled for some time before the Mexican payments crisis. The number of countries in arrears on international payments had risen from fifteen in 1975 to thirty-two at the end of 1981, and the number of developing countries reported by the World Bank as obtaining debt relief had risen from six in 1980 to thirteen in each of the years, 1981 and 1982.[2]

According to the IMF (International Monetary Fund), the total indebtedness of more than 130 developing countries and territories amounted to $849 billion at the end of 1982, the year when a serious debt problem became generally recognized. By the end of 1986, the figure had risen to $1,114 billion. As shown in Table 3–1, official agencies of the debtor countries guaranteed repayment of most of this debt (including, of course, the indebtedness of the agencies themselves). Still, a substantial portion is the debt of private parties without any such guarantee.

The guarantees have not sufficed to ensure punctual payments. As the table indicates, debt-servicing problems have recently afflicted countries accounting for more than half of the total debt. These countries either incurred arrears during 1985 or arranged a rescheduling of their debt payments during the period from end-1983 to end-1986. Moreover, the total indebtedness of this group of countries increased between 1979 and 1986 at about the same percentage rate as the indebtedness of the countries without such problems.

Of special significance is developing-country indebtedness to commercial banks. Following the Mexican payments crisis, the fear arose that major banks might be forced into insolvency by an inability to collect interest or principal on this debt. It is estimated that about half of developing-country debt at end-1986 was owed to commercial banks;[3] well over half of this debt probably was owed by problem debtors (countries with recent debt-servicing problems).[4]

A major part of the lending to developing countries has been by commercial banks in the United States. For U.S. banks with significant foreign operations, claims on the developing countries at the end of 1986 amounted to more than $108 billion, or nearly 7 percent of their total assets and 94 percent of their total shareholders' capital. (See Table 3–2.) The potential threat to solvency from developing-country defaults has been much greater for the nine largest U.S. banks, for their loans to the developing countries at end-1986 were equivalent to nearly 154 percent of their total capital. Viewed as a collective, then, these nine banks would have been bankrupted if something like two-thirds of their loans to the developing countries had clearly become worthless in 1986.

This threat seemed much greater during and immediately after the 1982 crisis, partly because bank capital then was even less adequate

Table 3–1. External Debt of Developing Countries, by Class of Creditor, End of Year, 1979–86[a] (in billions of U.S. dollars).

	1979	1980	1981	1982	1983	1984	1985	1986
All developing countries								
Total debt	534	634	748	849	900	949	1,019	1,114
Short-term	109	145	180	204	188	192	174	170
Long-term	425	489	568	644	712	757	845	943
Unguaranteed[b]	79	93	116	133	130	128	130	133
Guaranteed[b]	346	396	452	511	582	629	715	811
To official creditors	169	192	217	246	272	298	341	400
To financial institutions	140	163	190	214	258	276	317	344
To other private creditors	37	40	45	51	52	54	57	66
Developing countries with recent debt-servicing problems								
Total debt	318	384	462	527	547	570	593	634
Short-term	58	84	104	120	94	96	71	68
Long-term	260	300	358	407	453	475	523	566
To official creditors	81	94	109	125	144	161	184	213
To financial institutions[c]	99	115	136	153	188	200	228	239
To other private creditors[d]	80	91	113	129	120	114	111	115

Note: Detail may not add to totals shown because of rounding.

[a]Excludes debt owed to the International Monetary Fund.

[b]By an official agency of the debtor country.

[c]Covers only public and publicly guaranteed debt.

[d]Includes all unguaranteed debt on the presumption that this is owed mainly to private creditors.

Source: International Monetary Fund, *World Economic Outlook*, October 1987, World Economic and Financial Surveys (Washington, D.C.: IMF, 1987), pp. 104–07.

Table 3–2. U.S. Bank Claims on Developing Countries, 1978–86.

End of Year	All U.S. Banks with Significant Foreign Banking Operations			Nine Money Center Banks		
	Billions of Dollars	As Percent of Total Bank Assets	As Percent of Total Bank Capital[a]	Billions of Dollars	As Percent of Total Bank Assets	As Percent of Total Bank Capital[a]
1978	72.3	8.8	158.7	47.9	11.3	239.5
1979	81.8	8.7	164.3	54.6	11.2	249.3
1980	96.8	9.1	169.8	63.5	12.0	264.6
1981	115.8	9.9	184.7	74.0	13.1	283.5
1982	128.3	10.2	181.7	82.0	13.9	282.8
1983	132.9	9.9	167.6	84.7	14.6	268.9
1984	129.9	9.2	140.9	83.8	14.2	228.3
1985	119.0	7.8	112.9	78.3	12.6	185.1
1986	108.6	6.7	93.5	71.7	11.2	153.5

Note: Data are for domestic and foreign offices of the banking organizations and cover only cross-border and nonlocal currency lending.

[a]Capital includes equity, debentures, and reserves for loan losses.

Source: U.S. Board of Governors of the Federal Reserve System, "Country Exposure Lending Survey," Statistical Release E.16(126), various issues; and staff of the Board of Governors.

to absorb massive defaults by the developing countries. (See Table 3–2.) In February 1983, Paul Volcker, then Chairman of the Board of Governors of the Federal Reserve System, summarized the danger:

> The situation that emerged last year was unique in its scope and potential effects. It involved several major debtors at the same time, and threatened to spread to others, weak and strong alike. It is this potential for cascading liquidity pressures, undermining the stability of the financial system, that has demanded prompt and forceful action . . . to protect the stability of the financial system as a whole and our own economy. . . . The international financial system is not separable from our domestic banking and credit system. The same institutions are involved in both markets. A shock to one would be a shock to the other. . . . We are talking about dealing with a threat to the recovery, the jobs, and the prosperity of our own country, a threat essentially without parallel in the postwar period.[5]

If the economies of creditor countries such as the United States were threatened, so were the economies of the debtors. Not only would debtor-country exports have suffered as a result of any industrial-country recession sparked by developing-country defaults, but such serious defaults would have severely discouraged new bank lending to the developing countries for years, further depressing their economies. While the imminence and severity of the threat diminished after 1983, the threat remained.

Essentially, then, the problem is how best to restore the creditworthiness of the developing countries with debt-servicing problems. A rough idea of the degree to which that creditworthiness has been impaired can be obtained by examining the discounts at which bank loans to such countries are traded in the secondary market. Table 3–3 provides some data of this sort for early December of 1987. Each of the countries listed was classified by the World Bank as a major borrower, that is, as owing more than $17 billion in long-term debt at end-1985. As indicated in the table, buyers were willing to pay little more than half of the original loan value in order to acquire loans made to Chile, Mexico, or Venezuela, and loans to Argentina and Brazil were selling for even larger discounts.

Thus, the international debt problem has been both sizable and persistent. Why? What went wrong? Unforeseen changes in the world economy played an important role. In addition, many observers believe that both borrowers and lenders failed to exercise due prudence. Finally, some analysts cite the curtailment of bank lending after the Mexican crisis.

Table 3-3. Trading Prices for Selected Sovereign Debt, 10 December 1987 (in cents per U.S. dollar of original loan value).

Country	Price Quotation Range
Argentina	36–38
Brazil	45–47
Chile	60–61
Mexico	51–53
Venezuela	57–60

Source: Bernard J. Wolfson, "Sovereign Debt Trading Prices Expected to Slide Further in '88," *Journal of Commerce*, 15 December 1987.

CHANGES IN THE WORLD ECONOMY

Although marked differences exist among the developing countries, the fact that debt rescheduling has been widespread suggests a common underlying cause or set of causal factors. One such cause is slack demand for developing-country exports as a result of recession and sluggish economic growth in the industrial countries. Because of recessions during the early 1980s, total demand in the industrial countries grew at an annual average rate of only 2.2 percent from 1979 through 1986, compared to a rate of nearly 3.5 percent during the period 1969–79. In 1982, the year of the Mexican payments crisis, demand in the industrial countries declined 0.3 percent.[6]

Partly because of slow growth in demand, the prices of what many developing countries sold to the rest of the world declined after 1980, and declined further than the less flexible prices of the items they imported. For problem debtors, export prices fell by 18 percent in relation to import prices over the years 1981–86, meaning that those countries would have had to increase the volume of their exports by about this percentage just to maintain the same inflow of goods from the rest of the world.[7] By contrast, the same countries had enjoyed a marked rise in their terms of trade—in the ratio of their export prices to import prices—over the previous decade. Thus, slower world economic growth made it harder for the developing countries to earn the foreign exchange needed to service their debts. The total dollar value of developing-country exports had increased at an annual average rate of nearly 24 percent from 1969 to 1980, but then *decreased* at an annual average rate of 4.2 percent over the period 1981–86.[8]

Another cause of debt repayment difficulty was the sharp rise in interest rates during 1978–81 and the persistence of relatively high rates for some years thereafter. From a level of less than 7 percent during 1973–77, the average interest rate on new, long-term international loans to developing-country governments climbed to 11.1 percent in 1981, then declined irregularly to 8 percent in 1985.[9] Interest cost per dollar of indebtedness shot up for the developing countries after 1977 not only because interest rates went up, but because a marked decrease occurred in the proportion of debt for which interest rates were fixed over the long term, with the result that rates on much outstanding debt were revised upward. Of the total long-term public (or publicly guaranteed) debt of the developing countries, some 45 percent consisted of variable interest–rate loans in 1984, up from 25 percent in 1977.[10] This rise in the share of floating-interest debt reflected the effort of bank lenders to avoid getting locked into fixed rates of interest earnings that might later be exceeded by the interest rates the banks were obliged to pay their depositors. Bank loans accounted for nearly half of developing-country debt at the end of 1985.[11]

What was responsible for these extraordinarily high interest rates—rates that, on dollar-denominated obligations, reached record highs in the early 1980s? Part of the explanation is that prices in the industrial countries rose at double-digit or near double-digit rates during 1979–81, when the Organization of Petroleum Exporting Countries sharply raised oil prices. Faced with higher inflation, creditors demanded higher interest rates as compensation for the loss of purchasing power on the sums they loaned. Another reason for high interest rates was the adoption of anti-inflationary monetary policies that constrained the growth of lending in a number of industrial countries. In addition, fiscal policy changes in the United States after 1981 resulted in rapidly increasing federal budget deficits and greater borrowing demands, which also exerted upward pressure on interest rates.

The combination of high interest rates and slack demand made matters doubly difficult for debtors in many developing countries. For example, an exporter in Brazil might well have received fewer dollars for his goods at the same time that he required more dollars to service his outstanding debt. The estimated impact of these external shocks at the onset of the debt crisis in 1981–82 is shown in Table 3–4 for a

Table 3-4. Impact of External Shocks on the Balance of
Payments in Selected Developing Countries, 1981-82.

Country	Average Annual Percent of GNP
Argentina	− 6.4
Brazil	− 8.6
Chile	− 13.3
Colombia	− 8.3
Egypt	− 1.2
India	− 4.2
Indonesia	5.4
Ivory Coast	− 18.9
Jamaica	− 29.4
Kenya	− 19.0
Korea	− 21.7
Mexico	1.0
Morocco	− 9.7
Nigeria	3.8
Peru	− 5.6
Philippines	− 10.1
Tanzania	− 14.3
Thailand	− 10.1
Tunisia	1.9
Yugoslavia	− 10.0

Note: External shocks are defined as the impact on the balance of payments of: (a) changes in the terms of trade; (b) a decline in the growth rate of world demand for a country's exports; and (c) increases in interest rates. Data show the change from 1976-78 to 1981-82.

Source: World Bank, *World Development Report 1985* (New York: Oxford University Press, 1985), p. 56.

sampling of countries. Except for the countries that export oil, all experienced a negative net shock. Brazil's balance of payments with the rest of the world was worsened, from the 1976-78 level, by the equivalent of 8.6 percent of the nation's gross product—an experience that was fairly representative for the countries listed.

In addition to high interest rates and sluggish world demand, another factor sometimes cited as a cause of the debt problem is the increased flow of deposits into the commercial banks from oil-exporting countries whose oil revenues soared along with oil prices during 1979-80. Without this influx, it is said, the banks would have made fewer loans to the

Table 3–5. Total Liabilities of Banks in the United States and Liabilities to Oil-Exporting Countries, 1977–81.

End of Year	Total Liabilities of Insured Commercial Banks (billions of dollars) (1)	Liabilities to Oil-Exporting Countries (billions of dollars)[a] (2)	Column 2 as Percent of Column 1 (3)
1977	$1,260.1	$13.8	1.1
1978	1,420.9	13.7	1.0
1979	1,594.9	22.1	1.4
1980	1,748.1	22.3	1.3
1981	1,910.8	19.7	1.0

[a]Liabilities payable in U.S. dollars to Ecuador, Venezuela, Indonesia, Bahrain, Iran, Iraq, Kuwait, Oman, Qatar, Saudi Arabia, United Arab Emirates, Algeria, Gabon, Libya, and Nigeria.

Source: *Federal Reserve Bulletin*, various issues, Table 3.17; *Statistical Abstract of the United States, 1986* (Washington, D.C.: U.S. Bureau of the Census, 1985), Table No. 827.

oil-importing developing countries that later encountered payment difficulties. In fact, according to the published data, the inflow of funds from the oil-exporting countries was not very large in relation to the funds utilized by banks from other sources. As shown in Table 3–5, the year-end liabilities of banks in the United States to residents of the oil-exporting countries did indeed rise in relation to the banks' total liabilities between 1978 and 1979–80, but not beyond 1.4 percent of the total. For the bigger banks, the percentage may have been significantly higher, especially after taking into account the inflows from oil-exporting countries into these banks' numerous foreign offices.[12] But even if these "inflows" are considered large, they represented mainly a shift of preexisting deposits from non-OPEC to OPEC ownership, rather than an infusion of new cash into the banking system. In any event, being endowed with the wherewithal to make bad loans would hardly be sufficient excuse for making them. Thus, the inflow of "oil money" into the commercial banks in 1979–80 should not be treated as a major cause of the debt crisis, certainly not on a par with the worldwide economic slowdown and high interest rates.

IMPRUDENCE IN BORROWING AND LENDING

Are we to conclude, then, that the lenders and borrowers themselves bear no responsibility for their predicament, that they are the blameless victims of harsh external circumstances? Many analysts insist that numerous commercial banks and developing countries had blithely entered into loan agreements that were at best uneconomic, if not profligate.[13] The banks turned down the spigot only after the Mexican crisis in 1982 brought them to their senses. In short, both borrowers and lenders should have known better and could have weathered the external shocks much more easily if only they had been more prudent.

There is no disputing the fact that both total bank lending and net bank exposure to the developing countries increased at exceptional rates in the years leading up to the 1982 crisis. As shown in Table 3–1, total outstanding long-term loans to these countries by financial institutions increased from $140 billion at end-1979 to $214 billion at end-1982, or 15 percent per year. For countries that in recent years have had debt-servicing problems, the percentage rate of increase was similar. For U.S. banks with significant foreign operations, total outstanding loans to the developing countries grew from $82 billion to $128 billion from 1979 to 1982—or by 16 percent per year—while for the nine largest U.S. banks the total rose from $55 billion to $82 billion, or 14 percent per year. (See Table 3–2.) Not only did outstanding U.S. bank loans to the developing countries increase very rapidly, but they increased faster than total bank assets over these years, as shown by the second column in Table 3–2.

Nevertheless, to show that loan growth was rapid is not to prove that it was foolish in the light of what was generally known at the time. To be sure, in retrospect the managements of a number of banks came to regret lending so liberally to certain developing countries. Hindsight is better than foresight, especially when a recession is involved, for recessions have a way of converting seemingly sound loans into ones that any fool should have known would be unsound. On the other hand, booms do entail excesses, and many developing countries had been enjoying relatively high, if not booming, growth for some years prior to the 1982 recession. The relevant question, then, is not whether the banks and the developing countries might have been better off if there had been less lending—they certainly would have been. The relevant question is whether on the basis of the information available at the time they should have had the foresight to be a lot more conservative.

Several considerations suggest that, in general, such prescience should not have been expected. To begin with, it is natural for most developing countries to borrow from the rest of the world; if they truly are developing economies, they will offer profitable investment opportunities for foreign lenders and will attract net capital inflows, just as the United States did during its early development. Second, for many years prior to 1982 the losses experienced by banks on international loans had been proportionately lower than on domestic loans. Third, for a number of years before the 1982 recession, many developing countries had compiled much better records of economic growth than the industrial countries had.

Fourth, widely distributed forecasts by prestigious international organizations significantly underestimated the declines in economic growth rates that were to accompany the recession. For example, in June 1981 the IMF projected an output growth rate of 4.9 percent for the non-oil developing countries for 1981, whereas the actual rate turned out to be 3.1 percent. In April 1982 the growth rate projected for these countries for 1982 was 3.8 percent, whereas the actual was 1.7 percent. Similarly, at the end of 1981 the OECD projected a growth rate of 1.25 percent for the OECD countries for 1982, while the actual rate was −.5 percent.[14]

Fifth, not until 1982, or 1981 at the earliest, did the officially published statistics on "creditworthiness" clearly signify a distinct deterioration for the non-oil developing countries collectively—apart from the "deterioration" of 1974–78, which the world surmounted with little apparent difficulty. (See Table 3–6.) To be sure, the data initially published for 1981 (in parentheses) did show that the official monetary reserves of these countries in relation to their imports of goods and services had fallen to a comparatively low level and that debt service (payments of interest and principal) had come to claim a relatively large fraction of the receipts generated by exports. But these initial data also showed long-term external debt to be well below the highest levels attained in preceding years in relation to both exports and gross domestic production. With the benefit of hindsight, debt service as a percentage of exports was the most reliable indicator, but that fact was not so obvious in 1981 before the crisis erupted.

Sixth, if one can judge from the rate at which new loans were being made from 1979–82, official lenders shared the optimism of the commercial banks and other private lenders regarding the debt repayment capacity of the developing countries. Over this period, the year-to-year increases in developing-country long-term debt owed to official creditors were little different, in percentage terms, from the increases in such debt

Table 3-6.   Debt Indicators for Non-oil Developing Countries
Published by International Monetary Fund, 1973-82.

| Year | Official Reserves as Percent of Imports of Goods and Services | Long-term External Debt as Percent of | | Debt Service on Long-term External Debt as Percent of Exports of Goods and Services |
		Exports of Goods and Services	Gross Domestic Product	
1973	32	89	17	14
1974	22	81	16	12
1975	19	98	18	14
1976	24	103	21	14
1977	26	105	22	14
1978	27	111	24	17
1979	23	102	23	18
1980	18	93	22	16
1981	17(16)	103(96)	24(21)	21(21)
1982	17	109	25	22

Note: Reserves and debt are for end of year. Debt service consists of payments of interest and principal. Numbers in parentheses are estimates published in 1981; other data were published in 1982.

Source: International Monetary Fund: *World Economic Outlook* (June 1981), Occasional Paper No. 4 (Washington, D.C.: IMF, 1981), pp. 130, 133, 135; and *World Economic Outlook* (April 1982), Occasional Paper No. 9 (Washington, D.C.: IMF, 1982), pp. 169, 171, 173.

owed to private creditors. (See table 3-1.) It seems that official lenders perceived the need for restraint no more clearly than did the private lenders driven by business motives.

Finally, even though bank loans outstanding to the developing countries continued to rise rapidly in 1981 and 1982, the banks were not altogether oblivious to the gathering crisis, as they raised the risk premiums charged on loans to Brazil, Argentina, and Mexico well before the end of 1981, and well before debt repayment problems for these countries became widely publicized. (See Figure 3-1.) Later, of course, it became clear that this precautionary measure had been too late and too little.

Figure 3-1. Average Loan Rate Spreads (over London Interbank–Offered Rate) Charged to Selected Borrowing Countries, First-Quarter 1979 through Second-Quarter 1982.

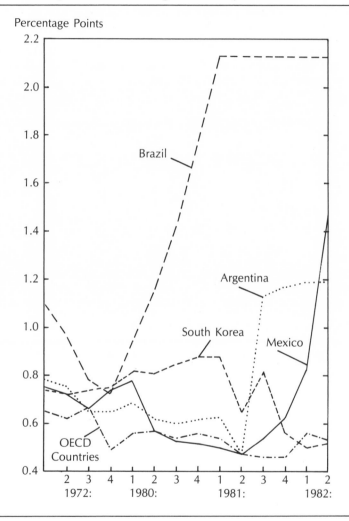

Percentage Points

Source: Andrew S. Carron, "Financial Crisis: Recent Experience in U.S. and International Markets," *Brookings Papers on Economic Activity 1982: 2, p. 413.*

FAULTY POLICIES IN DEVELOPING COUNTRIES

Aside from the question of whether the precrisis lending and borrowing should have seemed reasonable at the time, how circumspect were the developing countries in their economic policies more generally? Not surprisingly, data now available suggest that prudence within some of the borrowing countries was waning at about the time that the loan risk premiums were escalating. Aside from data now on hand for debt indicators such as those in Table 3–6, the data in Table 3–7 show that domestic saving and investment in the developing countries moved downward in relation to gross domestic product (GDP) from 1980 through 1982, while the share of consumption increased. It was as

Table 3–7. Consumption, Gross Domestic Investment, and Gross Domestic Saving, as a Percentage of Gross Domestic Product, for Selected Country Groupings and Years.

Country Group and Indicator	1973	1980	1981	1982
Developing countries				
Consumption	76.7	75.6	77.2	78.1
Investment	24.1	26.7	26.0	24.6
Saving	23.3	24.4	22.8	21.9
Low-income Asia				
Consumption	75.4	75.8	76.8	75.8
Investment	24.8	27.2	25.4	25.7
Saving	24.6	24.2	23.2	24.2
Low-income Africa				
Consumption	85.7	91.0	91.6	93.1
Investment	17.0	19.2	18.5	16.9
Saving	14.3	9.0	8.4	6.9
Middle-income oil importers				
Consumption	77.0	77.2	78.5	79.4
Investment	24.9	26.9	25.9	23.8
Saving	23.0	22.8	21.5	20.6
Middle-income oil exporters				
Consumption	76.8	71.0	74.0	76.4
Investment	22.3	26.7	27.6	25.4
Saving	23.2	29.0	26.0	23.6
Industrial-market economies				
Consumption	75.0	78.4	78.4	80.1
Investment	24.7	22.5	21.9	20.1
Saving	25.0	21.6	21.6	19.9

Source: World Bank, *World Development Report 1986* (Washington, D.C.: Oxford University Press, 1986), p. 157.

if loans from abroad were being used to finance relatively higher consumption rather than investment.

This inference must be qualified, however. As indicated in Table 3–7, similar declines occurred in saving and investment shares in the industrial-market economies. Was prudence on the wane in those countries as well? Perhaps, but a less subjective explanation can be offered. The pervasiveness of the relative declines in saving and investment suggests that the main cause of the declines was not growing recklessness but the worldwide decline in output and the severe recession that afflicted many countries during this period.

The recession, rather than general imprudence, was also largely responsible for the sharp deterioration in the developing countries' creditworthiness as measured by the conventional indicators. Consider the ratio of debt to exports in Table 3–8. This percentage rose smartly between 1980 and 1982, both for all developing countries and for countries with recent debt-servicing problems. One reason is that developing-country exports fell off—rather than increasing as usual— because of the recession in the industrial countries. Thus, total merchandise exports of the developing countries during 1981–82 averaged $47 billion less per year than the $631 billion figure for 1980.

As a crude experiment, suppose that these merchandise exports had remained at the 1980 level while all other international transactions of the developing countries during 1981 and 1982 were as reported. With the greater export receipts, the external debt of the developing countries would have increased less than it did, and the ratio of the lower debt to the higher exports would have been 95 percent in 1982—the "hypothetical" ratio in Table 3–8—rather than the 120 percent actually realized. Similarly, for problem debtors the 1982 ratio would have been 195 percent, rather than 241 percent. While these computations may give some idea of the immediate impact of the recession on the creditworthiness of the developing countries, the computations make no provision for the adverse impact of the considerable rise in interest rates, another factor beyond the control of any developing country.

All of this is not to say that faulty policies played no role in the gathering crisis. Even the hypothetical ratios shown in Table 3–8 are high by historical standards, especially the ratio for problem countries. Detailed examination of the circumstances of individual problem debtors clearly reveals that some became less than circumspect in their policies, and that lenders should have been more alert to that tendency.[15] By contrast, some other developing countries pursued more judicious

Table 3-8. External Debt Relative to Exports of Goods and Services, for Developing Countries.

Description	External Debt (billions of U.S. dollars)	Exports of Goods and Services (billions of U.S. dollars)	Debt as Percent of Exports
All developing countries			
Actual			
1979	534	587	91
1980	634	777	82
1981	748	788	95
1982	849	707	120
Hypothetical 1982[a]	754	791	95
Countries with recent debt-servicing problems			
Actual			
1978	242	135	180
1979	318	193	165
1980	384	253	152
1981	462	248	186
1982	527	219	241
Hypothetical 1982[a]	486	249	195

[a]Assumes that exports of *merchandise* were the same in 1981 and 1982 as in 1980.

Source: International Monetary Fund: *World Economic Outlook,* October 1987 (Washington, D.C.: IMF, 1987), pp. 78, 84, 104, 106, 109; and *World Economic Outlook,* October 1986 (Washington, D.C.: IMF, 1986), pp. 82, 103, 107.

policies and, partly because of those policies, avoided the necessity to reschedule their debt payments. This is persuasive evidence that the recession and higher interest rates were not solely responsible for the severity of the crisis.

More specifically, a number of developing countries in Asia suffered no debt crisis during this period, partly because they had not allowed their currencies to rise to unrealistically high values in the foreign exchange markets. Living more for the moment, some other governments had supported the foreign exchange values of their currencies (partly through purchases of their own currencies with borrowed foreign currencies) at levels that made imports seem cheap. The likelihood that their overvalued currencies would have to come down sharply became obvious to many residents of these countries, who converted substantial amounts of their own currencies into foreign currencies while the latter were still available at bargain rates. This "capital flight" was a powerful vote of no-confidence in government policy for the countries afflicted. The flight put growing downward pressure on the foreign exchange values of the currencies being sold, and those values eventually collapsed. Before the collapse, however, the afflicted countries considerably enlarged their gross indebtedness and also undermined their export industries, whose goods became less competitive when priced in overvalued currencies. Such countries were more vulnerable to the adverse external shocks and more prone to enter into the debt crisis.

Although capital flight is very difficult to measure, and difficult even to define with precision, a rough idea of the orders of magnitude can be gained from Table 3–9. For a number of the countries listed, capital fleeing the country over the period 1979–82 is estimated to

Table 3–9. Capital Flight and Gross Capital Inflows in Selected Countries, 1979–82.

Country	Capital Flight (billions of U.S. dollars)[a]	Gross Capital Inflows (billions of U.S. dollars)[b]	Capital Flight as a Percentage of Gross Capital Flows
Venezuela	22.0	16.1	136.6
Argentina	19.2	29.5	65.1
Mexico	26.5	55.4	47.8
Uruguay	0.6	2.2	27.3
Portugal	1.8	8.6	20.9
Brazil	3.5	43.9	8.0
Turkey	0.4	7.9	5.1
Korea	0.9	18.7	4.8

[a]Data are estimates. Capital flight is defined as the sum of gross capital inflows and the current account deficit, less increases in official foreign reserves. For some countries (notably Argentina and Venezuela), the estimate may overstate capital flight to the extent that unreported imports and normal portfolio investment abroad are included.

[b]Defined as the sum of changes in gross foreign debt (public and private) and net foreign direct investment.

Source: World Bank, *World Development Report 1985* (New York: Oxford University Press, 1985), p. 64.

have equaled more than 20 percent of the total capital flowing in.[16] In other words, rather than financing investment in the country, some of the capital flowing in merely served to finance an offsetting outflow. This recycling presented a special problem. A substantial portion of the funds flowing out were invested in assets yielding returns that were unreported to the developing-country governments or were otherwise immune from taxation by those governments, while, on the other hand, the same governments generally paid, or guaranteed payment of, interest on the funds flowing into their countries. It was as if a firm in a developing country had borrowed from abroad, with the aid of its government's guarantee of repayment, and then invested the proceeds of the loan abroad in a form that would yield no current return to the developing country.[17]

As noted above, countries with highly overvalued currencies were especially likely to suffer from capital flight. The contrast in exchange-rate behavior is illustrated by the experience of South Korea, on the one hand, and of Argentina and Mexico, on the other hand. For each country, the change in the real effective exchange rate reported in Table 3–10 measures the change in the average foreign exchange value of the currency after allowing for differing inflation rates between the country and its trading partners. Thus, the 51 percent appreciation in Argentina's effective exchange rate from 1978 to 1981 really means that Argentine *goods* became, on average, 51 percent more expensive in relation to foreign goods, after taking into account both the higher inflation in Argentina and the average change in the foreign currency prices quoted for its currency. Mexico suffered a smaller, but still significant, loss in competitiveness over the same period. In the subsequent adjustment, marked depreciations occurred in the foreign exchange rates of both the Argentine and Mexican currencies. On the other hand, South Korea, which avoided a debt crisis, experienced little change in its real effective exchange rate over this period. Similarly, as can be seen in Table 3–9, South Korea was much less troubled by capital flight than Argentina and Mexico were.

While currency overvaluation is the predominant cause of capital flight, it is not the only cause. In some developing countries, capital flight has been provoked by government controls that suppressed domestic interest rates below levels that could be earned abroad. Political instability and threats that assets might be immobilized, or even expropriated, have also given wings to capital.

Table 3-10. Real Effective Exchange Rates for Argentina, Mexico, and South Korea, 1978–83 (1978 = 100).

	Argentina	Mexico	South Korea
1978	100.0	100.0	100.0
1979	136.7	104.8	107.0
1980	161.2	114.1	98.0
1981	151.4	127.8	102.7
1982	108.1	92.6	104.3
1983	100.4	88.0	99.9

Note: Where the exchange-rate system entailed multiple rates, the official rate was used in the calculations.

Source: *World Financial Markets*, August 1987, p. 13; and staff of Morgan Guaranty Trust Company, New York.

Thus, evidence such as currency overvaluations and capital flight goes to prove that serious policy mistakes were made in some developing countries; lenders seem to have been less than alert to the likely consequences.[18] These factors must share responsibility for the debt crisis. Had there been no recession and no escalation of interest rates, the debt problem would not have become so grave, but would still have commanded the world's attention.

CURTAILMENT OF BANK LENDING

Once the Mexican payments crisis erupted, the commercial banks were reluctant to make new loans to many developing nations that were suddenly perceived, in the light of Mexico's difficulties, to be very poor risks. As shown in Table 3–11, bank loans outstanding to the developing countries increased by $52 billion in 1981, but by sharply diminishing increments in subsequent years. This curtailment of bank lending is commonly cited as an element or cause of the debt problem, because debtors who previously had been able to borrow from the banks, even to pay the interest they owed, were now put under pressure to come up with the money in some other way. According to one analyst, "The 1982 collapse of a reasonably competitive, if flawed, international capital market (at least for Latin America) constitutes the major external shock to the region during the early 1980s."[19]

Without question, the reduction in bank lending made life more difficult for the debtors. But a marked reduction in the extension of

Table 3-11. Changes in Outstanding Bank Claims
on Developing Countries, 1981–86.

Year	Billions of U.S. Dollars
1981	52
1982	38
1983	34
1984	17
1985	14
1986	5

Note: Data exclude claims on East European countries and bank-financed export credits officially guaranteed in the lending countries.

Source: Organization for Economic Cooperation and Development, *Financing and External Debt of Developing Countries: 1986 Survey* (Paris: OECD, 1987), pp. 54–55.

new bank loans was inevitable, given the circumstances already described in this chapter. The curtailment of bank lending was part and parcel of the debt problem, but less a cause of the problem than a consequence of the factors that gave rise to it.

DEALING WITH THE PROBLEM: SOME GENERAL CONSIDERATIONS

As already noted, the essence of the debt problem is how best to restore the creditworthiness of the developing countries that have fallen behind in servicing their debts. It is not possible to design a completely objective solution to this problem—a "scientific" solution free of normative or ethical considerations—because the problem involves the distribution of income and wealth. This is not to say that any proposed solution is as good as another, for some solutions might leave all concerned better off than other solutions would. Moreover, proposed solutions can vary sharply in their political acceptability. These factors suggest the need for compromise—for a bargained or negotiated attack on the problem rather than unilateral, extreme action.

This general principle can be readily illustrated. A debtor country in arrears could embark upon either of two extreme courses. The country could repudiate its debt, or it could undertake to eliminate its arrears forthwith. Neither extreme course is likely to serve the country—or its creditors—as well as an intermediate course of action negotiated with the country's creditors.

Consider first the option of repudiation. Because it can be very difficult, if not impossible, for creditors in one country to seize the assets of a defaulting debtor in another country, it might seem that struggling debtors would have strong incentive to repudiate. Such is not the case, however. Private debtors who fail to honor their obligations face the prospect of a curtailment of credit, and perhaps court proceedings as well. Governments that repudiated would bring upon their countries a drastic reduction in the availability of foreign credit, including credit for the financing of trade flows, and creditors might attach some assets held abroad by these governments, including some of their exports. Thus, it is not surprising that repudiations are virtually unheard of.

The other extreme option for the debtor country would be to attempt to eliminate all arrears, remaining current in its debt payments at all times. Thus, a debtor government that could not meet its scheduled payments might impose higher taxes. In some circumstances, such action would be entirely appropriate. But if the debtor country were in a recession or skirting one, as many were in the early 1980s, tax increases could well be counterproductive, depressing the country's economy even further and reducing rather than enlarging the government's revenues—an outcome that could lead to the replacement of the government itself by a new regime less conscientious about servicing the debt.

If debtors have good reasons to eschew radical courses of action, the same is true of their creditors. At one extreme, creditors could declare debtors to be in default as soon as payments became tardy. But it is hardly likely that creditors could seize enough assets of foreign governments to settle outstanding claims, and the abrupt cessation of lending that would accompany a declaration of default might well depress the debtors' economies, making it even more difficult for them to discharge their obligations. At the other extreme, creditors might forgive the overdue debt payments, at least for those debtors whose straits were most dire. To forgive the most hard-pressed debtors, however, would tempt all debtors to relax their efforts to meet their obligations; this "moral hazard" could be severe. Moreover, debt forgiveness, however appropriate for charitable institutions, has never been a noteworthy attribute of banks whose shareholders hope to realize a profit on their invested funds.

In sum, both borrowers and lenders have had powerful incentives to reject the most radical options available to them and to compromise by relaxing debt repayment schedules. In return for such debt rescheduling, and for some new lending, borrowing countries have pledged to undertake adjustment programs designed to improve their debt-servicing capacity. Thus, debt relief soon became central in mitigating the debt problem.

DEBT RELIEF ACCOMPANIED BY
ADJUSTMENT PROGRAMS

Debt relief, as defined by the World Bank, has taken several forms. Most sizable has been the rescheduling, or postponement to later years, of debt payments falling due in the near or medium term. (See Table 3–12.) Both commercial banks and official creditors have provided this kind of relief. In conjunction with such reschedulings, banks commonly have agreed to maintain or extend short-term credit lines and have also provided some new long-term loans.

Besides these kinds of relief, bridge loans have sometimes been arranged to enable a debtor country to meet its obligations until a rescheduling could be undertaken. For example, shortly after the eruption of the Mexican payments crisis in 1982, the U.S. Treasury Department and the Federal Reserve System extended several billion

Table 3–12. Aggregate Debt Relief Provided for Developing Countries, 1983–86 (in billions of U.S. Dollars).

Kind of Relief	1983	1984	1985	1986[a]
Debt rescheduling[b]				
By commercial banks	33.8	100.5	13.1	57.4
By official creditors	8.4	3.9	16.3	13.7
Total	42.2	104.4	29.4	71.1
New loan disbursements[c]	13.0	10.4	5.3	2.6
Short-term credit facilities[c,d]	27.9	36.7	35.0	35.0

[a]Provisional.

[b]Debt rescheduling with commercial banks is recorded in the year of agreement in principle; rescheduling with official creditors is recorded in the year in which the agreed minute is signed.

[c]Arranged in conjunction with debt rescheduling.

[d]Agreements to maintain or expand existing trade credit lines or to provide other short-term credits.

Source: World Bank, World Debt Tables, 1986–87 Edition (Washington, D.C.: 1987), p. xxii.

dollars in short-term credits to Argentina, Brazil, and Mexico, pending the arrangement of longer term lending programs. Much of this credit was arranged by the Bank for International Settlements (BIS), a "central bankers' bank," which marshaled very large sums for the same borrowers from other industrial nations as well as from the United States.

Negotiations between a debtor country and its creditors concerning debt repayment are usually conducted multilaterally, that is, with all creditors, or representatives of groups of creditors, present simultaneously at the negotiating sessions. Not only is this approach more efficient for the debtor than entering into separate debt-rescheduling negotiations with each of its many creditors, but the approach also facilitates uniformity of treatment of the creditors. Debts to governments, however, are renegotiated separately from debts to commercial banks.

A forum known as the Paris Club is employed for renegotiating debts to governments, as well as officially insured private export credits. An informal intergovernmental group, the Paris Club is chaired by an official of the French treasury. In a fairly typical case, interest as well as principal coming due within the next twelve to eighteen months would be rescheduled to be repaid within the next eight to ten years.

For renegotiation of debts to commercial banks not covered by export credit insurance, developing countries meet with ad hoc bank advisory committees. Given the popularity of internationally syndicated lending before the debt crisis, it is not uncommon for hundreds of banks to share in the loans being rescheduled. Only the major creditor banks are directly represented on the committee formed for a particular negotiation, but any agreement proposed by the committee does not go into effect until it is signed by a specified proportion of creditors and until other conditions are met, such as the payment of arrears. Normally, only principal, not interest, is rescheduled. Any new loans, in addition to loans rescheduled, have usually been shared by the banks in proportion to their loans already outstanding. Although bank loans are thus renegotiated separately from official loans, the Paris Club in its agreements prohibits debtor countries from entering rescheduling arrangements with banks on terms less favorable to the countries than those granted by the club itself.[20]

Rescheduling has been widespread. In 1986 the World Bank reported that countries entering rescheduling agreements after 1982 accounted for somewhat more than half of all external debt owed by the developing countries.[21] According to the Organization for Economic Cooperation and Development (OECD), between mid-1982 and end-April 1987, at least thirty-five countries had their bank debt rescheduled, sometimes repeatedly.[22] Interest rates charged on rescheduled loans declined over this period both because rates declined in the industrial countries and because lenders reduced the margins, or spreads, that they added to the rates they themselves paid for the funds that they loaned.[23]

As noted above, debtor governments have pledged, in exchange for debt relief, to undertake adjustment programs designed to enhance their debt-servicing capacity. The IMF has played a key role in the design and oversight of these adjustment programs. As a rule, creditors have been unwilling to reschedule debt until the debtor government has reached an agreement with the IMF on an adjustment program; and banks' new loan disbursements have usually been linked to the government's execution of adjustment policies.[24]

In general, adjustment programs have aimed at reducing the debtor country's imports in relation to its exports, thus making more foreign exchange available for the servicing of debt. While the details of the programs have varied from country to country and from time to time, the programs have often included devaluation of the domestic currency in terms of foreign currencies; reduction in the growth of the domestic money supply and domestic credit and an accompanying increase in domestic interest rates; and a more restrictive fiscal policy entailing diminished government spending and higher taxation. These measures operate to reduce domestic spending on imports and to free resources for export production, which is rendered more attractive.

Although the IMF is widely identified with such debtor adjustment programs, it has influenced the lending policies of creditors as well. For example, in late 1982 the IMF informed the creditor banks of Argentina and Mexico that no new IMF financing for those countries would be forthcoming unless the banks also put up new money—which they did. Had the IMF attached no such condition, the proceeds of its loans could have gone to repay the bank creditors rather than to support adjustment programs, an outcome the IMF sought to preclude.

In addition to their traditional collaboration with the IMF, commercial banks had embarked by the mid-1980s on a similar collaboration with the World Bank, linking some of their lending to structural and sectoral reforms to be carried out in debtor countries with the support of the World Bank. In some cases, the commercial banks tied their new loan disbursements to performance under both IMF- and World Bank-supported programs.[25] Thus, these two international institutions were playing pivotal roles in financing and adjustment efforts designed to restore creditworthiness.

GROWING DEBTOR RESISTANCE:
THE BAKER PLAN

The adjustment programs that developing countries were called upon to adopt, in exchange for debt relief, generally entailed reductions in domestic spending and, for the near term, in economic growth. Only by cutting back on their domestic absorption of resources could these countries quickly diminish their imports and release more of their own production for exports. Slow growth in industrial-country demand for many developing-country exports made the adjustment more difficult.

As time passed, resentment of such adjustment programs mounted in the debtor nations, and some openly became less cooperative. Thus, in a new departure, President Alan Garcia of Peru announced on 28 July 1985 that his government would limit payments on the country's foreign debt to 10 percent of the country's export earnings; moreover, his government would no longer be willing to include the IMF (or its proposed adjustment programs) in debt negotiations with Peru's creditors.[26] Two months later, President Jose Sarney of Brazil proclaimed, "Brazil will not pay its foreign debt with recession, not with unemployment, nor with hunger;" and President Garcia declared, "We are faced with a dramatic choice: it is either debt or democracy."[27]

Mindful of these developments, U.S. Treasury Secretary James A. Baker III acknowledged the importance of economic growth in the debtor countries in a major address in Seoul, Korea, on 8 October 1985. Speaking before the joint annual meeting of the World Bank and the IMF, Baker focused mostly on methods for promoting growth of output rather than for restraining demand. Creditor countries were exhorted to maintain markets open to developing-country exports and to promote sustained growth in aggregate demand. Debtor countries were urged to allow market forces to work more freely within their economies and, to this end, to adopt structural reforms such as the liberalization of trade, relaxation of barriers against investment inflows, and the improvement of tax codes and labor market regulations. To support the debtors' efforts, the major multilateral development banks, particularly the World Bank, were urged to make $9 billion in new loan disbursements to fifteen heavily indebted countries over the following three years, while the commercial banks were asked to come forth with new loans of $20 billion for the same countries, over the same period.[28] By mid-December 1985, general support for this "Baker Plan" had been expressed by the IMF and the World Bank, as well as by commercial banks holding 90 percent of the loans outstanding to developing countries.[29]

Execution of the Baker Plan was slow in starting, and modest. Both debtors and creditors showed signs of growing "debt fatigue," and debtors fell further into arrears. On 20 February 1987, the government of Brazil announced a suspension of interest payments on some $68 billion owed to foreign commercial banks.[30] A few days later, Ecuador's government, which had stopped paying interest in January on $5.4 billion owed to private creditors, stated that the suspension would continue until June; in March the government extended the suspension indefinitely and broadened it to cover debt totalling $8.3 billion.[31] In more dire straits, the government of Bolivia had paid no interest on its foreign debt since 1983.[32]

In recognition of such developments, Citicorp, the parent of Citibank, announced in mid-May 1987 that it would deduct $3 billion from its current income and transfer that amount to its reserves against which future loan losses could be charged.[33] The action was the first open, formal indication by a major creditor that its loans to the less developed countries were not likely to be fully collectible even in the long run. Following the Citicorp announcement, the *New York Times* proclaimed, "Death of 'Baker Plan' on Debt Seen," and other major U.S. banks soon also made sizable additions to their loan loss reserves.[34]

Having summarized the general strategies for dealing with the debt problem from 1982 through 1987, let us next consider the nature of the adjustment process itself in greater detail.

THE BALANCE-OF-PAYMENTS ADJUSTMENT PROCESS

To become better able to service their foreign debt, the problem debtors would have to improve their balances of trade; surpluses earned on merchandise trade could be used to pay interest on the debt. The data in Table 3–13 indicate that countries with recent debt-servicing problems incurred a trade deficit of nearly $25 billion in 1981, but had converted this deficit to a surplus almost as large by 1983. But as the table shows, the trade surpluses earned from 1983 to 1986 were not nearly sufficient to cover the interest payments, which therefore had to be financed largely from other sources, including additional borrowing from abroad. This borrowing from abroad is essentially equal to the current account deficit, which fell sharply after 1982.

Table 3-13. Current Account Transactions of Developing Countries with Recent Debt-Servicing Problems, 1979–86 (in billlions of U.S. dollars).

Category	1979	1980	1981	1982	1983	1984	1985	1986
Exports (f.o.b.)	153.3	199.8	189.9	169.5	169.8	183.6	175.6	157.2
Imports (f.o.b.)	163.9	204.2	214.4	177.6	147.9	148.8	140.7	139.9
Trade balance	−10.6	−4.4	−24.5	−8.0	21.9	34.8	34.8	17.3
Services, net	−32.4	−45.8	−56.7	−66.8	−55.4	−55.6	−52.9	−52.4
(Interest payments portion)[a]	−23.6	−37.2	−51.4	−60.5	−55.3	−60.4	−58.0	−53.4
Goods and services balance	−42.9	−50.2	−81.1	−74.9	−33.5	−20.8	−18.1	−35.0
Unrequited transfers	7.8	7.6	8.8	8.2	10.0	10.1	11.6	12.2
Current account balance	−35.1	−42.6	−72.3	−66.7	−23.5	−10.7	−6.5	−22.8

Note: Detail may not add to totals shown because of rounding.

[a]Including dividends and other investment income payments not related to foreign direct investment.

Source: International Monetary Fund, *World Economic Outlook*, October 1987, World Economic and Financial Surveys (Washington, D.C.: IMF, 1987), p. 84.

Two other features of these data are highly significant. First, not a penny of the improvement in the trade balance from 1981 to 1986 was attributable to an increase in exports. On the contrary, exports decreased in value, so that huge reductions in imports more than accounted for the entire improvement in the trade balance. The decrease in value of exports was attributable entirely to a decline in the price received for them, as their quantity grew by an estimated 8.5 percent over these five years.[35]

Second, as new loan disbursements received from creditors (counted as part of the current account deficit) fell substantially below the net interest paid those creditors, the incentive to maintain the interest payments became much weaker. As previously noted, perhaps the most powerful motivation for a developing country to avoid default is the fear of discouraging new lending. This motivation is diluted if the country finds that a suspension of its interest payments would much more than compensate for a termination of new lending at rates then current or likely in the foreseeable future. This conclusion holds *a fortiori* if the country has had to reduce its consumption and its imports, rather than expand its output and its exports, to meet its interest payments.

The import reductions of 1981–86 could not be accomplished without restraining domestic growth. As shown in Table 3–14, growth in GDP slowed markedly in the problem debtor countries with the onset of the world recession and the debt crisis, and GDP growth per capita slowed even further, turning negative during 1981–83. In 1986, real GDP per capita in these countries was nearly five and one-half percentage points below the 1980 level. While some of this decline represented a correction of the earlier economic boom, some resulted from the obstacles, internal and external, that these countries faced in expanding their exports.

The slowdown in economic growth in the problem debtor countries was due largely to a slowdown in their rates of domestic investment, as gross investment fell from 25 percent to 19 percent of their GDP between 1981 and 1986.[36] By contrast, the share of GDP that went to satisfy consumption was fairly well maintained.[37] Had the reverse been true, living standards would have declined even more in the short run, but in return for higher living standards in the future. Thus, the nature of the macroeconomic adjustment in the problem debtors did not augur well for their longer term growth.

Tables 3–15 and 3–16 offer more detailed information on the adjustment process in three key countries—Argentina, Brazil, and Mexico.

Table 3-14. Annual Percentage Changes in Real GDP and Real GDP Per Capita in Developing Countries with Recent Debt-Servicing Problems, 1969–86.

Year	In Real GDP	In Real GDP Per Capita
Average 1969–78[a]	5.5	3.1
1979	5.3	2.9
1980	4.2	1.9
1981	0.1	−1.9
1982	−0.3	−2.6
1983	−1.9	−3.9
1984	3.0	0.9
1985	2.7	0.7
1986	3.5	1.5

[a]Compound annual rates of change.

Source: International Monetary Fund, *World Economic Outlook*, October 1987, World Economic and Financial Surveys (Washington, D.C.: IMF, 1987), pp. 44–45.

Collectively, these three have accounted for almost one-quarter of the external debt of all less developed countries, and for more than two-fifths of the external debt of developing countries with recent debt-servicing problems.[38] In each table, items that add to net exports are given a positive sign, those that reduce net exports a negative sign. Also, all magnitudes represent changes measured at constant price levels.

As shown in Table 3–15, each country expanded the volume of its net exports of goods and services between 1981 and 1986, even though each also increased its net outlays for a major services category, namely, factor income payments to foreigners for debt servicing and other purposes. For each country, import quantity reductions (given a positive sign) made a much greater contribution toward raising net exports than did growth in exports. Again, such an adjustment is much less comfortable than one dominated by export expansion.

Further evidence on the nature of the adjustment is presented in Table 3–16. This table is based on a well-known accounting constraint: a nation can expand its net exports only by increasing its output of goods and services or by reducing its domestic absorption of goods and services. More precisely, the nation must increase its output by more than its domestic absorption, or reduce its absorption by more than its

Table 3-15. Change in Net Exports of Argentina, Brazil, and Mexico, in Constant Prices, by Major Component, 1981-86.

Country	Exports of Goods and Nonfactor Services (increase [+]) (1)	Imports of Goods and Nonfactor Services (increase [-]) (2)	Net Factor Income Payments Abroad (increase [-]) (3)	Net Exports of Goods and Services: Sum of Columns 1-3 (increase [+]) (4)
Argentina (thousands of domestic currency at 1970 prices)	+0.2	+0.8	0.0	+1.0
Brazil (millions of domestic currency at 1980 prices)	+85.3	+264.3	-58.4	+291.2
Mexico (billions of domestic currency at 1970 prices)	+36.4	+86.4	-7.8	+115.1

Note: Detail may not add to totals shown because of rounding.
Source: World Bank staff.

output. Either course of action allows the nation to boost its exports in relation to its imports, although the more pleasant course obviously is to expand output faster than absorption.

Of the three major debtors listed in Table 3-16, only Brazil was able to take this more pleasant course between 1981 and 1986. Only Brazil enlarged its domestic absorption, expanding both domestic consumption and domestic investment; a still larger expansion of output produced an increase in its net exports. In both Argentina and Mexico, the level of domestic absorption declined. For Argentina, the decline in absorption accounted for virtually the entire increase in the quantity of net exports, as its GNP showed little change. For Mexico, the picture is even starker: output actually decreased, and the nation managed to raise its net exports only by shrinking its domestic absorption by more than its output.

Table 3-16. Change in Net Exports of Argentina, Brazil, and Mexico, in Constant Prices, by Output and Absorption, 1981–86.

| Country | Gross National Product | | Domestic Absorption of Resources | | Statistical Discrepancy (increase [–]) (5) | Net Exports of Goods and Services: Sum of Columns 1-5 (increase [+]) (6) |
	Gross Domestic Product (increase [+]) (1)	Net Factor Income Payments Abroad (increase [–]) (2)	Total Consumption (increase [–]) (3)	Gross Domestic Investment (incease [–]) (4)		
Argentina (thousands of domestic currency at 1970 prices)	+0.1	0.0	0	+0.8	0	+0.9
Brazil (millions of domestic currency at 1980 prices)	+2,660.7	–58.4	–2,220.7	–24.3	–66.0	+291.2
Mexico (billions of domestic currency at 1970 prices)	–31.9	–7.8	+36.8	+113.4	+4.6	+115.1

Note: Detail may not add to totals shown because of rounding.
Source: World Bank staff.

The composition of the reductions in absorption is also noteworthy. As mentioned above, sustained reductions in domestic investment do greater damage to the prospects for long-term growth than do reductions in consumption. In Argentina, all—and in Mexico, most—of the reduction in absorption was attributable to a reduction in domestic investment rather than in consumption. Adverse though it may be for long-term growth, this outcome is not surprising, because reductions in aggregate consumption are especially difficult if per capita consumption is already low and the population is growing. A pie already too small must be made smaller still and must be divided among even more claimants. Thus, from 1981 to 1986 the volume of goods and services consumed *per person* fell by 8 percent in Argentina, and by 18 percent in Mexico. By contrast, Brazilians enjoyed an increase of 10 percent in their per capita consumption, a sharp reminder that not all developing countries are alike.[39]

To explain just how the reductions in Argentine and Mexican absorption were brought about would require rather detailed examinations of the two economies. Short of such detailed study, some general observations can be made. First, total income (roughly equivalent to GNP)—out of which consumption is largely financed—remained virtually constant in Argentina and decreased in Mexico. Second, both countries suffered severe deteriorations in the terms on which they traded with the rest of the world, as the prices of their exports dropped in relation to the prices of what they imported. Thus, a unit of their exports would not purchase nearly so large a quantity of imports for domestic use in 1986 as in 1981. (Total absorption thus diminished on this count, although consumption did not decline as a percentage of income.) For Argentina, export prices declined by 30 percent in relation to import prices; for Mexico, whose oil exports had commanded artificially high prices in 1981, the decline was a chilling 60 percent.[40]

From this brief survey, it is clear that the adjustment occurring between 1981 and 1986 was harsh for a number of developing countries, although some suffered relatively little. Partly because of the depressed state of many developing economies in 1986, the adjustment process had to be judged incomplete at that time. Further evidence on the need for additional adjustment is presented in the next section.

SOME INDEXES OF PROGRESS

If the solution to the debt problem includes restoration of creditworthiness, progress on the problem cannot be appraised without some index of creditworthiness. As might be expected, lenders have long computed such indexes, which take the form of ratios used as indicators of "country risk," or of future debt-servicing difficulties. Among such indicators are those reported in Table 3–6 and in the first three columns of Table 3–17.

Before jumping to conclusions on the basis of these indicators, one should consider their shortcomings. Debt indicators resemble the leading economic indicators used to forecast business cycles, in that they constitute measurement without much underlying theory but nonetheless are widely watched. In particular, they fall far short of being reliable, automatic signalers of impending problems.

The ambiguity surrounding these indicators can easily be illustrated by reference to the oldest and most popular one, the debt service ratio. This indicator is defined as debt service payments (interest and principal) divided by earnings from exports of goods and services. The assumption is that the higher the ratio, the less capacity a country has to service additional debt. In fact, a country rarely is called upon to service its foreign debt solely from current export earnings, as foreign creditors typically reinvest rather than collect most of scheduled

Table 3–17. Debt Indicators and Balance-of-Payments Errors and Omissions, for Countries with Recent Debt-Servicing Problems, 1979–86.

Year	External Debt[a] as Percent of:		Debt Service[b] as Percent of Exports of Goods and Services	Errors and Omissions (billions of U.S. dollars)
	Exports of Goods and Services	Gross Domestic Product		
1979	165	33	28	− 4.7
1980	152	33	25	− 16.5
1981	186	38	33	− 18.1
1982	241	44	40	− 17.0
1983	255	48	36	− 8.1
1984	246	48	36	2.4
1985	267	49	37	− 5.3
1986	310	51	43	1.1

[a]Long- and short-term at end of year, but excluding debt owed to IMF.

[b]Interest payments on total debt plus amortization payments on long-term debt only.

Source: International Monetary Fund, *World Economic Outlook*, October 1987, World Economic and Financial Surveys (Washington, D.C.: IMF, 1987), pp. 95, 109–13.

principal payments and make additional investments as well if the country seems creditworthy. Moreover, a rising ratio may not signify a falling debt-servicing capacity, nor a falling ratio a rising capacity. For example, a country in outright default and paying no debt service would have the lowest possible ratio of service actually paid. Thus, the World Bank has found "no clear link between high debt service ratios and countries that have had to reschedule their debt."[41]

More generally, all indicators like the debt service ratio provide only half-truths about the capacity of a country to assume additional debt. Differences observed in these ratios between countries do not necessarily signify differences in creditworthiness, because nations differ in their relative ability to employ capital productively; moreover, any one country will differ in this respect over time. Thus, it is not surprising that neither simple nor sophisticated statistical techniques have been very successful in using such indicators to forecast debt-servicing problems.

In spite of such caveats, it is hard to avoid being somewhat discouraged by the numbers displayed in the first three columns of Table 3–17. By all three of the indicators used, the creditworthiness of the developing countries with recent debt-servicing problems deteriorated, rather than improved, between 1982 and 1986. Thus, after four years of struggle, these countries seemed to have become even less creditworthy than at the onset of the debt crisis.

Another index of creditworthiness is the magnitude of capital flight, some estimates for which were presented in Table 3–9 for the years 1979–82. By definition, flight of capital from a country signifies a sharp loss of investor confidence—a fear that large losses would be incurred on funds held within the country. The greater the flight, the less creditworthy the country, in the eyes of many investors.

It is not possible to measure capital flight directly, because one cannot know what part of a capital outflow is inspired by fear of large loss rather than by more mundane investment motivations. Indeed, the flight may not be recorded at all, because the investors involved often seek to shift their funds without detection, employing channels that elude normal reporting requirements in order to evade government restraints or public criticism. Paradoxically, this very evasiveness has been the basis for more than one measure of capital flight, the most traditional being the "errors and omissions" item in the balance-of-payments accounts. When the transactions that have been reported or that can be estimated fail to "balance out" in the balance of payments, the difference is ascribed to "errors and omissions," which represents erroneous measurement or simple omission of transactions. Large swings in the magnitude of errors and omissions have long been thought to consist of unreported capital movements. Thus, these swings may provide a crude barometer of capital flight, although not a precise, comprehensive measure.[42]

From the data on errors and omissions in Table 3–17, it seems that capital flight may have peaked in 1981–82 and may have subsided in succeeding years, perhaps even vanishing by 1986. While these data are more encouraging than the other data in the table, the cessation of capital flight is hardly a hearty endorsement of a nation's creditworthiness. Much more impressive would be the return of the capital that had flown, a development that might generate some relatively large positive numbers for errors and omissions.

Progress in restoring creditworthiness can also be evaluated against earlier projections of that progress. The usefulness of such an exercise may go beyond merely providing a measure of progress against expectations. Provided that a projection seemed reasonable at the time it was prepared, an examination of the reasons it did not materialize could be helpful in designing policy for the future.

A standard source of forecasts relating to creditworthiness is the International Monetary Fund. The IMF projections are of special interest here not only because that organization played an important role in the attack on the debt problem but because it issued an analysis in 1987 of the reasons that an earlier projection fell wide of the mark. This analysis is reproduced in Table 3–18.

As the table shows, in April 1984 the IMF projected that external debt would amount to 132 percent of exports of goods and services for the non-oil developing countries at the end of 1987. The 132 percent represented a significant, although not dramatic, improvement from the figure of nearly 150 percent that had been reported for 1983.[43] In October 1987, however, the IMF expected the debt ratio to be 170 percent, or thirty-eight percentage points higher than the 1984 forecast.

Among the reasons for this net error, insufficient data on external debt accounts for a full fourteen percentage points; in other words, the existence of a sizable chunk of external debt had been unknown or unreported to the IMF at the time the 1984 projection was made. Obviously, then, better data were needed if lenders and borrowers were to deal adequately with the debt problem, and the data revisions reported by the IMF signified progress on this front, if not on the debt problem itself. Another thirteen percentage points of the error were attributable

Table 3-18.   Revision in IMF Projection of 1987 Debt Ratio
for Non-oil Developing Countries. [a]

Description	Percentage Points
April 1984 projection	132
October 1987 projection	170
"Error" in projection	38
Projection error due to:	
Data revisions [b]	14
Underlying forecast error	24
Forecast error due to:	
Valuation of debt [c]	13
New borrowing	−5
Price of exports	19
Volume of exports	−3

[a]The debt ratio is defined here as external debt outstanding as a percentage of exports of goods and services.

[b]Reflects primarily the improved accounting of external debt statistics.

[c]Reflects primarily the effects of exchange-rate changes.

Source: International Monetary Fund, World Economic Outlook, October 1987, World Economic and Financial Surveys (Washington, D.C.: IMF, 1987), p. 25.

to depreciation of the dollar, which had not been projected and which raised the dollar value of debt denominated in nondollar currencies; a smaller offsetting error, tending to reduce the debt, resulted from lower new borrowing by the non-oil developing countries than had been projected. A huge, unexpected drop in the prices of goods exported by these countries contributed another nineteen percentage points toward the net error, with a higher than expected volume of exports providing a slight offset.

It is important to note that none of the forecast error was attributable to a shortfall of gross output below the level that had been projected in 1984. On the contrary, for the non-oil developing countries the 1987 projection showed a level of gross output for 1987 that was two percentage points higher than projected in 1984, while for the industrial countries the 1984 and 1987 projections were identical. Thus, the IMF's projected improvement in the debt ratio failed to materialize even though output was growing somewhat faster than expected. This development posed a formidable challenge for international economic policy.

The foregoing appraisals of progress have focused on the restoration of creditworthiness for the debtor countries. As noted near the beginning of this chapter, a closely related matter is the threat to the solvency of the commercial banks that had loaned heavily to these countries. By the standard accounting measures, this threat diminished substantially between 1982 and 1986. For U.S. banks with significant foreign banking operations, outstanding loans to developing countries declined from nearly 182 percent of total capital to about 94 percent, while for the nine largest U.S. banks the decline was from 283 percent to about 154 percent. (See Table 3–2.) Although these data are based on accounting, or "book," values rather than on market values, it seems safe to conclude that more progress had been made in restoring the creditworthiness of these banks than of the developing countries.

As this is written, then, it is hard to demonstrate much progress in restoring the creditworthiness of the problem debtor countries. Their debt to banks was selling at huge discounts in the secondary markets, and for the entire group of countries, the most popular indicators of country risk had registered a deterioration between 1982 and 1986. Moreover, their output per capita was still somewhat below the level of 1982 and was growing very slowly.

REMEDIES

Since progress in restoring the creditworthiness of problem debtors was slow to materialize, the question arose whether new approaches were in order.[44] In fact, some modestly helpful innovations had been launched, and other proposals, some far-reaching, had been aired. Few, if any, of the proposed remedies contemplated a complete abandonment of previous approaches toward the debt problem. It was still envisioned that debtor countries would have to pursue the main lines of adjustment that had been prescribed by the IMF, the Baker Plan, and the World Bank, and lenders were still being urged to contribute at least the sums called for under the Baker Plan. In this section we consider first some limited, evolutionary innovations, then more radical schemes for easing the debt problem.

One financial market innovation that gained increasing usage as time passed was the debt swap.[45] It allows creditor banks to modify or reduce their claims on debtor countries and often serves to reduce the countries' external indebtedness. The swap can take three basic forms, sometimes combining them: debt-debt, debt-equity, and debt-local currency.

In a debt-debt swap, a U.S. bank might transfer some of its claims on Argentina to a European bank in exchange for claims on Chile. The U.S. bank would include a cash payment if the market value of the Argentine debt transferred was less than that of the Chilean debt acquired. Typically, a bank engaging in such swaps has done so in order to reduce the geographic dispersion of its claims, preferring to concentrate on those countries where it enjoys a competitive advantage, although swaps have also been undertaken for tax or liquidity reasons. Such swaps redistribute developing-country external debt among the holders, but entail no change in the total debt.

By contrast, debt-equity swaps convert externally held debt into externally held equity. Such swaps are made possible by the willingness of some developing-country governments to buy back their outstanding debt with local currency, on the condition that the local currency then be invested in the country. As an incentive for these swaps, the amount of local currency that the governments pay for their debt is substantially greater than the creditors could obtain by first selling the debt (which is denominated in foreign currency) in the secondary market at the prevailing discounts and then selling the foreign currency proceeds in the foreign exchange market in return for local currency. The governments do not pay local currency equivalent to the full face value of their debt, but their discount is considerably less than that taken in the secondary market.

The debt-equity swap allows the debtor country to reduce its external debt at some discount without expending scarce foreign exchange. It is possible, however, that at least some of the foreign investment involved in the swap would have been made even without the swap incentive. In that case, to acquire local currency without the swap the foreign investor would have supplied the country with foreign exchange that the country fails to receive under the swap arrangement. Even more to the point, if an incentive is required to attract foreign investment, the country could offer that incentive directly to the foreign investor—apart from any swap arrangement—thereby ensuring an inflow of additional foreign exchange. The swap arrangement does, however, allow the creditor banks to reduce their holdings of developing-country debt.

Debt–local currency swaps can be used to repatriate flight capital. They offer debtor-country residents the opportunity to obtain their local currencies in exchange for their countries' foreign currency–denominated debt, which the residents can purchase in the secondary market with the funds they have placed abroad. No questions are asked about how the funds got abroad, or whether taxes were paid on the income they yielded.

While these swap transactions attracted much publicity, as of mid-1987 they had made only a dent in the debt problem. By one informed estimate, about $5 billion of developing-country foreign currency debt had been replaced through swaps—not a large sum by comparison with the indebtedness of the problem debtors.[46]

Aside from swaps, a number of other financial market innovations had been proposed by 1987. One is especially interesting because it strove to surmount a thorny obstacle to new lending to the problem debtor countries. New bank lending had been discouraged by being denied any priority for repayment over outstanding, imperiled loans, even though new loans might otherwise have been very good investments, perhaps even boosting economic growth sufficiently to improve prospects for repayment of loans previously outstanding. Thus, the recommendation was made that new bank loans to problem debtors be given priority of repayment, or seniority, over bank loans already outstanding, and to facilitate this innovation, that most new bank lending to the problem debtors take the form of purchases of bonds issued by these countries.[47]

To some observers, such relatively limited proposals seemed woefully inadequate to bring about a satisfactory resolution of the debt problem. In their eyes, the problem was not mere temporary illiquidity, to be finessed through reschedulings and other attainable adjustments, but widespread insolvency, such that many outstanding loans would not be fully repaid with interest, even over the long run. From this more pessimistic camp came recommendations for bolder action involving explicit debt forgiveness.

A fairly typical recommendation of this sort called for the governments of the creditor nations to establish an international corporation that would buy problem debt from the banks at a discount and then seek to collect only this discounted value, or slightly more, from the debtor countries.[48] More specifically, the corporation would issue long-term bonds to the banks in exchange for developing-country debt, the debt being priced at a discount below the face value. The debtor countries would be relieved from paying off their debt to the extent of this discount (or most of it). If the corporation failed to collect enough on the developing-country debt to discharge its bond obligations, the creditor nation governments would make up the difference. Thus, the banks would dispose of problem loans—accepting losses—and the liabilities of the problem debtors would be reduced; both developments could stimulate new lending.

Difficulties would arise in implementing such a scheme. At precisely what discounts should the corporation offer to purchase the debt? Some indication could be obtained from prices quoted in the secondary market, but this market might be handling too small a volume of transactions to provide fully adequate guidance. Once the corporation did offer a particular discount for specific debt, some banks might be unwilling to sell at that discount, and the value of their debt holdings would then rise if the corporation acquired enough discounted debt from other banks to improve the creditworthiness of the problem debtors. Such an outcome could be unfair to those banks that did sell to the corporation at its discount, and to obviate such unfairness it might be necessary to require participation by all banks. But compelling the banks to enter into debt forgiveness would likely deter their future lending just as fully as debtor repudiation would.

The fairness issue arises not only with respect to the banks but also with respect to the developing countries. Having purchased debtor-country debt at a discount, the corporation would pass along to the debtors most of the benefit of that discount. Should the discount that is passed along to a country be based merely on the secondary market price for its debt, along with other customary indicators of creditworthiness, or should factors such as the country's per capita income, and the change therein, be taken into consideration?[49]

The moral hazard problem must also be confronted. If debtor countries could benefit from discounts on their debt linked to discounts in the secondary market or to other creditworthiness indicators, those countries would have an incentive to pursue policies that worsened their perceived creditworthiness, at least in the short run. Finally, any plan for debt forgiveness that might entail a notable U.S. government contribution seemed in 1987 unlikely to gain acceptance in the United States, where the struggle to reduce the federal budget deficit continued and where opposition was strong to bailing out big banks on their foreign debts.

Thus, in 1987 substantial difficulties stood in the way of explicit and sweeping debt forgiveness. On the other hand, nonconfrontational, or "conciliatory," defaults may have become more likely.[50] The immediate incentive for problem debtors to pay interest on a timely basis had become rather dubious, as their annual interest payments had for years run substantially in excess of the sums that they could borrow (as measured by their current account deficits), and their overall rate of economic growth remained very low. Also, the incentive had diminished for commercial banks to make new loans out of which the interest due them could be paid, because the fraction of their capital imperiled by possible developing-country defaults had been significantly reduced. With the banks in much better position to absorb nonpayment of interest, and with the debtor countries in poorer position to make those payments, the near-term outlook seemed rather gray, but not black.

SUMMARY

During the 1980s, the world economy faced a crisis in the form of a widespread failure by developing-country debtors to pay their foreign debts on schedule. The chief immediate fear was that major commercial banks in industrial countries might be forced into insolvency by their inability to collect payments due, perhaps igniting a financial panic as depositors rushed to withdraw their funds from all banks rumored to be threatened. Were such developments to provoke a recession in the industrial countries, the developing economies would find it even harder to make the export sales needed both for expansion and for servicing their debts. Moreover, developing countries that could not meet the interest payments on their outstanding debt were unlikely as time passed to receive new bank loans that might contribute to their economic growth. Thus, how best to restore the creditworthiness of the problem debtor countries became a crucial problem.

The causes of the debt problem are fairly well identified, although their relative importance is the subject of debate. An important role was played by adverse changes in the world economy, including a sharp rise in interest rates during 1978–81 and recessions in the industrial countries during the early 1980s. The rapid increase of developing-country indebtedness in the years before the crisis suggests that another causal factor was bad judgment, or imprudence, on the part of both borrowers and lenders. In particular, some developing countries promoted serious overvaluations of their currencies, and both borrowers and lenders seemed generally to miscalculate the likely consequences.

Both debtors and creditors had good reasons to avoid reacting to the debt problem with extreme, unilateral measures, such as repudiation by the debtors or declarations of default or debt forgiveness by the creditors. Instead, the primary strategy for coping with the problem became the rescheduling, or postponement to later years, of debt payments falling due, accompanied by debtor agreements to undertake adjustment programs designed to enhance their debt-servicing capacity. In the event, the problem debtor countries did quickly convert their aggregate foreign trade deficit into a surplus. The surplus was not sufficient, however, to meet their interest payments, most of which had to be financed out of other sources, including some additional borrowing from abroad. Unfortunately, the 1981–86 improvement in these countries' trade balances came entirely from import reductions accompanied by slower economic growth, rather than from export expansion.

Although no foolproof measure of a nations' creditworthiness has been devised, measures that are widely employed indicate a deterioration in the creditworthiness of the problem debtors between 1982 and 1986. An improvement projected by the IMF for the years 1984–87 also failed to materialize, even though the world economy grew as rapidly as the IMF had expected. On the other hand, the threat to the solvency of the creditor commercial banks substantially diminished between 1982 and 1986, as outstanding bank loans to the developing countries declined dramatically in relation to the banks' capital.

The lack of readily measurable progress in restoring the creditworthiness of the problem debtors, and the depressed levels of their per capita production, stimulated fresh interest in innovative proposals to remedy the problem. No suggested remedy was free of difficulties, however, and by the end of 1987 nothing of great moment had been adopted. Creditor commercial banks were in better position to absorb defaults than at the onset of the crisis, and problem debtors had less incentive to avoid default, as their annual interest payments had mounted substantially above the amounts that they could borrow.

NOTES

1. International Monetary Fund, *Annual Report on Exchange Arrangements and Exchange Restrictions, 1987* (Washington, D.C.: IMF, 1987), pp. 17–18, and IMF, *Annual Report on Exchange . . . 1981*, p. 22.
2. IMF, *Annual Report on Exchange . . . 1982*, p. 27; World Bank, *World Debt Tables*, 1982–83 Edition (Washington, D.C.: World Bank, 1983),

p. viii. Poland is counted among those obtaining debt relief in 1981 and 1982.

3. Organization for Economic Cooperation and Development, *Financing and External Debt of Developing Countries: 1986 Survey* (Paris: OECD, 1987), p. 55.

4. For example, Table 3–1 shows that countries with recent debt-servicing problems accounted for 239/344, or 69 percent, of developing-country, long-term, guaranteed debt held by private financial institutions.

5. Paul Volcker, Statement before the Committee on Banking, Finance and Urban Affairs, U.S. House of Representatives, 2 February 1983.

6. International Monetary Fund, *World Economic Outlook,* October 1987, World Economic and Financial Surveys (Washington, D.C.: IMF, 1987), p. 40.

7. Ibid., p. 69.

8. Ibid., p. 63.

9. World Bank, *World Debt Tables,* 1986–87, p. 3, and World Bank, *World Debt Tables,* 1983–84, p. 3.

10. Ibid.

11. OECD, *Financing and External Debt* (1987), p. 54.

12. Thus, of the total 1980 year-end liabilities of major foreign branches of U.S. banks, 9.3 percent were owed to customers in the oil-exporting countries. See U.S. Board of Governors of the Federal Reserve System, "Geographical Distribution of Assets and Liabilities of Major Foreign Branches of U.S. Banks," Statistical Release E.11(121), 18 March 1982.

13. See, for example, Jeffrey D. Sachs, "International Policy Coordination: The Case of the Developing Country Debt Crisis," Working Paper No. 2287 (Cambridge, Mass.: National Bureau of Economic Research, 1987), pp. 10–17; and Rudiger Dornbusch, "Our LDC Debts," Working Paper No. 2138 (Cambridge, Mass.: National Bureau of Economic Research, 1987), pp. 9–19.

14. *OECD Economic Outlook* 30 (December 1981): 12; *OECD Economic Outlook* 41 (June 1987): 156; IMF, *World Economic Outlook* (1981), Occasional Paper No. 4, p. 112; IMF, *World Economic Outlook,* (1982), Occasional Paper No. 9, p. 144; IMF, *World Economic Outlook,* (1984), Occasional Paper No. 32, p. 30.

15. Sachs, "International Policy Coordination . . . ," pp. 10–17; Dornbusch, "Our LDC Debts," pp. 9–19; Jeffrey D. Sachs, "External Debt and Macroeconomic Performance in Latin America and East Asia," *Brookings Papers on Economic Activity,* 1985: 2, pp. 523–48; and World Bank, *World Development Report 1985* (New York: Oxford University Press, 1985), pp. 43–70.

16. For a compilation of other estimates, see Robert Cumby and Richard M. Levich, "On the Definition and Magnitude of Recent Capital

Flight," Working Paper No. 2275 (Cambridge, Mass.: National Bureau of Economic Research, 1987).

17. For interesting analyses of capital flight, see Michael Deppler and Martin Williamson, "Capital Flight: Concepts, Measurement, and Issues," in IMF, *Staff Studies for the World Economic Outlook,* (August 1987), World Economic and Financial Surveys, pp. 39–58; Alain Ize and Guillermo Ortiz, "Fiscal Rigidities, Public Debt, and Capital Flight," *International Monetary Fund Staff Papers* 34 (June 1987): 311–32; Mohsin S. Khan and Nadeem Ul Haque, "Capital Flight from Developing Countries," *Finance and Development* 24 (March 1987): 2–5; Jonathan Eaton, "Public Debt Guarantees and Private Capital Flight," Working Paper No. 2172 (Cambridge, Mass.: National Bureau of Economic Research, 1987); John T. Cuddington, *Capital Flight: Estimates, Issues, and Explanations,* Princeton Studies in International Finance No. 58, (Princeton, N.J.: Princeton University, 1986); World Bank, *World Development Report 1985,* pp. 63–65.

18. Even the currency overvaluations of the early 1980s, however, were partly attributable to the external shocks. The need for depreciations of developing-country currencies would not have been so great in the absence of higher interest rates and recession in the industrial countries.

19. Carlos F. Diaz-Alejandro, "Latin American Debt: I Don't Think We Are in Kansas Anymore," *Brookings Papers on Economic Activity,* 1984: 2, p. 356.

20. A discussion of institutional arrangements for debt relief and the components of relief is presented in World Bank, *World Debt Tables,* 1986–87, pp. xxii–xxv.

21. World Bank, *World Debt Tables,* 1985–86, p. xxii.

22. OECD, *Financing and External Debt* (1987), p. 57.

23. Maxwell Watson, et al., *International Capital Markets: Developments and Prospects,* World Economic and Financial Surveys (Washington, D.C.: International Monetary Fund, 1986), pp. 56–57.

24. Ibid., pp. 18, 58; K. Burke Dillon and Gumersindo Oliveros, *Recent Experience with Multilateral Official Debt Rescheduling,* World Economic and Financial Surveys (Washington, D.C.: International Monetary Fund, 1987), p. 3.

25. Watson, et al., *International Capital Markets,* p. 58.

26. Alan Riding, "Peru's New Chief to Limit Payments on Foreign Debt," *New York Times,* 29 July 1985.

27. Alan Riding, "Latin Debtors Resisting Austerity, Citing Political Pressures at Home," *New York Times,* 26 September 1985.

28. James A. Baker III, Secretary of the Treasury of the United States, Statement before the Joint Annual Meeting of the International Monetary Fund and the World Bank, 8 October 1985, Seoul, Korea.

29. Clyde H. Farnsworth, "IMF Says Banks Back Baker Plan," *New York Times,* 16 December 1985.

30. Alan Riding, "Brazil to Suspend Interest Payments to Foreign Banks," *New York Times,* 21 February 1987; and Alan Riding, "Brazil Keen on Starting New Talks," *New York Times,* 23 February 1987.

31. "Ecuador Wants Further Delay," *New York Times,* 26 February 1987; and Linda Chavez, "Ecuador Suspends Payment on Debt Following Quakes," *New York Times,* 14 March 1987.

32. "Is Anybody Paying?" *Economist,* 14 March 1987.

33. Eric N. Berg, "Citicorp Accepts a Big Loss Linked to Foreign Loans," *New York Times,* 20 May 1987.

34. Peter T. Kilborn, "Death of 'Baker Plan' on Debt Seen," *New York Times,* 26 May 1987; and Phillip L. Zweig, "Major Banks Face Worst Quarter Ever," *Journal of Commerce,* 22 June 1987.

35. IMF, *World Economic Outlook,* October 1987, p. 65.

36. Ibid., p. 46; see the row labeled, "countries with recent debt-servicing problems."

37. World Bank, *World Development Report 1987,* p. 174; see data for "highly indebted countries" for the years 1980–86.

38. World Bank, *World Debt Tables,* 1986–87, pp. 206, 286, 338; and IMF, *World Economic Outlook,* October 1987, pp. 104, 106.

39. Per capita consumption measures were computed from data supplied by World Bank staff.

40. Computed from terms of trade data supplied by World Bank staff.

41. World Bank, *World Development Report 1985,* p. 45.

42. For a fuller explanation of the "errors and omissions" item, also known as the "statistical discrepancy," see Norman S. Fieleke, *What Is the Balance of Payments?* (Boston: Federal Reserve Bank of Boston, 1985), pp. 9–10.

43. IMF, *World Economic Outlook* (April 1984), Occasional Paper No. 27, p. 219.

44. See Jan S. Hogendorn, *Economic Development* (New York: Harper & Row, 1987), pp. 158–61, 167–68, for a broad survey of suggested new approaches.

45. David L. Roberts and Eli M. Remolona, "Debt Swaps: A Technique in Developing Country Finance," in Richard A. Debs, David L. Roberts, and Eli M. Remolona, *Finance for Developing Countries* (New York: Group of Thirty, 1987), pp. 15–40.

46. Ibid., p. 19.

47. William R. Cline, *Mobilizing Bank Lending to Debtor Countries,* Policy Analyses in International Economics 18 (Washington, D.C.: Institute for International Economics, 1987), pp. 11–18.

48. For brief summaries and critiques, see Cline, *Mobilizing Bank Lending,* pp. 88–91; and Stanley Fischer, "Resolving the International Debt

Crisis," Working Paper No. 2373 (Cambridge, Mass.: National Bureau of Economic Research, 1987), pp. 34–39.

49. For a proposal that would index debt forgiveness to change in per capita income, see Jeffrey Sachs, "Managing the LDC Debt Crisis," *Brookings Papers on Economic Activity,* 1986: 2, especially pp. 424–27.

50. Anatole Kaletsky, *The Costs of Default* (New York: Priority Press Publications, 1985), especially pp. 63–67.

4 THE UNITED STATES IN DEBT

On 24 June 1986, the U.S. Department of Commerce released data showing that the United States had become a net debtor in 1985, for the first time since 1914.[1] Reactions varied. According to President Reagan, the country's new debtor status was not cause for concern, but showed that the economy had been strong enough to attract foreign investment. By contrast, some private analysts worried that the U.S. standard of living would suffer as the debt increased and the nation had to pay growing amounts of interest to foreign creditors.[2]

What is the magnitude of U.S. indebtedness, and how rapidly is it growing? Why has the United States become a net debtor, and what are the likely consequences? If the rise in U.S. indebtedness must be slowed or stopped, how can the task best be accomplished?

THE MAGNITUDE OF U.S. INDEBTEDNESS

The Commerce Department 1985 data that made the news are summarized in Table 4–1, along with data for other years. By the end of 1985, the net international investment position of the United States had turned negative by nearly $112 billion, meaning that foreign assets in the United States exceeded U.S. assets abroad by that amount.[3] During the following year, U.S. net indebtedness increased to some $264

Table 4-1. International Investment Position of the United States at Year-end, 1970–86 (in billions of dollars).

Year	U.S. Assets Abroad (1)	Foreign Assets in the United States (2)	Net International Investment Position of the United States (column 1 less column 2) (3)
1970	165.4	106.9	58.5
1971	179.0	133.5	45.5
1972	198.7	161.7	37.0
1973	222.4	174.5	47.9
1974	255.7	197.0	58.7
1975	295.1	220.9	74.2
1976	347.2	263.6	83.6
1977	379.1	306.4	72.7
1978	447.8	371.7	76.1
1979	510.6	416.1	94.5
1980	607.1	500.8	106.3
1981	719.8	578.7	141.1
1982	824.9	688.0	137.0
1983	873.9	784.3	89.6
1984	896.1	892.5	3.6
1985	949.4	1,061.3	−111.9
1986[a]	1,067.9	1,331.5	−263.6

Note: Detail may not add to totals shown because of rounding.
[a]Preliminary.
Source: *Survey of Current Business:* 66 (June 1986): 28; and 67 (June 1987): 40.

billion. The transition from creditor to debtor status was swift and dramatic; the United States had attained its peak as a creditor nation as recently as 1981, with a positive net international investment position of $141 billion.

Major components of the change in the investment position during 1986 are reported in Table 4–2. By far the largest component is capital flows; foreigners loaned or invested about $213 billion in the United States, $117 billion more than U.S. residents invested in foreign countries. Aside from such capital flows, rising securities prices increased the value of stocks and bonds held both in the United States and abroad, with foreign assets in the United States increasing by $28 billion more

Table 4-2. The U.S. Net International Investment Position: Summary of Changes During 1986 (in billions of dollars).

	U.S. Assets Abroad (1)	Foreign Assets in the United States (2)	Net International Investment Position of the United States (column 1 less column 2) (3)
Position at end of 1985	949.4	1,061.3	−111.9
Changes in 1986 attributable to:			
Capital flows	96.0	213.4	−117.4
Price changes	8.7	36.8	−28.1
Exchange-rate changes	11.8	2.9	8.9
Other changes	2.1	17.1	−15.0
Total changes	118.5	270.2	−151.7
Position at end of 1986 [a]	1,067.9	1,331.5	−263.6

Note: Detail may not add to totals shown because of rounding.

[a]Preliminary.

Source: *Survey of Current Business* 67 (June 1987): 39.

than U.S. assets abroad on this count. Also, the 1986 rise in the dollar exchange rate of many other currencies boosted the dollar value of foreign currency–denominated stocks and bonds held by U.S. residents. On balance, such exchange-rate changes made a positive contribution of nearly $9 billion to the U.S. net investment position.

This measurement of the U.S. position may be substantially in error, as the Commerce Department itself points out. On the one hand, some U.S. claims on foreigners are understated because of certain measurement conventions or difficulties. For instance, U.S. official gold holdings—deemed, like U.S. holdings of foreign currency, to be a claim on foreigners—are valued at a most conservative $42.22 per ounce. Revaluing this gold stock at $400 per ounce—some $50 below the market price at this writing—would raise the reported value of U.S. assets abroad at year-end 1986 by nearly $94 billion.[4] Similarly, U.S. direct investments abroad are carried at their original book value rather than at their higher current market value.

On the other hand, other measurement problems probably result in an understatement of the value of foreign assets in the United States.

For years the United States has been receiving from abroad very large net receipts that cannot be traced to specific transactions—the so-called "statistical discrepancy" in the balance of payments. Some, perhaps most, of these net receipts—which totaled $23 billion in 1986—may well have been generated by "capital account" transactions, particularly by foreign investment in the United States. Thus, some understatement of foreign assets in the United States seems likely. Such an understatement would, of course, tend to lower the reported net indebtedness of the United States below its true value, while the likely understatement of U.S. assets abroad would have the opposite effect.

While some part of the large unidentified receipts in the U.S. balance of payments has surely taken the form of foreign investment in the United States, it would almost certainly be a mistake to attribute all of these net receipts to such capital account transactions. Much evidence exists that a significant portion of the receipts has been generated not by capital account but by current account transactions, such as the sale of U.S. goods and services abroad, or the charging of interest on U.S. loans to foreigners. Insofar as the unidentified receipts have resulted from current account transactions, the reported value of U.S. net indebtedness requires no upward revision.

Some of the most interesting evidence of unreported current account receipts comes from comparisons of data collected by different nations. For example, Canada's recorded imports of U.S. merchandise have consistently exceeded the merchandise exports to Canada recorded by the United States. In large part, the discrepancy has been due to underreporting of U.S. exports, as many U.S. firms, especially truckers, have failed to file export documents with U.S. customs officials before moving goods into Canada. As a result, U.S. exports to Canada have at times been understated by nearly 20 percent. Because trade between the two nations surpasses that between any other two, the dollar amount of the understatement had been sizable; for example, after consulting with Canadian officials, U.S. officials raised the reported value of U.S. exports to Canada in 1986 by more than $10 billion.[5]

Other evidence indicates that the United States is not alone in underreporting current account receipts. If one adds up all the current account balances reported for the nations of the world in any recent year, one obtains a very large overall deficit, amounting to some $70 billion in 1985, for instance.[6] Since one nation's international deficit must be the surplus of some other nation or nations, the grand total of all current account balances should, of course, be zero, if recordkeeping were perfect and internationally consistent. Thus, it seems that the under-reporting of current account receipts is a fairly widespread phenomenon. Further analysis indicates that the reporting problem lies primarily with investment income—especially income from securities and bank accounts—and with income generated by transportation services, rather than with merchandise exports.[7] No doubt, the United States shares in this underrecording, especially of investment income, in view of the sizable foreign investments by its residents.

Inaccuracies of this sort can have unfortunate consequences, for errors in statistics can lead to errors in both market judgments and government policy. For example, overstatement of the U.S. deficit on foreign trade or of U.S. international indebtedness could lead to unwarranted depreciation of the dollar in the foreign exchange markets or to new protectionist measures by the U.S. government. On balance, however, it is hard to say whether the published measure of the U.S. net international investment position is significantly in error. Some considerations suggest an understatement, others an overstatement.

The transition of the United States from creditor to debtor status is not to be explained by transactions with a particular country or region. On the contrary, the U.S. position turned more negative (or less positive) with all major areas for which U.S. data are regularly published. As shown by Table 4–3, through 1986 the biggest swing was with Western Europe.

If the United States has become a sizable net debtor, which countries are the creditors? Unfortunately, data on net international investment position—or "net external assets," as the measure is generally called

Table 4–3. Net International Investment Position of the United States at Year-end, by Area, 1981 and 1986, (in billions of dollars).

Area	1981	1986	Change
Western Europe	−51.9	−280.1	−228.2
Japan	−1.7	−64.7	−63.0
Canada	66.3	48.8	−17.5
Latin American republics and other Western Hemisphere	100.3	25.3	−75.0
Other	28.2	7.1	−21.1
Total	141.1	−263.6	−404.7

Note: Detail may not add to totals shown because of rounding.

Source: *Survey of Current Business* 67 (June 1987): 39; and U.S. Commerce Department staff.

outside the United States—are officially published by only a few countries; moreover, steps have not been taken to assure the comparability of the few national measures that are published. Limited as they are, data collected by the West German central bank, depicted in Figure 4–1, show that as U.S. net indebtedness rose, so did the net creditor positions of Japan, West Germany, and the United Kingdom. Japan recorded the largest growth in net creditor position, but the United Kingdom and West Germany also had substantial gains. These three countries, along with Switzerland (for which official data are not available), probably were the major creditors among the industrial countries in 1985. Still larger net creditor positions were presumably held by some members of the Organization of Petroleum Exporting Countries, especially Saudi Arabia and Kuwait.[8]

Once the United States became a net debtor, it became fashionable to compare its indebtedness with that of the less developed countries. U.S. indebtedness, it was widely reported, had come to exceed the

Figure 4–1.   Net External Assets(+) of Selected Major Industrial Countries at Year End, 1983 and 1985.

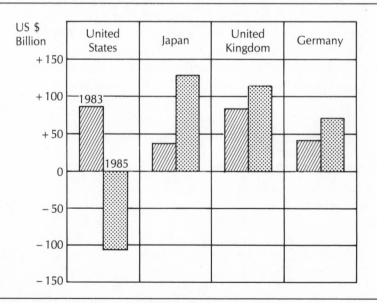

Note: The recording of external assets and liabilities is subject to some uncertainty and is probably not complete in all cases.

Source: *Monthly Report of the Deutsche Bundesbank* 38 (October 1986): 32.

indebtedness even of Brazil, then the leading debtor among the developing nations. The comparison, however, was of apples with oranges. For one thing, the gross debt of the less developed countries was being compared with U.S. debt *net* of U.S. assets abroad. Such comparison is sometimes defended on the grounds that the external assets of developing countries typically are relatively small or, when privately owned, are beyond the control or influence of developing-country governments. The argument has merit, but to ignore all such assets is extreme.[9]

If measured gross, on roughly the same basis as less developed country debt is measured, the U.S. external debt came to $753 billion at the end of 1985, the year during which the nation became a net debtor. This amount greatly exceeded the gross external debt of any less developed country. Indeed, the total external debt of all the capital-importing developing countries then amounted to only about 25 percent more than the U.S. debt.[10]

In any event, by any conventional measure U.S. indebtedness exhibited a remarkable increase. We shall examine some explanations for the U.S. external deficit and then consider the possible repercussions of the deficit. Explanations can be classified into those that emphasize "supply-side" factors, "demand-side" factors, or both.

SUPPLY-SIDE EXPLANATIONS: PRICE COMPETITIVENESS

The large trade and current account deficits that have ballooned U.S. net debt (Table 4–4) are often taken to signify a loss of U.S. "competitiveness." Although exponents of this viewpoint are seldom clear on what they mean by competitiveness, they commonly refer to factors that underlie the aggregate supply of U.S. goods—factors such as technology, capital formation, research and development, and the quality of management and the labor force. Thus, to enhance U.S. competitiveness, action has often been proposed to upgrade the education of the work force (especially in math and science), to grant more favorable tax treatment to investment in capital equipment, to relax the antitrust laws so that firms could pool their research efforts, to provide better patent protection for new inventions, and so on.

In other countries, the term *competitiveness* has similar supply-side connotations. In France, for example, much attention was given to a 1987 book alleging that France had lost competitiveness because of a

Table 4–4. U.S. Balances on Selected Components of International Current Account Transactions, 1970–86 (in billions of dollars)

Year	Balance on Merchandise Trade (1)	Balance on Services (2)	Balance on Unilateral Transfers (3)	Balance on Current Account (columns 1 plus 2 plus 3) (4)
1970	2.6	3.2	−3.4	2.3
1971	−2.3	4.7	−3.9	−1.4
1972	−6.4	4.7	−4.1	−5.8
1973	.9	10.3	−4.1	7.1
1974	−5.5	14.9	−7.4	2.0
1975	8.9	14.1	−4.9	18.1
1976	−9.5	19.0	−5.3	4.2
1977	−31.1	21.6	−5.0	−14.5
1978	−33.9	24.1	−5.6	−15.4
1979	−27.5	32.7	−6.1	−1.0
1980	−25.5	34.9	−7.6	1.9
1981	−28.0	42.3	−7.5	6.9
1982	−36.4	36.7	−9.0	−8.7
1983	−67.1	30.3	−9.5	−46.2
1984	−112.5	17.7	−12.2	−107.0
1985	−122.1	21.1	−15.3	−116.4
1986	−144.3	18.6	−15.7	−141.4
1987[a]	−159.2	12.0	−13.5	−160.7

Note: Detail may not add to totals shown because of rounding.

(−) Signifies deficit.

[a]Preliminary.

Source: *Survey of Current Business* 67 (June 1987): 54–55 and staff, U.S. Department of Commerce.

slothful work force. Entitled *Lazy France*, the book reported that the average worker put in 1,550 hours a year at the office or factory in France compared to 1,850 hours in the United States, 2,000 in Japan, and more than 2,700 in Korea.[11] Evidently, concern about competitiveness is not confined to the United States.

Analyses of competition among suppliers commonly divide it into two broad categories: price competition and nonprice competition, the former being the chief concern of this section. Perhaps the best single index of a nation's changing overall price competitiveness is the change in its real exchange rate, that is, the change in its average price level relative to the average foreign price level after taking into account the change in the average foreign currency price of its currency. Thus, a nation's price competitiveness will be impaired by a rise in its domestic prices relative to foreign prices, unless there is an offsetting decline in the foreign currency price of its currency.

Although analysts differ on precisely how to measure the real exchange rate, all widely used measures show big swings in U.S. price competitiveness during the period of deterioration in the U.S. trade and current account balances. In general, the indexes suggest that the United States lost much price competitiveness between 1980 and 1985, but then rapidly regained the lost ground. For example, the index plotted as a solid line in Figure 4-2 shows a rise in U.S. relative prices of 37 percent (after incorporating nominal exchange-rate change) from 1980 to 1985, followed by a decline to approximately the 1980 level by the end of 1987. The "nominal" index plotted in the chart represents only the change in the foreign currency price of the dollar. Clearly, it was this nominal exchange-rate change, rather than changes in domestic or foreign prices, that accounted for the large swings in U.S. overall price competitiveness over this period.

It is widely agreed that the loss of U.S. price competitiveness between 1980 and 1985 contributed substantially to the increase in the U.S. trade deficit. But what caused the loss of price competitiveness? A number of factors could be responsible, not all of them supply-side in nature. Here a supply-side factor—productivity change—is considered; other factors are discussed in a subsequent section.

Changes in the productiveness of a country's resources can have an important influence on the country's price competitiveness. If productivity rises, other things remaining equal, the money cost and price of a unit of output can fall. Did productivity grow less rapidly in the United States than in other countries during the period of decline in U.S. price competitiveness?

To address this question, one should turn to a measure of the output yielded by a unit of all productive factors combined, including labor, land, and capital. Unfortunately, such measures of total factor productivity are extraordinarily difficult to construct. Consequently, international productivity comparisons are commonly based on indexes of output per input of labor in manufacturing, as listed in Table 4-5.

Figure 4-2.   Weighted Average Foreign Exchange Value of
U.S. Dollar, 1980–87 (in terms of forty other currencies
weighted according to manufactures trade; based on
monthly averages of daily rates).

Index (1980–82 = 100)

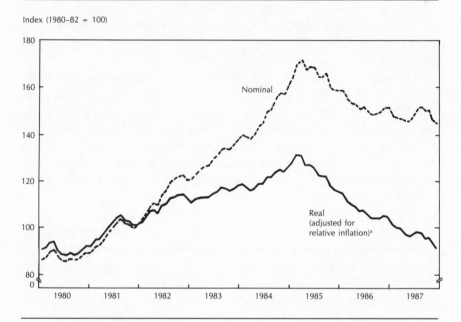

aInflation measured in terms of wholesale prices in manufactures excluding food and fuel.
Source: Morgan Guaranty Trust Company.

The table indicates that output per labor-hour in manufacturing did indeed grow less rapidly in the United States than in several other industrial countries during the years 1980–85. Of the seven countries listed individually, Japan and the United Kingdom enjoyed the highest rates of growth (33.4 percent and 32 percent, respectively) over this period, well above the rate in the United States. The United States did, however, surpass Canada, West Germany, and Italy.

Aside from such bilateral comparisons, how did the United States perform by comparison with its major industrial competitors as a group? As shown in the last column, eleven foreign industrial countries achieved an average increase of about 24 percent over the period 1980–85, compared to an increase of 22.5 percent in the United States. This differential hardly seems significant. Moreover, the U.S. lag in labor productivity

Table 4-5.   Output per Labor-Hour in Manufacturing in Selected Industrial Countries, 1970-86 (Indexes: 1980 = 100).

Year	United States	Canada	Japan	France	West Germany	Italy	United Kingdom	Eleven Countries[a]
1970	79.7	77.0	52.8	62.1	65.6	62.2	78.4	64.1
1971	84.1	82.4	55.9	65.4	68.1	64.1	82.1	67.5
1972	87.8	86.5	61.4	69.4	72.7	69.4	87.6	72.5
1973	92.1	92.0	67.7	73.4	77.3	77.8	94.0	78.4
1974	89.3	93.4	70.5	76.1	80.5	81.5	95.8	81.1
1975	91.6	90.2	71.5	79.0	83.0	77.9	93.6	81.2
1976	95.8	96.5	76.9	84.8	88.9	84.6	97.8	86.9
1977	98.6	101.8	81.5	89.3	92.1	85.5	98.3	90.5
1978	100.1	103.0	88.0	94.4	94.9	88.1	99.8	94.3
1979	100.0	103.9	93.6	98.5	99.6	94.5	100.7	98.2
1980	100.0	100.0	100.0	100.0	100.0	100.0	100.0	100.0
1981	102.2	104.8	103.7	103.9	102.2	103.5	105.2	103.9
1982	104.4	102.2	110.0	110.3	103.7	105.6	111.7	107.1
1983	110.5	108.9	116.0	115.0	109.7	108.3	120.9	113.4
1984	116.5	112.2	124.3	119.5	113.7	115.2	127.3	119.2
1985	122.5	114.8	133.4	123.5	118.7	117.0	132.0	124.3
1986	127.0	114.2	137.1	125.8	121.0	118.4	135.9	126.3

[a]A trade-weighted average of Canada, Japan, France, West Germany, Italy, the United Kingdom, Belgium, Denmark, the Netherlands, Norway, and Sweden, but excluding in 1986 Belgium and the Netherlands, for which data are not available at this writing. The weights reflect the relative importance of each country as a U.S. manufacturing trade competitor as of 1980.

Note: The data relate to all employed persons, including the self-employed, in the United States and Canada, and to all employees (wage and salary earners) in the other countries. Although the indexes relate output to the hours of persons employed in manufacturing, they do not measure the specific contributions of labor as a single factor of production. Rather, they reflect the joint effects of many influences, including new technology, capital investment, capacity utilization, energy use, and managerial skills, as well as the skills and efforts of the work force.

Source: U.S. Department of Labor News: USDL 87-237, 15 June 1987; and USDL 87-333, 3 August 1987; and staff of U.S. Bureau of Labor Statistics.

growth was far greater during the 1970s, before the major deterioration in U.S. price competitiveness took place. Between 1970 and 1975, labor productivity in manufacturing rose by 15 percent in the United States, and by nearly 27 percent in the eleven foreign industrial countries; between 1975 and 1980, the increase was only 9 percent in the United States, and 23 percent in the eleven other nations.

It is clear that the loss of U.S. price competitiveness during 1980–85 should not be attributed to the relative U.S. record on labor productivity in manufacturing over these years. To be sure, higher U.S. productivity growth could, in principle, have yielded lower U.S. inflation and, other things being equal, a smaller rise in the U.S. real exchange rate than that shown in Figure 4–2. The relative U.S. record on labor productivity in manufacturing, however, was extremely good during 1980–85 by comparison with the previous decade.

SUPPLY-SIDE EXPLANATIONS: NONPRICE FACTORS

Supply-side explanations of the U.S. trade and current account deficits relate not only to the price competitiveness of U.S. suppliers but also to nonprice competition. U.S. firms were often said to have lost competitiveness because their products had become inferior in quality to foreign brands. Automobiles provide a good illustration. During the first half of the 1980s, surveys showed that U.S. consumers and engineers both considered foreign-brand cars generally to be of higher quality than U.S. cars. Consumers buying foreign cars were more likely to be satisfied with their purchase and to report a low frequency of repairs than were the buyers of U.S. cars.[12]

In addition, U.S. firms were criticized for failing to tailor products to the preferences of foreign purchasers and for failing to mount aggressive, long-term marketing efforts in foreign lands. On the other hand, Japanese firms have been acclaimed for their success in these areas. To illustrate, one remarkable account contrasts the tactics of the Japanese with their American and European rivals in the Chinese market during the 1980s.[13] Japanese firms were more willing to sacrifice short-term profit for the sake of building market share. Japanese personnel were better trained in the Chinese language, worked longer hours, lived in poorer housing, and served longer assignments in China than did their American counterparts. It was not uncommon for Japanese employees to leave their families in Japan and accept housing in cramped rooms in inferior Chinese hotels.

Because such reports are so common, it may well be that U.S. competitiveness did lag in terms of quality and other nonprice considerations. How much weight to attach to these various nonprice dimensions is impossible to quantify with any precision. However, other evidence suggests that, whatever the shortcomings of U.S. firms, the worldwide performance of U.S. management did not degenerate as the U.S. trade deficit began to mushroom early in the 1980s.

Some of the most revealing evidence on the relative performance of U.S. management has to do with the record of multinational firms headquartered in the United States. By and large, management has more scope to influence the operations of a multinational firm than a national firm. With activities in more than one country, the multinational firm is not chained to local customs, regulations, or labor force. Management can shift activities of the firm from one nation to another as circumstances warrant, taking advantage over time of the best that each nation has to offer for the overall success of the firm. Thus, one may gain more insight into the international competitiveness of U.S. management by examining the performance of U.S.-based multinationals than by examining only the performance of U.S. firms.

Summary data on performance in export markets for manufactures are presented in Table 4–6. As shown by line 4, the overall share of U.S.-based multinationals—including exports by U.S. parents as well as by their majority-owned foreign affiliates (MOFAs)—increased somewhat between 1966 and 1984, the latest year for which data are available at this writing. From these numbers, one might argue that U.S. management was holding its ground in the international arena. By comparison, the first line shows that all U.S. manufactured exports, expressed as a share of the world total, declined from 1966 to 1977, rose from 1977 to 1982, and then declined slightly between 1982 and 1984 (a period when the U.S. trade deficit also increased sharply). Thus, the United States as a nation experienced some loss in competitiveness by this indicator between 1982 and 1984, but the rising market share of U.S. multinationals tends to exonerate U.S. management. It is especially interesting that the U.S. multinationals maintained their market share between 1982 and 1984 by raising the share of their MOFAs to compensate for a decline on the part of the U.S. parents.

Table 4-6. Shares (as a Percentage) in Value of World Manufactures Exports.[a]

	1966	1977	1982	1983	1984
United States	17.5	13.3	14.3	13.7	14.0
U.S. Multinationals					
Parents	11.0	9.2	9.5	9.1	9.2
MOFAs[b]	8.2	9.7	9.7	9.9	10.3
Parents and MOFAs	17.7	17.6	17.7	17.7	18.1

[a]The "world" is here defined as all market economies.

[b]Exports by majority-owned foreign affiliates (MOFAs) as percent of exports by all countries except the United States.

Source: Robert E. Lipsey and Irving Kravis, "The Competitiveness and Comparative Advantage of U.S. Multinationals, 1957–1984," *Banca Nazionale del Lavoro Quarterly Review* 161 (June 1987): 151.

COMPETITIVENESS, COMPARATIVE ADVANTAGE, AND AGGREGATE SUPPLY

Apart from its *overall* competitiveness, the United States, like any other nation, has *comparative* advantages and disadvantages in particular activities or industries. That is to say, by comparison with the rest of the world, the nation excels in some activities relative to others. One rough-and-ready index of this relative excellence is known as "revealed comparative advantage," measured here by the industrial distribution of U.S. exports relative to that of the world. Thus, if machinery constitutes a larger share of U.S. exports than of world exports, the United States is said to have a comparative advantage in the production of machinery.[14]

As Table 4–7 indicates, the United States has indeed possessed a comparative advantage in the production of machinery, and also in chemicals and transport equipment. For each of these broad industry categories in 1982, the ratio of U.S. exports in the category to total U.S. manufactured exports was more than 100 percent of the ratio of world exports in the category to total world manufactured exports. Comparative U.S. disadvantages existed in foods, metals, and other manufacturing. Comparative advantages and disadvantages of this sort will, of course, be present regardless of the size of a nation's trade deficit or surplus; they should not be confused with the nation's overall competitiveness as

Table 4–7. Industry Share in Total U.S. Manufactured
Exports as a Percentage of the Industry Share in World
Manufactured Exports, 1982.

Industry	Percent
Foods	67
Chemicals	113
Metals	64
Machinery	142
Nonelectrical	164
Electrical	111
Transport equipment	117
Other manufacturing	73

Source: Robert E. Lipsey, "Changing Patterns of International Investment in and by the United States," in Martin Feldstein, ed., *The United States in the World Economy* (Chicago: University of Chicago Press, 1988), p. 496.

measured by other indicators, such as the nation's real exchange rate or its share of world exports.

Perhaps the best summary indicator of a nation's overall supply-side competitiveness is the share of world output that the nation supplies. Measures of this share are not precise; it is difficult to construct accurate comparisons of the outputs of different countries, partly because the composition and the price structure of output vary from country to country. Nonetheless, such comparisons are regularly made by the Organization for Economic Cooperation and Development (OECD), whose membership includes twenty-four countries, nearly all of them industrialized.

In Table 4–8, which draws on the OECD data, it can be seen that the United States held its own with respect to gross output between 1981 and 1986, a period during which the U.S. trade balance registered a huge decline. Nor did the United States suffer by comparison with other OECD countries in terms of output per capita (a measure of economic well-being). Thus, at least by comparison with other countries, the United States did not display a serious aggregate "supply-side" problem during these years of deterioration in its trade balance.

If the supply side cannot be held responsible for the U.S. external deficits, what is to blame? After all, it is clear that the nation lost overall price competitiveness as the deficits began to increase. The answer may lie in the *relation* between aggregate U.S. supply and demand and, more precisely, in the forces that influence that relationship.

Table 4–8. U.S. and OECD Gross Domestic Product and U.S. Trade Balance, 1981–86.

Year	U.S. GDP as Percent of OECD GDP		U.S. GDP Per Capita as Percent of OECD GDP Per Capita		U.S. Merchandise Trade Balance (billions of dollars; balance-of-payments basis)
	At Current Prices and Exchange Rates	At 1980 Prices and Exchange Rates	At Current Prices and Exchange Rates	At 1980 Prices and Exchange Rates	
1981	39	35	132	120	−28.0
1982	41	34	138	117	−36.4
1983	42	35	143	118	−67.1
1984	45	35	152	120	−112.5
1985	46	35	154	119	−122.1
1986	39	36	131	120	−144.3

Note: For 1986, underlying GDP data are provisional, and underlying population data are for 1985.

Source: *Survey of Current Business* 67 (June 1987): 54–55; Organization for Economic Cooperation and Development, *National Accounts, 1960–85,* Vol. 1 (Paris: OECD, 1987), pp. 109, 113; and *Main Economic Indicators,* February 1988: 174–75.

Table 4-9. Real GNP and Real Domestic Demand in the United States and Other OECD Countries, 1981–86.

| | Real GNP | | | | Real Domestic Demand | | | |
| | Level (1980 = 100) | | Percent Change from Preceding Year | | Level (1980 = 100) | | Percent Change from Preceding Year | |
Year	United States	Other OECD	United States	Other OECD	United States	Other OECD	United States	Other OECD
1981	101.9	101.2	1.9	1.2	102.2	99.8	2.2	-0.2
1982	99.4	102.1	-2.5	0.9	100.3	100.6	-1.9	0.8
1983	103.0	104.1	3.6	2.0	105.4	102.0	5.1	1.4
1984	109.6	107.8	6.4	3.6	114.1	104.8	8.3	2.7
1985	112.6	111.4	2.7	3.3	118.0	107.8	3.4	2.9
1986	115.4	114.2	2.5	2.5	122.1	111.7	3.5	3.6

Source: OECD Economic Outlook 41 (June 1987): 2–3; and OECD Economic Outlook 41, Statistics on Microcomputer Diskette (June 1987).

AGGREGATE SUPPLY AND DEMAND

The total output supplied by a nation's productive resources can fall short of the output demanded, or absorbed, by the residents of the nation. The gap is filled by net imports from abroad. Although the output supplied by the nation may be growing rapidly, total demand within the nation may be growing even faster, so that the nation's trade and current account deficits with the rest of the world expand (unless there are offsetting price changes, such as import price reductions). To stem the growth of the deficit, the nation must retard the growth of its demand (that is, its absorption or expenditure) or accelerate the growth of its output.

The United States in the mid-1980s was such a nation. The data in Table 4–9 reveal that domestic demand grew faster than gross national product in the United States in every year from 1983 through 1986, a period during which dramatic increases occurred in the country's deficits on international trade and current account. Note that in most years U.S. output grew faster than output in other OECD countries as a group; however, U.S. demand grew even faster by comparison with demand in other OECD countries.

It seems, then, that the U.S. external deficits did not result from "supply-side" problems, certainly not from supply-side problems *alone*. Demand, or more precisely, the changing relationship between demand and supply, seems a more promising subject for analysis. In what follows, some explanations involving both demand and supply are considered. Foreign as well as U.S. demand and supply are relevant, since some of what the United States supplies goes to satisfy foreign demand, while some of U.S. demand is satisfied by foreign supply.

UNFAIR FOREIGN TRADING PRACTICES

One explanation often advanced for the U.S. trade deficit is unfair foreign trading practices. The playing field is said to be tilted against the United States. (Apparently, teams never change goals on this field!)

This explanation involves references to both demand and supply. Although it is foreign rather than U.S. demand and supply that have allegedly been manipulated, the impact would have been to increase U.S. net imports. On the supply side, other nations have been charged with subsidizing or "dumping" their exports in world markets, thus lowering their supply prices and stealing both U.S. and foreign markets from U.S. suppliers. On the demand side, other nations are accused of imposing barriers against U.S. exports, thereby reducing demand for them.

To be sure, unfair trading actions do occur, and national governments, including the U.S. government, commonly undertake to shield firms within their borders against injury from such practices. In the United States, the law provides U.S. industries with remedies against import competition from dumped or subsidized merchandise, as well as against other practices deemed unfair. *Dumping* is defined as the sale of foreign merchandise at prices below those charged in the foreign producers' home market, or below the foreign cost of production. The antidumping statutes provide for the imposition of antidumping duties to offset such price-cutting when a determination is made that a domestic industry is being materially injured—or threatened with such injury—by the dumped imports, or that the establishment of the industry is being materially retarded by such imports. Similarly, "countervailing" duties are imposed to offset foreign subsidies upon a determination by U.S. authorities that, because of subsidized import competition, a U.S. industry is being materially injured—or threatened with such injury—or the establishment of the industry is being materially retarded.[15]

During 1986, the United States imposed new antidumping duties on fourteen products from thirteen countries, and imposed new countervailing duties on ten products from nine countries. At the end of the year, antidumping duties were in force on 122 products from thirty-two countries, and countervailing duties were levied on sixty-two products from twenty-five countries.[16] Other actions were taken against practices that the United States deemed unfair on grounds other than those covered under the antidumping or countervailing duty laws.[17]

Therefore, while unfair foreign trading practices may have operated to increase U.S. imports, it is plain that U.S. firms availed themselves of the provisions of U.S. law in order to stem such increases. The burden of proof rests with those who suggest that U.S. imports were bloated by unfair foreign trading practices in spite of the legal remedies that U.S. firms invoked against such practices. Unfair foreign trading practices were to be found long before the U.S. trade deficit began to surge in the early 1980s, and it remains to be shown that those practices intensified so as to contribute substantially to the deficit.

Another difficulty with attributing the increased U.S. deficit to unfair foreign trading practices is that the increase was distributed widely across both commodity categories and geographic areas. This fact is documented in Tables 4–10 and 4–11. It seems most unlikely that

Table 4–10. U.S. Merchandise Trade, by Major Trading
Partners or Areas, 1980 and 1986 (in billions of dollars)

Country or Area	1980	1986	
		Actual	Allocated on Basis of 1980 Shares[a]
Canada			
U.S. exports	41.6	57.0	41.6
U.S. imports	42.9	70.3	63.3
Balance	−1.3	−13.3	−21.7
Japan			
U.S. exports	20.8	26.4	20.8
U.S. imports	31.2	80.8	46.1
Balance	−10.4	−54.4	−25.3
West Germany			
U.S. exports	11.4	10.3	11.4
U.S. imports	11.7	24.5	17.3
Balance	−0.2	−14.3	−5.9
Mexico			
U.S. exports	15.2	12.4	15.2
U.S. imports	12.6	17.2	18.6
Balance	2.7	−4.8	−3.4
United Kingdom			
U.S. exports	12.8	11.1	12.8
U.S. imports	9.8	15.1	14.5
Balance	3.0	−4.0	−1.7
OPEC			
U.S. exports	17.4	10.5	17.4
U.S. imports	55.6	18.9	82.1
Balance	−38.2	−8.4	−64.7
Rest of the world			
U.S. exports	105.1	96.7	105.1
U.S. imports	86.0	141.9	126.9
Balance	19.1	−45.1	−21.8
Total, all areas			
U.S. exports	224.3	224.4	224.4
U.S. imports	249.8	368.7	368.7
Balance	−25.5	−144.3	−144.3

Note: Detail may not add to totals shown because of rounding.

[a]Each area is allocated the same fraction of total 1986 U.S. exports and imports as in 1980.

Source: *Survey of Current Business* 67 (June 1987): 60–62.

Table 4-11. U.S. Merchandise Trade, by Major End-Use Category, 1980 and 1986 (in billions of dollars).

End-Use Category	1980	1986 Actual	1986 Allocated on Basis of 1980 Shares[a]
Food, feeds, and beverages			
Exports	35.7	22.6	35.7
Imports	18.1	24.0	26.7
Balance	17.6	− 1.4	9.0
Industrial supplies and materials			
Exports	71.9	64.0	71.9
Imports	133.3	102.8	196.7
Balance	− 61.4	− 38.8	− 124.8
Capital goods, except automotive			
Exports	74.2	79.8	74.2
Imports	31.2	75.4	46.1
Balance	43.0	4.4	28.1
Automotive vehicles, parts, and engines			
Exports	17.5	25.4	17.5
Imports	27.9	78.1	41.2
Balance	− 10.4	− 52.7	− 23.7
Consumer goods (nonfood), except automotive			
Exports	16.6	14.5	16.6
Imports	34.4	77.8	50.8
Balance	− 17.8	− 63.3	− 34.2
All other, including balance-of-payments adjustments			
Exports	8.2	18.1	8.2
Imports	4.8	10.6	7.1
Balance	3.4	7.5	1.1
All categories			
Exports	224.3	224.4	224.4
Imports	249.8	368.7	368.7
Balance	− 25.5	− 144.3	− 144.3

Note: Detail may not add to totals shown because of rounding.

[a]Each category is allocated the same fraction of total 1986 U.S. exports and imports as in 1980.

Source: *Survey of Current Business* 67 (June 1987): 64.

virtually all major trading partners of the United States would simultaneously have intensified unfair practices in their trade with the nation.

Table 4-10 presents aggregate data on trade between the United States and each of its five leading trade partners, listed in order of magnitude of total U.S. trade with them in 1986. Similar data are shown for OPEC and for the rest of the world. Together, the five leading trade partners accounted for 55 percent of U.S. international trade (exports plus imports) in 1986; if OPEC is added, that share rises to 60 percent. Clearly, the U.S. trade balance deteriorated markedly from 1980 to 1986 with every listed area but OPEC, from which U.S. imports of petroleum declined dramatically.

To identify the areas with which the U.S. trade position deteriorated more than proportionately, the last column of Table 4–10 shows what the value of U.S. exports and imports with each area would have been in 1986 if each area had retained the same percentages of total U.S. exports and imports as in 1980. Comparison of the last two columns reveals that the U.S. trade balance worsened not only actually, but disproportionately (the 1986 "actual" exceeds the "allocated"), with all listed areas except OPEC and Canada. While the greatest actual deterioration was with the "rest of the world," the greatest disproportionate deterioration, amounting to $29 billion, was with Japan.

The deterioration in the U.S. trade balance was distributed widely across commodity categories as well as across geographic areas. As indicated in Table 4–11, aside from the "all other" category the balance worsened between 1980 and 1986 in every major commodity category except industrial supplies and materials, a category influenced by the decline in oil imports. The greatest deteriorations, in order of importance, occurred in consumer goods, automotive vehicles, parts, and engines, and capital goods. Especially noteworthy is the decline of the surplus in capital goods, a category in which U.S. surpluses had come to be taken for granted. Even so, the largest deficits in 1986 were in consumer goods and automotive items.

More than proportionate deteriorations occurred in foods, feeds, and beverages, capital goods, automotive vehicles and parts, and consumer goods. For each of these categories, the actual 1986 deficit was larger—or the actual 1986 surplus was smaller—than it would have been if the category had accounted for the same percentage of total exports and imports as in 1980. (See last two columns of Table 4–11.) It is remarkable that total U.S. exports actually declined between 1980 and 1986, while imports increased in every category but industrial supplies and materials.

Thus, the pervasiveness of the deterioration in the U.S. trade balance makes it unlikely that unfair foreign trading practices played a major role. Does this conclusion hold even for U.S. trade with Japan? The issue is raised most often with regard to Japan, partly because the U.S. deficit with that nation increased so sharply and amounted to more than one-third of the total U.S. deficit in 1986. While precise explanation of trade flows is very difficult, quantitative studies have concluded that the increase in the U.S. deficit with Japan was attributable mainly, or perhaps fully, to factors such as changes in prices, incomes, and the yen-dollar exchange rate. Any impact of unfair trading practices was adjudged to be decidedly secondary.[18]

Japan's record is not without blemish, however. In particular, evidence has been marshaled that Japan has offered some formidable "invisible" barriers to international trade. An invisible barrier is a system or regulation that applies to both domestic and foreign producers, but that works, perhaps unintentionally, to reduce the share of imports in domestic consumption. Government procurement policies, the wholesale and retail distribution systems, the setting of product standards, and the testing of products against these standards have commonly been alleged to constitute formidable invisible barriers in Japan. According to one investigation, if Japan's invisible barriers had been reduced to levels corresponding to those in the United States and the European Economic Community in the early 1980s, Japan's manufactured imports might have increased by 27 percent (equivalent to a rise of 7 percent in the country's total imports), with at least half of the increased imports coming from the United States. At the same time, the investigation points out that such an increase would be far too small to eliminate the U.S. trade deficit with Japan. Thus, the conclusion remains that the deficit was generated mainly, if not totally, by causes other than unfair trading practices.[19]

If unfair foreign trading practices are an improbable explanation of the U.S. trade and current account deficits, what other explanations might be more convincing? This matter is taken up next.

PROBABLE CAUSES OF THE U.S. TRADE AND CURRENT ACCOUNT DEFICITS

In its 1985 annual report, the Council of Economic Advisers identified three factors as the *immediate* causes of the U.S. trade deficit: (1) the appreciation of the dollar in the foreign exchange markets after mid-1980;

(2) the more rapid expansion of real income and demand in the United States than in the rest of the world after 1982; and (3) the reduced demand for imports by the less developed countries that began to experience severe difficulty in servicing their debt and in obtaining new loans after mid-1982. According to the council, the third factor accounted for somewhat less than 25 percent of the increase in the deficit between 1980 and 1984; the second factor accounted for a full 25 percent; and the first accounted for most of the increase.[20]

But what explains these factors themselves? The debt-servicing difficulties of the developing countries were the subject of the preceding chapter and will not be considered again in detail here. This chapter has already taken note of the other two factors; explanations for them are offered here, with most attention given to the appreciation of the dollar.

The dollar's value will rise in the foreign exchange markets if the demand for dollars exceeds the supply at prevailing exchange rates. During the early 1980s, one important development that led to increased demand for dollars, relative to the supply, was an increase in net borrowing from abroad by U.S. residents. Foreign currency balances were exchanged into dollar balances to accommodate this increase in U.S. borrowing, thereby bidding up the price of the dollar. The increased U.S. borrowing was caused largely by changes in federal fiscal policy, especially the shift toward deficit in the budget, which occurred at a time when U.S. monetary policy was relatively restrictive.

The key role played by government fiscal policy in inducing borrowing from abroad is suggested by an important accounting relationship: private domestic investment can be funded out of either the country's private saving or government saving, or out of funds loaned by foreigners. If government saving decreases without a compensating increase in private saving, private investors must tap foreign saving more heavily if they are to sustain their outlays.

The relative magnitudes involved in this accounting relationship for the United States are shown in Table 4–12, where private domestic investment in the fourth column is equal to the sum of its sources of financing, itemized in the first three columns. A negative number in one of the first three columns means that saving is being absorbed, on balance, rather than being made available for private domestic investment. Thus, in 1975 foreigners borrowed from current U.S. saving, rather than lending out of their own saving. Government in the United States also borrowed to finance a deficit in 1975; consequently, out of private saving amounting to 19 percent of GNP, only 13.7 percent was left for private

Table 4-12. Major Categories of Saving and Investment as a Percentage of GNP for the United States, 1970-87.

Year	Gross Private Saving + (1)	Government Saving + (2)	Net Investment (lending) by Foreigners = (3)	Gross Private Domestic Investment (4)
1970	16.2	-1.0	-0.5	14.7
1971	17.3	-1.8	-0.1	15.6
1972	16.8	-0.3	0.2	16.7
1973	18.0	0.6	-0.6	17.6
1974	17.3	-0.3	-0.4	16.3
1975	19.0	-4.1	-1.4	13.7
1976	18.0	-2.2	-0.5	15.6
1977	17.8	-1.0	0.4	17.3
1978	18.2	0.0	0.5	18.5
1979	17.8	0.5	-0.1	18.1
1980	17.5	-1.3	-1.5	16.0
1981	18.0	-1.0	-0.3	16.9
1982	17.6	-3.5	0.0	14.1
1983	17.4	-3.8	1.0	14.7
1984	17.9	-2.8	2.4	17.6
1985	16.6	-3.3	2.9	16.0
1986	16.1	-3.5	3.4	15.8
1987	15.0	-2.4	3.5	16.0

Note: Detail may not add to totals shown because of statistical discrepancy.

Source: U.S. Board of Governors of the Federal Reserve System, Macrodata Library.

investment within the United States (after adjustment for problems of measurement, known as the statistical discrepancy).

In 1982, the government deficit increased sharply in relation to GNP and remained large by historical standards through 1986 and into 1987. Over the same six years, private saving as a percentage of GNP declined, rather than rising to compensate for the greater government dissaving. Thus, private investment was increasingly financed by U.S. borrowing from abroad, as can be seen in Table 4-12. The borrowing from abroad allowed total U.S. demand, or spending, to increase faster than U.S. output.

This net borrowing from abroad, it should be noted, is essentially the same as the current account deficit in the U.S. balance of payments. Although the government deficit and the current account deficit are thus related in an accounting sense, the sizes of the two deficits can still vary independently of each other, or inversely. On occasion, inverse variation does occur. For example, from 1971 to 1972 the government deficit diminished while net borrowing from foreigners (the current account deficit) expanded.

Such inverse variation is not likely when the government deficit changes dramatically in response to a change in government policy, as was the case in the United States in 1982, when a major federal tax reduction began to take effect even as spending on federal programs was being accelerated. While views differ regarding the short-run impact of government deficits, the dominant theory is that such a policy-induced surge in government borrowing in a country will put upward pressure on interest rates (adjusted for expected inflation) in that country, thereby attracting foreign investment. As foreign investors acquire the country's currency in order to invest there, they bid up the price of that currency in the foreign exchange markets. The higher price of the country's currency will discourage foreigners from purchasing its goods but will encourage residents of the country to use their now more valuable currency to purchase foreign goods, so that the country's current account will move toward deficit (or toward a larger deficit). In addition, any increase in the country's total spending resulting from the enlarged government deficit will go partly for imports and for domestic goods that would otherwise be exported, also worsening the current account balance. Again, to return to one of our central themes, we can see from this brief description that the deterioration of the current account balance is associated with an increase in the country's total demand relative to the country's output.

Figure 4–3 supports the view that an increase in the government deficit tends to increase the current account deficit at least over the medium run. The government deficit represented in this chart has been adjusted to exclude the effects of the business cycle; for example, any declines in tax revenues occurring because of recessions have been added back to the recorded level of government receipts, reducing the recorded deficit. Such adjustments are warranted because our interest is in deficits that tend to add to the preexisting level of borrowing and spending, rather than in deficits that merely offset a decline in aggregate borrowing and spending elsewhere in the economy. Since cyclically adjusted data are

Figure 4–3.   The Current Account and Federal Budget
Deficits of the United States.

Billions of Dollars

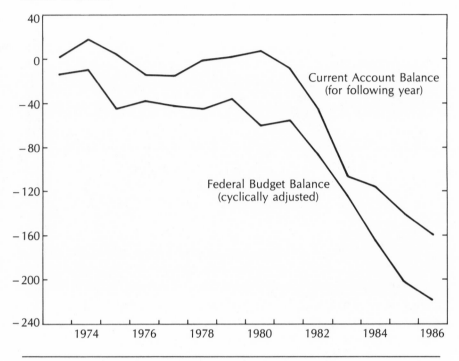

Source: *Survey of Current Business* 66 (March 1986): 14, 67 (June 1987): 54–55, 67 (August
1987): 4, and 68 (February 1988): 24.

not available for state and local government deficits, Figure 4–3 uses
data for the federal deficit, which has been the focus of concern. Also,
the federal deficit for each year is matched with the current account
deficit for the following year, on the assumption that some time is required for an increase in the federal deficit to influence the current account deficit.

As noted above, a change in the federal deficit is presumed to affect
the current account deficit partly through its impact on the dollar price
of foreign exchange. Figure 4–4 suggests that the hypothesized relationship between the government deficit and the exchange rate did indeed prevail over the period 1973–85, although the relationship is rather
loose. In this case, the government deficit for each year is paired with

Figure 4-4. The Real Exchange Rate and the Federal Budget Deficit of the United States, 1973–87.

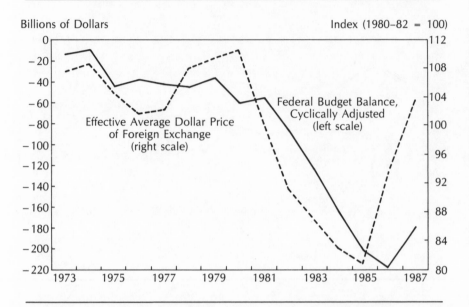

Source: *World Financial Markets*, June/July 1987, p. 16, and staff of Morgan Guaranty Trust Company; *Survey of Current Business* 66 (March 1986): 14, 67 (August 1987): 4, and 68 (February 1988): 24.

the exchange rate for the same year, with no lag, on the common assumption that exchange rates react promptly to stimuli, or even anticipate them (but then affect the current account with a lag). Also, the dollar price of foreign exchange, rather than the foreign exchange price of the dollar, is plotted; therefore, a downward movement signifies appreciation of the dollar.

Although Figures 4–3 and 4–4 are suggestive, strong conclusions should not be drawn from them alone. The exchange rate and the current account are influenced not just by the government deficit but by other factors as well.[21] Other factors likely to have contributed significantly to the dollar's appreciation during the early 1980s—and thus to the current account deficit—were an anti-inflationary U.S. monetary policy, U.S. tax law changes and deregulation that enhanced the after-tax profitability of investing in the United States, and the easing of restrictions over capital outflows from Japan.[22] The net flow of capital into the United States was also fostered by the loss of investment appeal on the part of the less developed countries that could not meet the interest payments on their debt.

If net capital flows into the United States increased so rapidly during the early 1980s, what form did these inflows take? As shown in Table 4-13, privately owned capital generally accounted for the great bulk of the inflows; foreign net purchases of U.S. securities consistently were relatively large, as were inflows through U.S. banks. In 1986, the private inflows were substantially augmented by inflows of officially owned capital, as more than $30 billion of dollar holdings in the United States were

Table 4-13.   Capital Transactions in the U.S. Balance of Payments, 1980–86 (in billions of dollars).

Type of Transaction	1981	1982	1983	1984	1985	1986
Private capital, net	− 22.6	− 19.9	35.4	85.8	106.3	84.3
Securities, net	4.1	5.1	10.1	30.8	63.9	75.8
Foreign net purchases	9.8	13.1	16.9	35.6	71.4	79.1
U.S. Treasuries	2.9	7.0	8.7	23.0	20.4	8.3
U.S. corporate bonds	2.1	2.8	2.2	13.9	46.6	53.8
U.S. corporate stocks	4.8	3.3	6.0	− 1.3	4.3	17.0
U.S. net purchases of foreign securities	− 5.7	− 8.0	− 6.8	− 4.8	− 7.5	− 3.3
Direct investment, net	15.6	16.2	11.6	22.5	1.8	− 3.0
Foreign direct in U.S.	25.2	13.8	11.9	25.4	19.0	25.1
U.S. direct investment abroad	− 9.6	2.4	− .4	− 2.8	− 17.3	− 28.0
Net flows reported by U.S. banks	− 42.0	− 45.4	20.4	22.7	39.7	18.3
Other	− .3	4.2	− 6.6	9.7	.9	− 6.8
Official capital, net	− 5.3	− 7.5	− .4	− 5.6	− 7.8	33.1
Total reported capital flows, net	− 27.9	− 27.4	35.1	80.2	98.5	117.4
Statistical discrepancy	19.9	36.1	11.2	26.8	17.9	23.9
Current account balance	6.9	− 8.7	− 46.2	− 107.0	− 116.4	− 141.4

Note: Minus sign indicates an outflow.

Source: *Survey of Current Business* 67 (June 1987): 54, 55, 72; and U.S. Department of Commerce staff.

acquired by foreign monetary authorities, some of whom had sold their own currencies in exchange for dollars in an effort to limit their currencies' appreciation in the foreign exchange markets. Inflows of officially owned capital were even larger in 1987, according to preliminary data.

Having considered the causes of the U.S. current account deficit, we turn now to the consequences. These can be divided into two categories: past and future. Our chief concern will be with consequences for the United States, rather than for the rest of the world.

DEINDUSTRIALIZATION?

To some observers, the large U.S. external deficits connote something more alarming than reduced U.S. competitiveness; they connote the "deindustrialization" of America. According to this school, U.S. manufacturing not only has lost ground in export markets, but has been in retreat before a flood of competing imports. Strong action has, therefore, been recommended, to preserve the viability of domestic industry.

The pervasiveness of any such problem across American industries is hard to judge, largely because the pertinent Census Bureau data (relating U.S. exports and imports to domestic production by product category) become available only with a long lag. But rough approximations to the desired Census Bureau data can be constructed, and Table 4–14 presents such approximations for manufacturing industries for 1986, as well as for 1980. In this table, industries are listed in order of the size of 1986 exports less competing imports, expressed as a percentage of the industry's shipments.[23]

From column 1 it is clear that a number of major U.S. manufacturing industries were exporting a sizable fraction of the products that they shipped in 1986, in spite of the huge overall U.S. trade deficit. Moreover, the value of imports that competed with these particular industries was commonly less than the value of the industries' exports. The producers of aircraft parts boasted the greatest relative surplus of exports over competing imports in 1986, followed by agricultural chemicals and complete aircraft. Several other chemical-producing industries are also near the top of the list, as are the makers of some machinery and equipment.

By contrast, industries listed at the bottom of the table were experiencing intense import competition. Both for "kitchen articles and pottery" and "other leather products" (which includes leather footwear, gloves, purses, and luggage), the value of competing imports less the industry's exports was greater even than the value of total industry shipments. Very high import penetration had also occurred in radios and television sets, and in ophthalmic goods, watches, and clocks. These four import-competing industries encountered extremely sharp increases in import competition after 1980. The excess of competing imports over exports as a percentage of shipments rose by 101 percentage points for kitchen articles and pottery, by ninety-five percentage points for other leather products, by sixty percentage points for radios and television sets, and by fifty-two percentage points for ophthalmic goods, watches, and clocks. These percentages, as reflected in the rankings shown in the last column of the table, are the worst of those recorded for the seventy-three industries. At the other end of the spectrum, the industries with the leading rankings in the last column not only held their own but advanced internationally against the rising tide of imports, as their exports rose by more than competing imports over the six-year period.

While such extreme industry values are interesting, they fail to represent the experience of the great mass of American industry. A better measure of that experience is provided by the median—the "middle" value, or that industry value with half the values above it and the other half below it. For example, for the industry with median rank in column 7 (the building paper industry), the difference between exports as a percantage of shipments and competing imports as a percentage of shipments shifted in favor of imports by five and one-fifth percentage points between 1980 and 1986; competing imports increased by more than exports for sixty-eight of the seventy-three industries. On the other hand, as shown in column 3, exports were equal to or greater than competing imports in 1986 for twenty-three of the industries, and for the median industry (in this case, the building materials and wire products industry), competing imports exceeded the industry's exports by only 2.3 percent of the industry's shipments, hardly an alarming statistic.

Increases in the share of the U.S. market supplied by foreign producers may or may not be associated with actual declines in domestic employment. To be sure, the typical U.S. industry would produce more output and employ more people if it were subjected to less foreign competition, other things being equal. But if demand is growing for the kinds of things an industry produces, the industry's output and employment can rise along with competing imports. More generally, other factors besides foreign competition play a role in determining an industry's employment and general health, and a rise in the measured intensity of foreign competition is not necessarily cause for concern.

Table 4-14. U.S. Manufactured Exports, Imports, and Exports Less Imports, by Industry, 1986 and 1980 (all as a percentage of shipments).

Industry, in Order of Size of Column 3	1986			1980			Rank of Industry According to Column 3 Less Column 6
	Exports (1)	Competing Imports (2)	Exports Less Competing Imports (3)	Exports (4)	Competing Imports (5)	Exports Less Competing Imports (6)	(7)
1. Aircraft parts	23.6	8.9	14.6	24.5	7.2	17.3	26
2. Agricultural chemicals	18.9	6.4	12.5	21.2	4.7	16.5	32
3. Complete aircraft	15.8	3.9	12.0	27.3	2.8	24.5	53
4. Fats and oils	14.0	3.5	10.4	20.6	3.0	17.6	42
5. Construction, mining, and material-handling equipment	23.6	15.2	8.4	33.7	4.1	29.6	65
6. Tobacco manufactures	8.4	.5	7.9	9.0	.8	8.2	6
7. Machine shops	7.6	0.0	7.6	6.0	0.0	6.0	2
8. Other chemical products	12.2	5.2	7.1	15.3	2.5	12.7	40
9. Shipbuilding and tanks	7.5	.6	6.9	8.1	0.0	8.1	15
10. Steam engines and turbines	18.1	11.6	6.5	35.2	6.6	28.7	66
11. Industrial chemicals, except pigments	17.8	11.6	6.2	15.9	7.1	8.8	25
12. Ordnance	11.6	5.5	6.1	15.6	3.4	12.2	41
13. Scientific and engineering products	16.7	11.0	5.8	20.1	6.6	13.5	44
14. Office and computing machines	26.9	24.0	2.9	26.7	7.8	18.9	61

15. Railroad equipment	21.2	18.8	2.4	5.6	4.6	1.1	3
16. Service-industry machinery	6.8	5.0	1.8	13.2	1.6	11.5	48
17. Drugs, soaps, and toiletries	5.5	4.4	1.0	6.5	2.7	3.8	27
18. Household furniture	.9	.4	.5	1.7	.1	1.6	14
19. Meat products	4.1	3.7	.4	3.2	4.0	-.8	4
20. Paperboard containers	.8	.4	.4	.9	.1	.8	7
21. Newspapers, books, and periodicals	1.7	1.6	.1	2.1	1.2	1.0	11
22. Electrical transmission and distribution equipment	4.7	4.6	.1	7.1	3.6	3.5	29
23. Metal cans, barrels, and drums	1.1	1.1	0.0	1.3	.4	.9	12
24. Wood buildings and mobile homes	.3	.5	-.2	2.2	.1	2.1	22
25. Paints and related products	3.8	4.1	-.3	3.4	2.4	1.0	17
26. All other foods	3.7	4.0	-.4	5.6	4.3	1.3	18
27. Other publishing and printing	.5	.9	-.4	1.1	.7	.4	10
28. Dairy products	1.0	1.4	-.4	.8	1.4	-.6	5
29. Knitting mills	.6	1.1	-.5	1.1	.3	.8	16
30. Die-cut paper and board	.2	1.0	-.8	.4	.7	-.4	8
31. Paving and roofing materials	.4	1.2	-.8	.7	.4	.3	13
32. Other paper products	2.0	3.0	-1.0	3.0	1.6	1.4	24
33. Iron and steel foundries	.9	2.0	-1.1	1.4	.4	1.0	21
34. Other rubber and plastics products, n.e.c.	4.2	5.6	-1.4	5.6	4.2	1.4	28
35. Wood containers	1.4	3.5	-2.2	1.5	1.9	-.3	20
36. Glass containers	.4	2.7	-2.3	1.0	1.0	0.0	23
37. Building materials and wire products	2.4	4.8	-2.3	5.0	2.6	2.4	35

Table 4-14. continued

Industry, in Order of Size of Column 3	1986			1980			Rank of Industry According to Column 3 Less Column 6 (7)
	Exports (1)	Competing Imports (2)	Exports Less Competing Imports (3)	Exports (4)	Competing Imports (5)	Exports Less Competing Imports (6)	
38. Other fabricated metal products	5.1	7.8	-2.7	6.7	5.0	1.7	34
39. Electrical industrial apparatus	7.6	10.6	-3.0	14.0	5.4	8.6	51
40. Communication equipment	5.9	9.0	-3.1	7.4	6.6	.8	30
41. Other electrical machinery	12.3	15.9	-3.6	15.7	9.5	6.2	49
42. Other stone, clay, and glass products	3.2	7.2	-4.0	4.6	3.8	.8	36
43. All other wood products	5.3	9.5	-4.1	8.7	8.8	-.1	33
44. Miscellaneous equipment	5.3	10.0	-4.7	6.9	6.2	.7	39
45. Floor-covering mills	2.0	6.9	-4.8	5.6	5.1	.5	38
46. Farm machinery and equipment	11.1	16.2	-5.1	14.1	11.1	3.0	45
47. Other durable goods	5.1	10.2	-5.1	8.7	5.7	3.1	46
48. Broad-woven fabrics and other textiles	4.2	10.3	-6.1	6.8	5.6	1.2	43
49. Beverages	1.1	7.5	-6.4	1.4	7.0	-5.6	9
50. Building paper	4.0	10.7	-6.7	2.3	3.8	-1.5	37
51. Other petroleum products	3.4	10.6	-7.2	1.5	7.0	-5.5	19
52. Pulp and paperboar mills, except building paper	8.2	15.6	-7.4	12.3	15.7	-3.4	31

53. General industry machinery	25.1	32.5	−7.4	28.6	13.1	15.5	67
54. Internal combustion engines	18.4	27.4	−9.0	23.3	14.1	9.2	63
55. Photographic goods	12.4	22.3	−10.0	15.3	10.7	4.5	55
56. Household appliances	5.5	17.0	−11.5	9.6	7.9	1.7	54
57. Electronic components	18.6	30.5	−12.0	20.9	17.7	3.2	59
58. Special industry machinery	11.6	24.3	−12.7	18.2	15.9	2.3	57
59. Cutlery, hand tools, hardware	6.7	19.6	−12.9	12.2	13.3	−1.1	52
60. Leather, industrial products, and cut stock	17.4	32.8	−15.4	13.2	13.3	−.1	60
61. Tires and tubes	3.4	19.8	−16.4	5.9	12.8	−6.9	47
62. Blast furnaces, steel mills	1.8	19.9	−18.2	4.3	11.7	−7.4	50
63. Nonferrous metals	8.1	28.7	−20.6	15.0	18.2	−3.3	62
64. All other furniture	2.0	25.4	−23.4	2.8	11.3	−8.5	56
65. Metalworking machinery	16.5	40.1	−23.6	17.6	15.7	1.9	68
66. Other transportation equipment	6.5	30.2	−23.7	8.3	35.7	−27.5	1
67. Motor vehicles and parts	8.9	35.8	−26.9	12.0	23.8	−11.8	58
68. Apparel and related products	2.2	33.4	−31.2	3.6	14.5	−10.9	64
69. Miscellaneous personal goods	9.5	70.0	−60.6	14.9	30.8	−15.9	69
70. Ophthalmic goods, watches, and clocks	9.6	102.1	−92.6	10.1	50.3	−40.2	70
71. Radio and television	8.3	101.7	−93.4	16.1	49.2	−33.1	71
72. Other leather products	3.2	135.9	−132.7	3.2	41.2	−38.0	72
73. Kitchen articles and pottery	14.1	206.3	−192.2	8.4	99.4	−91.0	73

Note: Detail may not add to totals shown because of rounding.

Source: U.S. Bureau of the Census: EA675, U.S. Exports, 1980; EM575, U.S. Exports, December 1986; IA275, U.S. Imports for Consumption and General Imports, 1980; IM175, U.S. Imports for Consumption and General Imports, December 1986; and Census Bureau staff.

In fact, recorded changes in employment by industry are not closely correlated with changes in the degree of net import competition over the period 1980–86. As illustrated in Figure 4–5, little relationship exists between the percentage-point change in exports less competing imports as a percentage of an industry's shipments, on the one hand, and the percentage change in industry employment, on the other hand.[24]

Figure 4–5.   Exports Less Competing Imports and Insured Employment for Seventy-three Manufacturing Industries, 1980–86.

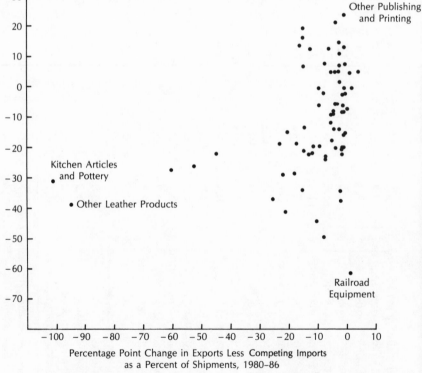

Percent Change in
Employment, 1980–86

Percentage Point Change in Exports Less Competing Imports
as a Percent of Shipments, 1980–86

Source: 1980 employment data from U.S. Bureau of Labor Statistics computer tape; 1986 employment data were estimated (see appendix to this chapter); other data from Table 14.

Thus, the evidence examined here offers only marginal support for the view that employment trends were most adverse in the industries experiencing the sharpest rises in net import competition.

Even though changes in reported employment are not closely associated with changes in net import competition for the great mass of industries, such an association might exist for the industries with the largest numbers of employees. If one is concerned, however, with the relationship between foreign competition and *aggregate* U.S. economic performance, that relationship is more appropriately analyzed with aggregate data for the entire economy than with data for individual industries. Now, at the aggregate level, just as at the industry level, total output and employment would have been higher if exports had been greater, or competing imports smaller, other things being equal. But once this point is granted, how did the U.S. economy in fact perform under the intensified foreign competition?

The answer is perhaps best conveyed by aggregative data on the production of goods and services. Because goods are generally more transportable than services, firms that produce goods usually are subject to more foreign competition than are firms that produce services. According to the data in Table 4-15, the production of U.S. goods grew faster than either U.S. GNP or the production of U.S. services after the 1981–82 recession, and the growth of goods production over this period compares favorably with that during previous recent expansions.[25] By this measure, then, U.S. goods producers did well, even with the

Table 4-15. Percentage Changes in U.S. Real Output During Recessions and the Succeeding Expansions.

Period (Year and Quarter)	Goods	Services	Structures	Total GNP
1969:4 to 1970:4 (recession)	– 3.3	1.6	2.4	– 0.4
1970:4 to 1973:4 (expansion)	17.6	12.0	12.7	14.5
1973:4 to 1975:1 (recession)	– 7.8	3.0	– 18.9	– 4.3
1975:1 to 1980:1 (expansion)	25.2	18.7	28.1	22.4
1980:1 to 1980:3 (recession)	– 3.6	.8	– 10.4	– 2.3
1980:3 to 1981:3 (expansion)	5.8	1.3	2.5	3.3
1981:3 to 1982:4 (recession)	– 7.3	1.2	– 6.3	– 3.2
1982:4 to 1987:4 (expansion)	30.3	15.5	27.6	22.7

Source: U.S. Board of Governors of the Federal Reserve System, Macrodata Library.

heightened foreign competition; evidently, the growth of total U.S. demand was rapid enough to accommodate a substantial rise in U.S. production as well as in U.S. imports. (During recessions, of course, goods output actually declines, while services output continues to grow.)

Thus, neither the detailed industry data nor the aggregative data indicate that U.S. producers have suffered greatly from the increased trade deficit. Contrary to a common view, rising import competition need not signify unemployment and plant closings. To be sure, import competition can have an adverse effect on an industry's employment. Rising import competition by itself, however, is likely to be a misleading indicator of industrial health—especially when domestic demand is growing rapidly, for at such times both domestic production and imports can increase. In any event, at this writing, the "deindustrialization" of America by foreign competition is more nearly myth than substance.

A MODERATING INFLUENCE

Although the U.S. external deficits have not been destroying American industry, they have exercised a moderating influence. As already noted, U.S. output would have grown even more rapidly in the absence of those deficits; the result might well have been an overheated economy, with appreciably higher inflation and interest rates.

This conclusion is supported by the data in Table 4–9. The growth rate of U.S. real domestic demand in the years 1983 through 1986 was high by historical standards—and extraordinarily high in 1983 and 1984, the two years of greatest increase in the U.S. trade and current account deficits. Indeed, the 8.3 percent growth in U.S. domestic demand in 1984 was the highest since 1951. Had the United States been unable to acquire additional goods and services from abroad to help satisfy this surging demand, the nation could have experienced "bottlenecks"—if not more general shortages—as well as an acceleration of inflation. Even with the huge increase in its net imports, the U.S. economy expanded its output in 1984 by 6.4 percent, which was, again, the fastest rate of growth since 1951. Partly because of the availability of imported goods, this rapid expansion took place without any rise in overall inflation as measured by the GNP deflator. To be sure, the nation's high rate of unemployment—7.4 percent in 1984—also militated against rising inflation. But the unemployment rate did fall steadily after 1983, and by end-1986, according to some authorities, was at or near the level at which it would no longer serve to restrain inflation.[26] This level would have been reached much sooner without the increase in net imports.

It also seems clear that interest rates would have been higher in the United States had the nation been foreclosed from borrowing abroad. As reported in Table 4–12, gross private saving in the United States declined from 1981 to 1987 even though government dissaving had risen to unusually high levels; the nation stepped up its foreign borrowing to help offset these developments. Without the availability of foreign financing, U.S. interest rates would have risen so as to choke back the level of private domestic investment to the lower level of financing provided from domestic sources alone. Even with the net inflow of foreign capital, U.S. interest rates, both short- and long-term, reached record heights in the early 1980s.[27]

Thus, the near-term consequences of its external deficits seem to have been decidedly beneficial for the United States. What about the longer term?

THE COMING ADJUSTMENT

Both common sense and experience testify that neither individuals nor nations can incur debt without regard to ability to repay. But it would be a gross exaggeration to suggest that the United States in 1987 was facing an imminent debt crisis. By no conventional statistical indicator was the nation in such desperate straits.

In this kind of analysis, it is common to distinguish between liquidity and solvency risk. Although countries do not declare bankruptcy, a country is insolvent if it is unable, either for economic or political reasons, to meet its debt obligations over the long term. By contrast, illiquidity means that a country cannot meet its obligations coming due in the near term, but can discharge those obligations, with accrued interest, in the longer run, along with the rest of its obligations.

To assist in evaluating such risks, analysts have developed various indicators of the burden of international indebtedness. Although these indicators are crude, they can help to signal emerging distress.[28] Some widely used indicators focus on the share of a country's output or income that is owed to its creditors. Others focus on the share of export earnings that is absorbed by payments to creditors, recognizing that some significant fraction of those earnings must remain to pay for imports.

According to the data in Table 4–16, by comparison with other countries the U.S. position at end-1986 was extremely strong by one measure, but not so strong by the other measures presented. Gross external debt as a percentage of GNP was lower for the United States than for any of the other countries or country groups; no alarm was being sounded by this indicator. Nor was gross external debt as a percentage of exports very high by comparison with other countries. On the other hand, payments made by the United States to its creditors loomed relatively large in relation to the nation's export receipts, although much lower than payments to creditors by the triad of Argentina, Brazil, and Mexico, whose debt repayment difficulties have received so much publicity. On balance, one could hardly make the case from such indicators that the United States was threatened with a debt crisis, especially since the indicators fail to take into account the relatively large foreign assets held by U.S. residents.

Table 4–16.   Selected Debt Burden Indicators for the United States and Other Areas, 1986.

	Gross External Debt as Percent of		Debt Service on Gross External Debt as Percent of Exports of Goods and Services [a]	
	GNP or GDP	Exports of Goods and Services	Interest Alone	Total Debt Service
United States	11.9	135.6	16.5	76.9
Canada	42.5	142.6	12.4	56.9
Western Europe	37.3	98.4	9.8	53.2
Eastern Europe	16.1	132.5	8.5	60.5
Africa	52.2	254.5	13.6	72.4
Latin America	78.6	304.7	23.1	78.5
Argentina, Brazil, and Mexico	68.1	434.5	39.6	119.5
Asia and Pacific	45.0	154.1	9.0	39.1
Middle East	55.4	130.7	8.4	62.3

Note: For country groups, the value shown is the median.

[a]Net private transfers (where positive) are included in exports of goods and services.

Source: *Morgan International Data*, December 1987: Tables A–5 and A–7.

One key difference between the United States and the countries that have suffered debt repayment problems in recent years is that the great bulk of U.S. external debt has been denominated in U.S. rather than foreign currency.[29] Unlike debtors in these other countries, U.S. debtors generally have not had to acquire foreign exchange with which to service their external debts. Were this practice to continue, U.S. debtors would be unlikely to experience more difficulty in meeting their external obligations than in meeting their obligations to domestic creditors. In other words, any debt crisis encountered by the United States would be a general crisis, imperiling resident as well as foreign creditors, rather than an exclusively international crisis. Only a most unlikely development, such as systematic lending by foreigners to unsound U.S. businesses, or limitations by the U.S. government on U.S. payments to foreign creditors, would generate a peculiarly international problem. On the other hand, should U.S. external debt come to be denominated largely in foreign currencies, a depreciation of the dollar against those currencies would, of course, increase the number of dollars that U.S. debtors were obliged to repay; and a sharp depreciation could provoke a debt crisis that was initially concentrated in the international sector.

The fact that U.S. external debt was owed overwhelmingly in dollars does not mean that the debt imposed no burden, nor does the improbability of an external debt crisis mean that the United States could continue along the path taken in 1985–86. Some data relevant to this issue can be found in Table 6–2. Column 6 shows the accumulated net current account deficit (–) or surplus for each of fourteen industrial countries over the thirty-four–year span from 1952 to 1985, while the last column shows the ratio of that accumulated deficit or surplus to the gross saving done by the country during 1985. The largest negative ratio, –4.4, signifies that the nation with this ratio, Ireland, would require about four and one-half years of saving at its 1985 rate in order to pay back its net foreign debt incurred on current account over the years 1952–85. If Ireland's ratio seems rather high, the other negative ratios are much lower, and the general impression is one of conservatism among industrial countries in the accumulation of net debt. Even if a nation were inclined to borrow without limit, others generally would not lend to it beyond its perceived capacity to service its debt. The moral for the United States—for which the ratio had become –0.7 by end-1986—is that it would be unable to continue incurring such relatively large current account deficits in the long run, even if its government deficit remained large.

The long run, however, could be rather long. Some elementary computations are illuminating. At this writing, the U.S. current account deficit is approaching 3.5 percent of U.S. GNP, and GNP is about $4.5 trillion at an annual rate. Suppose that the current account deficit continued to run at 3.5 percent of GNP, and that nominal GNP increased by 6 percent each year, a fairly modest rate by recent historical standards. Also suppose that the average interest rate, or more generally, the average rate of return, earned by foreigners investing in the United States were 8 percent per annum. Finally, since the United States reportedly received nearly $21 billion more in interest and other income payments from foreigners than it made to them in 1986 (even though the data showed the nation then to be a net debtor), we shall suppose that the United States did not in fact become a net debtor until the time of this writing.

On these assumptions, the fourth column of Table 4–17 shows how net interest earned by foreigners would rise as a percentage of U.S. GNP over a fifty-year period. After a half-century, this interest burden would amount to about 4.7 percent of U.S. GNP. More likely, if U.S. net debt did rise markedly in relation to GNP, foreigners would demand higher interest rates to compensate for the reduced creditworthiness of the nation (the seemingly greater risk of lending to it). Thus, the percentages in the fourth column would climb initially at a faster pace than shown, then at a slower pace as foreigners became reluctant to extend additional loans. Indeed, to contemplate a net foreign debt for the United States amounting to more than half its GNP, as this scenario does, might seem beyond the realm of reason. As the data in Table 4–16 suggests, such ratios did obtain for gross (and presumably net) external debt at the end of 1986 for a number of countries, but most were less developed, with much smaller economies, than the United States. Moreover, net interest ratios approaching the highest levels shown in column 4 of Table 4–17 would likely translate into something like two-fifths of U.S. exports of goods and services. In any event, our calculations are merely illustrations, not forecasts.

An interesting alternative is to assume that the U.S. current account deficit continued at an annual rate of about $150 billion—rather than rising with GNP—but to retain the other assumptions underlying the preceding computations. In this case, the net interest burden as a percentage of GNP would move upward for many years, as shown by the last column in Table 4–17, but would then decline (beginning with the eighteenth year, not shown in the table). This scenario seems much less threatening.

Table 4-17. Net U.S. Interest Burden from External Debt Under Differing Assumptions (in billions of dollars, unless otherwise noted).

Year	Nominal GNP (1)	Annual Current Account Deficit Assumed to Be 3.5% of GNP			Annual Current Account Deficit Assumed to be $150 Billion		
		Cumulative Current Account Deficit (2)	Net Interest on Cumulative Deficit (3)	Net Interest as Percent of GNP (4)	Cumulative Current Account Deficit (5)	Net Interest on Cumulative Deficit (6)	Net Interest as Percent of GNP (7)
1	$4,500	$157.5	$12.6	.28	$150	$12	.27
2	4,770	324.5	26.0	.55	300	24	.50
3	5,056.2	501.4	40.1	.79	450	36	.71
4	5,359.6	689.0	55.1	1.03	600	48	.90
5	5,681.1	887.8	71.0	1.25	750	60	1.06
6	6,022.0	1,098.6	87.9	1.46	900	72	1.20
7	6,383.3	1,322.0	105.8	1.66	1,050	84	1.32
8	6,766.3	1,558.8	124.7	1.84	1,200	96	1.42
9	7,172.3	1,809.9	144.8	2.02	1,350	108	1.51
10	7,602.7	2,076.0	166.1	2.18	1,500	120	1.58
20	13,615.2	5,793.7	463.5	3.40	3,000	240	1.76
30	24,382.7	12,451.7	996.1	4.09	4,500	360	1.48
40	43,666.7	24,375.0	1,950.0	4.47	6,000	480	1.10
50	78,198.7	45,727.9	3,658.2	4.68	7,500	600	.77

Note: Nominal GNP is assumed to increase by 6 percent annually. Interest rate is assumed to be 8 percent and is applied to the net debt outstanding at the end of each period, which is taken to be zero prior to year one.

Variations in the underlying assumptions would, of course, yield different hypothetical outcomes. What seems clear from the calculations presented is that the U.S. current account deficit must come down appreciably *in relation to U.S. GNP*. It is not so immediately obvious that the deficit must be reduced sharply from the level of about $150 billion per year that was attained after the end of 1986. With the deficit at this constant level, U.S. GNP presumably would eventually increase more rapidly than U.S. net indebtedness (the accumulated deficit), so that the net interest burden would begin to decline in relation to GNP well before reaching the level of 2 percent.

To suggest that the United States might continue to incur a sizable current account deficit is not to imply that the nation could avoid any adjustment in its external accounts. As U.S. net interest payments to foreigners increased with U.S. net indebtedness, the nation would have to generate increasing net surpluses on other current account transactions—essentially merchandise trade—in order to prevent the overall current account deficit from expanding. How this adjustment might take place is the topic of the next section.

THE NATURE OF THE ADJUSTMENT

The point has been made that total U.S. demand, or spending, increased faster than U.S. output, and that the nation is absorbing foreign saving to finance the gap. To reduce the imbalance, the United States must increase the rate of growth of its output or reduce the rate of increase in its spending. Alternatively, to prevent the imbalance from rising as interest payments to foreigners go up, the United States must increase the growth rate of its output of internationally traded goods or reduce the rate of increase in its spending on such goods.

To attempt to raise the growth rate of output above that recorded in 1985 through 1987 would be to court a marked rise in the rate of inflation. As already noted, by 1987 the U.S. economy was at or approaching "full employment," in the sense that further significant reductions in the unemployment rate would likely generate strong upward wage pressures.[30] Measures that raised output by raising productivity would not invite higher inflation. But raising the productivity of capital would tend to attract more investment from abroad, and as we have seen, investment from abroad works to enlarge rather than diminish the current account deficit. Therefore, policies designed to raise the rate of growth of output probably hold little promise for shrinking the external imbalances of the United States.

The nation could also attack these imbalances by restraining its spending. Slowing down the growth of consumption spending, private or government, would, of course, be equivalent to accelerating the pace of saving. Alternatively, if the course of saving were left unchanged, the economy could cut back on the growth of its private investment spending. Cutting back on investment in plant and equipment, however, would reduce the future growth of the nation's output.

To step up the rate of saving, the government could contract the budget deficit, either by cutting back its own spending programs or by raising taxes so that households would lower their consumption spending. If reduction of the budget deficit—and of the economic stimulus it provides—took place at a moderate pace, a recession need not ensue, since a goal of the deficit reduction would be to allow U.S. net exports, another stimulus, to expand more rapidly. One way that such deficit reduction could boost U.S. net exports would be by generating a depreciation of the dollar's foreign exchange value, just as enlargement of the deficit had generated an appreciation.

Thus, if U.S. spending must be constrained, cutting the federal budget deficit seems a relatively appealing strategy for cutting the international trade deficit. But are alternative or supplementary strategies available that do not rely on such direct attacks on spending? This economist is tempted to reply that there is no free lunch. Nonetheless, some other widely proposed remedies do have some merit.

One such meritorious strategy would be the adoption of more expansionary policies by countries with excess productive capacity and very low inflation, such as West Germany and Japan. Faster growth of demand in such countries would generally uplift U.S. exports, although the gains would be decidedly smaller than those from direct cuts in U.S. spending.

Another government strategy would be to do nothing at all—to take no action designed specifically to shrink the U.S. trade deficit, even in relation to GNP. As U.S. indebtedness mounted in relation to U.S. exports and GNP, investors would become more reluctant to lend to, or acquire net claims on, the United States, thus putting upward pressure on U.S. interest rates and downward pressure on the foreign exchange value of the dollar. Indeed, this process seemed to be under way late in 1986 and at times during 1987, as U.S. interest rates rose sharply in relation to rates in some other industrial countries even as the dollar dropped in value against the currencies of those countries. The higher

U.S. interest rates would discourage U.S. builders and other businesses from investing in new structures and equipment, and this reduced spending would help to improve the U.S. trade balance, albeit at the expense of future U.S. growth. Trade balance improvement would also be fostered by the depreciation of the dollar.

Just how dollar depreciation can improve the U.S. trade balance is a matter of some debate. One conceivable route is via a reduction in the purchasing power of U.S. money balances. A rise in the dollar price of foreign currency (dollar depreciation) tends to raise the dollar prices of foreign goods imported into the United States, as well as the prices of substitute goods produced within the country. Thus, the purchasing power of U.S. residents could be somewhat diminished, discouraging spending and improving the balance of trade.

Dollar depreciation typically has another related price effect that also is helpful. The depreciation-induced rise in the dollar price of imports, and of exports, encourages U.S. businesses to shift resources into the production of export goods and of goods that can substitute for imports, and away from the production of goods that do not move in international trade. The same price movements encourage U.S. consumers to switch their purchases away from the goods that move in international trade and toward nontraded goods. Again, the tendency is to improve the trade balance. And if the prices of nontraded goods decline, or rise more slowly than before the depreciation, the nation need not experience a marked rise in its overall rate of inflation.

Still another government strategy to reduce the trade deficit would be protectionism. Now, the U.S. trade deficit in 1987 was very large, and any U.S. import tariffs or quotas severe enough to have a sizable initial impact on the deficit would certainly have provoked foreign retaliation against U.S. exports. Even in the absence of retaliation, tariffs or quotas would not be very effective in decreasing the trade deficit unless they somehow reduced total U.S. spending. A tariff could reduce spending if the tariff reveneue were used by the government to cut back on its budget deficit, but other taxes would offer the same opportunity without the cost of an international trade war. Protectionism, therefore, is not a promising approach to the problem.

Of the various strategies considered, then, the most desirable would be a combination of federal deficit reduction, more expansionary policy in some other industrial countries, and tolerance of dollar depreciation. From 1985 through 1987, however, the main burden was placed on dollar depreciation—and during the latter part of the period, on higher U.S. interest rates that may well have been associated with the depreciation.

While the adjustment process under way in 1986 and 1987 was not ideal, the current account deficits incurred by the United States may well have been appropriate in the circumstances, for reasons already set forth. At worst, the deficits seem to have been a necessry evil, the evil being the sacrifice to be faced by the United States in its adjust-ment. As indicated in Table 4–12, the unusually high level of U.S. bor-rowing from abroad during the mid-1980s was not accompanied by an unusually high level of private domestic investment. The implication is that the increased borrowing from abroad went mainly or entirely to finance increased consumption. Unlike sound investment, consump-tion generates no return with which to repay a loan. Thus, to service its foreign debt, the United States will have to consume less than it other-wise would.

SUMMARY

Between 1981 and 1986, the U.S. international investment position dra-matically shifted from one of sizable net creditor to much more sizable net debtor, with further huge, debt-augmenting deficits in the offing. This transformation occurred even though the United States may have lost little or no competitiveness for "supply-side" reasons. In particular, U.S. labor productivity gains were virtually as great as those in other industrial nations; the performance of U.S.-based multinational firms suggests that U.S. management was maintaining its international competitiveness; and the United States did in fact maintain its share of world output.

Nor can unfair foreign trading practices explain much of the U.S. ex-ternal deficits. The deterioration in the U.S. trade balance was distributed widely across commodity categories, as well as across geographic areas. It seems most unlikely that virtually all major trading partners of the United States would simultaneously have intensified unfair practices in trade with the United States in virtually all major commodity categories.

A more plausible explanation of the U.S. external deficit focuses on (1) the more rapid expansion of real income and demand in the United States than in the rest of the world after 1982, and (2) the appreciation of the dollar in the foreign exchange markets after mid-1980, a develop-ment that reduced the price competitiveness of U.S. goods. Both of these factors stimulated greater growth in U.S. purchases of foreign goods than in foreign purchases of U.S. goods; both factors were themselves a result largely of the worldwide blend of monetary and fiscal policies, including the huge increase in the U.S. federal budget deficit. This increase in net federal spending boosted aggregate U.S. demand. Moreover, the increase in U.S. government borrowing associated with the budget deficit, coupled with an anti-inflationary U.S. monetary policy, tended to push up U.S. interest rates (adjusted for inflation), thus attracting investment by foreigners, whose purchases of dollar-denominated securities served to bid up the value of the dollar in the foreign exchange markets.

Contrary to a widespread impression, the U.S. trade deficits were not accompanied by a "deindustrialization of America." Following the 1981–82 recession, the production of goods grew faster than the production of services within the United States, and the growth of goods production compared favorably with that during earlier economic expansions. Thus, U.S. goods producers fared relatively well despite the increased U.S. trade deficit. Rather than destroying large segments of American industry, imports from abroad helped to satisfy the swiftly growing U.S. demand, without the development of shortages and rising inflation.

Although the net foreign debt of the United States soared with the trade deficit, at the end of 1987 no crisis loomed for the nation on indebtedness. Over the longer run, of course, foreigners would not be prepared to lend more and more to a nation whose indebtedness continued to rise in relation to its gross output and exports. Thus, the U.S. current account deficit must shrink in relation to the nation's output and exports, and the trade deficit in particular must be converted to surplus if the nation is to fund increasing net interest payments to its foreign creditors. The depreciation of the dollar that took place after February 1985 will contribute to this adjustment, as would further dollar depreciation and measures to reduce the federal budget deficit. The adjustment will not be painless for the United States, which will be obliged to consume less than it otherwise would.

APPENDIX: DATA USED IN TABLE 4–14
AND FIGURE 4–5

The authoritative source of detailed and comparable data on U.S. merchandise exports, imports, and output (shipments) is the Census Bureau's *U.S. Commodity Exports and Imports as Related to Output*. In this publication, data on shipments of products (as well as data on exports and imports) are classified by the kind of product involved rather than by the kind of industry that ships the product. For example, a plant's output might consist mainly of aluminum castings, so that the plant would be classified as part of the aluminum foundry industry, even though the plant also produced some copper castings. A classification of shipments by industry would combine the plant's copper shipments with its aluminum shipments, since the producing plant is classified in the aluminum industry, while the aforementioned Census Bureau publication would classify the plant's copper shipments along with other shipments of copper castings. At this writing, the latest available issue of this Census Bureau publication offers data no more recent than for the year 1982, so we have been obliged to employ shipments data classified by industry (including preliminary data for 1986). This industry classification is inferior to the product classification for purposes of comparing shipments with exports and imports—which are classified by kind of product—but the error involved is reduced by the fairly high degree of aggregation of industry shipments in this article.

As they were unavailable at this writing, data on insured employment by industry (four-digit SIC) were estimated for 1986; the estimation assumed essentially that insured employment at the detailed industry level (for which 1985 data had been published in *Employment and Wages: Annual Averages: 1985*), on the one hand, and total employment at a somewhat more aggregative level (for which both 1985 and 1986 data had been published in *Employment and Earnings*), on the other hand, would be linked by the same set of ratios in 1986 as in 1985.

SUGGESTIONS FOR FURTHER READING

For brief descriptions of balance-of-payments adjustment mechanisms and some estimates of their quantitative effects, see Andrew Dean and Val Koromzay, "Current-Account Imbalances and Adjustment Mechanisms," *OECD Economic Studies*, No. 8 (Spring 1987): 7–33; and Paul Krugman, *Adjustment in the World Economy*, Occasional Papers No. 24 (New York: Group of Thirty, 1987).

A comprehensive discussion of U.S. capital account transactions with the rest of the world is provided by Jeffrey A. Frankel, "International Capital Flows and Domestic Economic Policies," Working Paper No. 2210 (Cambridge, Mass.: National Bureau of Economic Research, 1987).

An argument that a "hard landing" was in store not only for the dollar but for the world economy is made by Stephen Marris, *Deficits and the Dollar: The World Economy at Risk*, Policy Analyses in International Economics 14 (Washington, D.C.: Institute for International Economics, 1985).
Also see the references cited in the notes to this chapter.

NOTES

1. "International Investment Position of the United States, 1985," U.S. Department of Commerce News, BEA 86–30, 24 June 1986; also see Russell B. Scholl, "The International Investment Position of the United States in 1985," *Survey of Current Business* 66 (June 1986): 26–35.
2. "U.S. Becomes Largest Debtor," *Journal of Commerce*, 25 June 1986.
3. Actually, the number first published was $107.4 billion; it was subsequently revised to $111.9 billion. See U.S. Department of Commerce News, BEA 86–30, 24 June 1986, for the original number.
4. See *Federal Reserve Bulletin* 73 (July 1987): A54, Table 3.12.
5. Bureau of the Census, *Reconciliation of United States–Canada Merchandise Trade, 1986* (Washington, D.C.: U.S. Bureau of the Census, 1986).
6. International Monetary Fund, *World Economic Outlook*, April 1987, World Economic and Financial Surveys (Washington, D.C.: IMF, 1987), pp. 103–06.
7. Ibid.
8. "External Assets of the Federal Republic of Germany in mid-1986," *Monthly Report of the Deutsche Bundesbank* 38 (October 1986): 30.
9. It should also be noted that the measure of the U.S. position in Tables 4–1, 4–2, and 4–3 includes equity as well as debt claims, while the customary measures of the debt of less developed countries do not include equity held by foreigners. For a discussion of these matters, see Barry Herman, "The United States as a Debtor Country: Indicators of Resource Transfer and Solvency," Working Paper No. 2 (U.N. Department of International Economic and Social Affairs, February 1987): 1–4.
10. Herman, "The U.S. as a Debtor Country," pp. 1–2; also see IMF *World Economic Outlook* (latest issue) for more recent data than Herman supplies on developing-country debt.
11. Steven Greenhouse, "New French Cause Célèbre: A Book Calling Nation Lazy," *New York Times*, 20 June 1987.
12. See, for example, Department of Commerce, *The U.S. Automobile Industry, 1982* (Washington, D.C.: U.S. Department of Commerce,

1983), pp. 49–51; and *Consumer Reports*, various issues evaluating automobiles.

13. Nicholas D. Kristof, "Japan Winning Race in China," *New York Times*, 29 April 1987.

14. For some defects of this measure, see Robert E. Lipsey and Irving Kravis, "The Competitiveness and Comparative Advantage of U.S. Multinationals, 1957–1984," *Banca Nazionale del Lavoro Quarterly Review* 161 (June 1987): 155.

15. Countervailing duties may be imposed in some cases merely upon the determination that a subsidy is being granted. See U.S. International Trade Commission, *Operation of the Trade Agreements Program, 1985*, Publication No. 1871 (Washington, D.C.: USITC, 1986), pp. 229–35 for an outline of U.S. law and procedures relating to the imposition of antidumping duties and countervailing duties.

16. USITC, *Operation of the Trade Agreements Program, 1986* (Publication No. 1995), pp. 5–4, 5–5, B-15–16, and B–19.

17. Ibid., pp. 5–3, and 5–6 through 5–13.

18. Jeffrey H. Bergstrand, "United States–Japanese Trade: Predictions Using Selected Economic Models," *New England Economic Review*, May/June 1986: 26–37; and C. Fred Bergsten and William R. Cline, *The United States–Japan Economic Problem*, Policy Analyses in International Economics 13 (Washington, D.C.: Institute for International Economics, 1985), pp. 45–46.

19. Dorothy Christelow, "Japan's Intangible Barriers to Trade in Manufactures," *Federal Reserve Bank of New York Quarterly Review*, Winter 1985–1986: 11–18.

20. U.S., President, *Economic Report of the President, February 1985* (Washington, D.C.: U.S. Government Printing Office, 1985), pp. 102–03.

21. Among these factors are resource discoveries, changes in tastes and technology, and differences in national growth rates. Changes in tastes and in technology, however, as well as growth trend differentials, generally exert their influence gradually over long periods, and major resource discoveries are rare. From year to year, movements in the real exchange rate and the current account are more powerfully influenced by business cycle fluctuations, by government controls, and by government monetary and fiscal policy, including changes in the government deficit such as those depicted in Figures 4–3 and 4–4.

22. Rachel McCulloch and J. David Richardson, "U.S. Trade and the Dollar: Evaluating Current Policy Options," in Robert E. Baldwin and J. David Richardson, eds., *Current U.S. Trade Policy: Analysis, Agenda, and Administration*, NBER Conference Report (Cambridge, Mass.: National Bureau of Economic Research, 1986), pp. 56–57; Martin S. Feldstein, "The View from North America," in C. Fred Bergsten, ed., *Global*

Economic Imbalances, Special Reports 4 (Washington, D.C.: Institute for International Economics, 1985), p. 7.

23. The appendix to this chapter describes in more detail some of the data used to assess the impact of foreign competition.

24. The simple correlation coefficient is 0.35, significant at the 0.05 level. Simple correlation rather than multiple regression analysis is used because the hypothesis to be tested is the popular view that rising net import competition generally signifies poor actual employment performance. The low correlation obtained here suggests that in a properly specified and estimated structural model, any negative employment impact of rising import competition would largely be offset by other factors, for the period 1980–86.

25. The data in Table 4–15 are adjusted for price change, unlike the individual industry data, which could not be so adjusted.

26. Michael L. Wachter, "Comment on Lawrence H. Summers's 'Why Is the Unemployment Rate So Very High Near Full Employment?' " *Brookings Papers on Economic Activity*, 1986: 2, pp. 390–91.

27. Bureau of the Census, *Historical Statistics of the United States, Colonial Times to 1970*, Part 2 (Washington, D.C.: U.S. Government Printing Office, 1975), pp. 1001–1004; and Bureau of the Census, *Statistical Abstract of the United States: 1987* (Washington, D.C.: U.S. Government Printing Office, 1986), pp. 492–93.

28. For further discussion of such indicators, see Chapter 3.

29. See, for example, *Survey of Current Business* 67 (June 1987): 73, 75.

30. Franco Modigliani, "The Real Trade Issue: In the Shadow of the Budget Deficit," *New York Times*, 1 March 1987.

5 THE INTERNATIONAL MONETARY SYSTEM
Out of Order?

On the subject of money, the nineteenth-century economist John Stuart Mill delivered a statement that was to become very widely quoted—and, eventually, criticized:

> There cannot, in short, be intrinsically a more insignificant thing, in the economy of society, than money; except in the character of a contrivance for sparing time and labour. It is a machine for doing quickly and commodiously what would be done, though less quickly and commodiously, without it: and like many other kinds of machinery, it only exerts a distinct and independent influence of its own when it gets out of order.[1]

This statement is the economic equivalent of the assertion that lethal weapons are harmful only if they get out of control. History is replete with illustrations of the proclivity of both money and weapons to get out of order, with consequences that are far from incidental. With respect to money, severe inflations are promoted by rapid increases in the supply of money, and recessions are often initiated or exacerbated by marked decelerations in the growth of the money supply.

At this writing, the world is free from both widespread inflation and widespread recession, but many analysts nonetheless believe that the international monetary system is sorely in need of repair. Exchange rates between national currencies are alleged to fluctuate excessively, and for long periods around the wrong levels. More fundamentally, the

165

system is said to lack an effective mechanism for coordinating national macroeconomic policies so as to prevent the emergence of major imbalances in international payments.

And just what is the international monetary system? It is the set of mechanisms by which payments are made across national boundaries, and by which imbalances in these payments—such as the 1986 U.S. current account deficit—are either financed or adjusted.[2] A key distinction between the international monetary system and the typical national system is that the national system utilizes only one currency, while in the current international system national currencies are exchanged for one another in the foreign exchange markets. Within each nation, the quantity of the national currency—and more generally, of domestic money—is regulated by the central bank or other national monetary authority; but at the international level, no supreme central bank presides over these national banks. Any disturbance affecting any currency in the world is registered in the international system, if only by a change in the foreign exchange value of that currency.

THE PAR VALUE SYSTEM

As recently as the early 1970s, the world employed an international monetary system that had been designed partly to avoid the major shortcomings now attributed to the current system. In particular, exchange-rate fluctuations in the earlier system were generally constrained to narrow bands, and significant exchange-rate changes were allowed only after much evidence had accumulated as to their suitability. Why, then, was this system relinquished? An examination of the reasons will prove helpful in appraising the present system and proposals for its reform.

The earlier system was codified in the original Articles of Agreement of the International Monetary Fund, an international agreement negotiated in 1944 at Bretton Woods, New Hampshire. The Bretton Woods agreement called for essentially fixed rates of exchange between national currencies, on the assumption that fixed exchange rates would foster international commerce and international cooperation. In order to maintain fixed exchange rates in the foreign exchange markets, most governments specified "par values" for their currencies in terms of the U.S. dollar; they then bought or sold their currencies in exchange for dollars whenever necessary to prevent the dollar values of their currencies from deviating from the par values by more than 1 percent.

With the values of other currencies thereby fixed in terms of the dollar, it was unnecessary for the United States to fix the value of the dollar in terms of other currencies. Instead, the obligation assumed by the United States was to fix the value of the dollar in terms of gold for purposes of transactions with foreign monetary authorities. The United States was to supply gold in exchange for dollars presented by these authorities—or to supply dollars in exchange for gold—at the official price of gold, originally set at $35 per ounce.

To make the par value system work, each government held a stock of international reserves—usually gold or dollars. A government could draw upon these reserves (or upon loans from the International Monetary Fund or other sources) to purchase its currency whenever necessary to stop a decline in the foreign exchange value of its currency. This outflow of reserves constituted a deficit in the country's overall balance of payments. If the currency subsequently tended to rise in value, the government would then reacquire reserves that it had previously paid out, and the country would realize a balance-of-payments surplus to offset the earlier deficit. Of course, such deficits and surpluses would not have been realized, and reserves would not have been necessary, if governments had not chosen to fix the values of their currencies in the foreign exchange markets. Instead, foreign exchange rates would have fluctuated freely.

The par value system worked reasonably well for more than two decades. By 1973, however, it had been abandoned, the victim of three related problems: liquidity, confidence, and adjustment.

THE PROBLEMS OF LIQUIDITY, CONFIDENCE, AND ADJUSTMENT

The problem of liquidity in the par value system was the problem of providing the appropriate amount of international reserves. Reserves were to be used to finance temporary deficits in international payments; such deficits could be expected to grow in size as the volume of international transactions increased, so that it was necessary for the volume of international reserves (liquidity) to grow over time. If reserves had not grown, countries would have found that they had less leeway to incur deficits in the short run while waiting for longer run corrective measures to take effect. In this case, governments probably would have resorted to harsh restrictions over international transactions in an attempt to prevent balance-of-payments deficits. On the other hand, if international reserves grew too rapidly, as they sometimes did in the system's later years, inflation was likely to result.

Under the par value system, nearly all of the growth in international reserves took the form of increases in the amounts of key currencies (especially the dollar) that were held by national monetary authorities, because these authorities as a group could not acquire enough gold from private suppliers at the fixed official price to meet their perceived need for international reserves. In fact, instead of purchasing gold, some central banks began sizable sales after 1965 in order to prevent the market price from rising much above the official price of $35 an ounce. In 1968, the participating central banks stopped these sales of gold to private parties and allowed the market price to fluctuate freely, although they maintained the official price at $35 per ounce for dealings among themselves.

Partly because of the lack of growth in their gold reserves, other countries were pleased for a number of years to run a balance-of-payments surplus with the United States, a surplus that added to their holdings of reserves in dollar form. Reserve growth in this form, however, proved to be unsatisfactory, largely because it led to a loss of confidence in the dollar. As foreign central banks purchased the dollar in order to support its price in the foreign exchanges, foreign official claims on the United States rose to more than $20 billion in 1970, while U.S. gold and other reserves amounted to only about $14 billion. The threat of a run on the bank led the Nixon administration, on 15 August 1971, to formally suspend its willingness to convert foreign official dollar balances into gold or other reserve assets.

This example dramatically illustrates the problem of confidence, which was the problem of avoiding a flight from one reserve asset, such as the dollar, into another reserve asset, such as gold. One obvious way to preclude such a flight would have been to have only one reserve asset. Another partial remedy would have been to stop fixing the price at which one reserve asset could be exchanged for another in dealings between central banks, instead using the market price for such dealings. The difficulty with price-fixing was that flights from one reserve asset into another were encouraged when the market price tended to diverge appreciably from the price fixed for official dealings. For example, after the market price of gold rose well above the official price in 1968, gold was no longer used in international payments. Somehow it went against a central banker's principles to transfer his gold to another central banker at a price far below the market price; instead, dollar balances were used.

The third major problem to arise under the par value system was the problem of adjusting, or eliminating, imbalances in international payments. The foremost illustration was the seeming inability of the United States to eradicate the deficit in its balance of payments. Indeed, the nation was running a huge deficit in the first half of 1971, just before the gold convertibility of the dollar was terminated.

Payments imbalances could have been reduced through timely exchange-rate changes, but exchange-rate change found little favor under the rules of the par value system, and even less favor under the body of custom that grew up beside those rules. The rules also discouraged the use of comprehensive government controls over international transactions. Since exchange-rate changes and controls were discouraged, the only respectable way for a government to eliminate a balance-of-payments surplus or deficit was to alter its monetary or fiscal policy. But governments generally preferred to use these policy tools to pursue full employment or to fight inflation, rather than to correct international imbalances. Therefore, the system was without an adequate balance-of-payments adjustment mechanism.

As a consequence, a number of governments gave up their attempts to fix exchange rates. The reason is nicely illustrated by the experience of the West German central bank in early 1973.[3] To limit increases in the value of the deutsche mark in the foreign exchange market, the West German central bank found itself selling large volumes of marks in exchange for U.S. dollars. The resulting increases in the stock of marks outstanding tended to boost inflation in West Germany at a time when the West German central bank was already very concerned about rising prices. After purchasing a daily record $2.6 billion on March 1, the central bank relinquished its efforts to control the foreign exchange value of the mark and began to focus instead on restraining inflationary pressures. Within a few months, the mark had risen sharply in value against the dollar.

A number of other countries experienced the same dilemma as West Germany, and by the spring of 1973 exchange-rate variation had clearly become a primary means of balance-of-payments adjustment. Now, if a currency were allowed to float perfectly freely in the foreign exchange market, the country whose currency it was would realize no overall balance-of-payments deficit or surplus whatsoever. The country would neither use reserves (incur a deficit) to prop up the price of its currency nor acquire reserves (accrue a surplus) in return for sales of its currency undertaken to suppress the price—although offsetting deficits and surpluses could, of course, still occur in the various *components* of the overall balance of payments (such as merchandise trade, securities purchases, and so on). In fact, no government did permit its currency to float perfectly freely, but the variation allowed in 1973 was still very large and plainly signaled the demise of the par value system.

A COMPOSITE SYSTEM

It was several years before the widespread practice of floating exchange rates received formal international sanction. In January 1976, a committee representing the 128 member countries of the IMF (International Monetary Fund) gave its blessing to proposals that would amend the IMF Articles of Agreement, both to legitimize the new exchange-rate flexibility and to make other fundamental changes. On 1 April 1978, these amendments entered into force.

While the current international monetary system differs from the par value system in several respects, by far the most important is the greater degree of exchange-rate flexibility. On the other hand, no government has gone to the extreme of allowing its currency to float freely; all continue to intervene in the foreign exchange markets, some more vigorously than others, in order to influence exchange rates for their currencies. In fact, at the end of 1986 the governments of 100 countries were fixing exchange rates for their currencies within fairly narrow, clearly specified ranges. Thirty-three of these governments were pegging the exchange rates of their currencies against the U.S. dollar, fourteen were pegging against the French franc, and fifty-three (including the members of the European Monetary System) were pegging against some currency, or group of currencies, other than the dollar or the franc. Fifty other governments, including most of the major industrial countries, were not fixing exchange rates for their currencies within any specified range, although they were prepared to intervene to influence those rates. Therefore, while exchange rates are much more flexible than under the par value system, substantial official intervention still occurs in the foreign exchange markets, and many governments still fix the rates of exchange for their currencies over fairly extended periods of time.[4]

The 1978 amendments to the IMF Articles of Agreement sanction these diverse exchange-rate practices. Might such diversity breed disorder? For example, suppose that the U.S. government became persuaded that the U.S. dollar should have a higher foreign exchange value, especially in deutsche marks, while the West German government held the opposite view. Would the West German authorities sell dollars for marks, while the U.S. authorities made offsetting sales of marks for dollars? The customary communication between central banks makes it very unlikely that such conflicting market intervention would occur merely by accident. However, if a frank and fundamental disagreement developed, how would the issue be resolved?

The amended Articles of Agreement do not offer a detailed formula for resolving such disputes, but they do include some general principles of good behavior that IMF members are expected to observe with respect to exchange rates. Specifically, each member agrees to cooperate to assure "orderly" exchange arrangements, especially by promoting orderly underlying economic and financial conditions and by refraining from exchange-rate manipulation designed either to prevent balance-of-payments adjustment or to gain unfair competitive advantage in international trade. Moreover, the IMF is charged with overseeing the adherence of its members to this code of good behavior and with spelling out the code in more detail. Accordingly, the IMF has added to the code the following principles:

> A member should intervene in the exchange market if necessary to counter disorderly conditions which may be characterized inter alia by disruptive short-term movements in the exchange value of its currency.
>
> Members should take into account in their intervention policies the interests of other members including those of the countries in whose currencies they intervene.[5]

The IMF has also adopted some guidelines to assist it in judging whether its members are adhering to the foregoing code. These "principles of surveillance over exchange rate policies" call for the IMF to be wary of the following developments:

> (i) protracted large-scale intervention in one direction in the exchange market;
>
> (ii) an unsustainable level of official or quasi-official borrowing, or excessive and prolonged short-term official or quasi-official lending, for balance of payments purposes;
>
> (iii) (a) the introduction, substantial intensification, or prolonged maintenance, for balance of payments purposes, of restrictions on, or incentives for, current transactions or payments, or
>
> (b) the introduction or substantial modification for balance of payments purposes of restrictions on, or incentives for, the inflow or outflow of capital;
>
> (iv) the pursuit, for balance of payments purposes, of monetary and other domestic financial policies that provide abnormal encouragement or discouragement to capital flows; and

(v) behavior of the exchange rate that appears to be unrelated to underlying economic and financial conditions including factors affecting competitiveness and long-term capital movements.[6]

If the IMF suspects a member country of violating the code of exchange-rate behavior, consultations are held with that member. In principle, a serious offender could be denied the right to borrow from the IMF and could eventually be expelled from the organization.

Thus, to bring about balance-of-payments adjustments, the current international monetary system relies much more heavily than its predecessor on exchange-rate change, although this reliance is not without rules. How does the current system deal with the other problems of liquidity and confidence, which also troubled the par value system?

With respect to liquidity, the stock of international reserves (measurable liquidity) was ample—perhaps too ample—when the par value system broke down. Moreover, governments do not require reserves to support the exchange values of their currencies if exchange rates are permitted to vary freely, and considerable variation is now allowed. It should also be noted that a government deemed creditworthy can always borrow dollars or other foreign exchange if its stock of owned reserves runs low.

The system does make specific provision for the creation of additional reserves if needed. The method is one that was introduced in 1969 and first employed in the twilight years of the par value system. The reserves created by this technique are known as special drawing rights (SDRs). SDRs are issued by the IMF upon the instruction of its member countries and are allocated among these countries in proportion to their financial contributions, or quotas, in the IMF. Although SDRs are nothing more than bookkeeping entries, participating governments have agreed to accept them as means of payment in settling international accounts. The value of an SDR in terms of currency is defined as the value of a "basket," which contained at the end of 1986, U.S. $.42 and specified quantities of four other currencies widely used in international commerce. A total of 21.4 billion SDRs were allocated in the course of two separate issuances, the first during the years 1970–72, the second during 1979–81.

If a government draws upon its allocation of SDRs to make international payments, it must pay net interest to the IMF on the SDRs so expended. The IMF, in turn, pays net interest to the governments that receive SDR transfers in addition to their original IMF allocations. Such interest payments serve a useful function. In their absence, governments generally would have an incentive to use SDRs, allocated to them at no cost, in order to pay for goods obtained from other countries. SDRs that paid no interest would find no willing holders. At this writing, the interest rate on the SDR is equal to a weighted average of the interest rates on prime domestic money market instruments in the five countries whose currencies are included in the SDR's valuation basket.

As noted in the previous section, one way of precluding a confidence problem, or a flight from one reserve asset into another, would be to have only one reserve asset. The 1978 amendments to the Articles of Agreement do include the objective of "making the special drawing right the principal reserve asset in the international monetary system,"[7] but very little progress has been made toward this objective. Of total international reserves as reported by the IMF, SDRs accounted for only 4.4 percent at the end of 1986. By far the largest reserve component continues to be countries' holdings of other countries' currencies, or of short-term assets denominated in those currencies. These foreign exchange holdings accounted for about four-fifths of all international reserves in 1986. Country holdings of reserve positions in the IMF and of gold account for the remainder of international reserves.[8]

Even though the SDR has not been installed as the principal reserve asset, progress has been made in solving the confidence problem. The fact is that the confidence problem stemmed not merely from the existence of more than one reserve asset but also from the effort to fix the price at which these assets were exchanged for each other. Flights from one reserve asset into another were encouraged when the market price tended to diverge appreciably from the officially fixed price, as happened with gold in 1968. This source of the confidence problem was eliminated when such price-fixing was abandoned, leaving central banks free to transfer all reserve assets among themselves for settlement of debts at market-related prices.

From this account, it is clear that the current international monetary system differs significantly from the par value system, but retains various features of that system. Most prominent among the retained features is that many exchange rates are still more or less fixed. Thus, the system is not at all "pure," but is a hybrid, or composite—combining the characteristics of both fixed and flexible exchange rates.

The variegated nature of the system, especially its permissiveness with respect to exchange-rate arrangements, has led to the allegation that it is in fact no system at all, but a nonsystem that invites chaos in international monetary affairs. More specifically, exchange rates are said to be much too volatile and to depart for long periods from their appropriate, or equilibrium, levels. Such criticisms merit careful consideration.

EXCHANGE-RATE VOLATILITY AND RISK

At the time the composite system was adopted, most economists expected it to put an end to the turmoil that had afflicted international financial markets under the par value system, especially during its latter years. No longer would a government feel obliged to intervene to defend an exchange rate that was under massive attack in the market, in a surrounding air of crisis and with the eventual sharp change in the exchange rate as the government yielded to market forces (as the West German central bank did in March of 1973). Now that exchange rates could respond promptly to market influences, they would typically change gradually as the underlying economic "fundamentals" changed, replacing the practice of less frequent, more abrupt changes. Sharp fluctuations from temporary disturbances would be prevented by stabilizing speculators, who would recognize the temporary nature of the disturbances, and who would buy or sell a currency before it fell or rose very much in order later to turn a profit as the currency returned to its longer run equilibrium level.

In the event, these expectations were not fulfilled.[9] Rather than diminishing, exchange-rate variability has been much greater under the composite system than under its predecessor. Nor has there been a trend toward reduced variability as experience has accumulated.

Exchange-rate variation can be measured in various ways. Since any currency exchanges for many other currencies, it is helpful to have an index that summarizes the changing value of a country's currency in terms of other currencies. For this purpose, the changes in value of a currency against other currencies are customarily weighted by the importance of those changes to the international trade of the country for which the index is being constructed. Such an index is said to measure change in the "nominal effective exchange rate."

This nominal index can be adjusted for differences between the rate of inflation in the country whose currency is being indexed and the trade-weighted average of inflation rates abroad. When so adjusted, the index is known as the real effective exchange rate and is commonly used as a measure of changing competitiveness. For example, a marked decline in a country's nominal effective exchange rate (that is, in the average foreign exchange price of the country's currency) would translate—unless offset by a rise in the country's inflation rate relative to inflation abroad—into lower prices for the country's goods relative to prices of foreign goods; the decline in the real exchange rate would indicate this increased competitiveness. On the other hand, if the decline in the country's nominal effective rate were accompanied by an offsetting rise in the country's relative inflation rate, the real exchange rate would remain constant, indicating no change in the country's overall price competitiveness.

Whether measured in nominal or in real terms, effective exchange rates for the seven major noncommunist industrial countries have displayed much greater variability since the collapse of the par value system. This variability is illustrated in Table 5–1: the weighted average of monthly changes in nominal effective exchange rates for these countries was 1.18 percent over the ten years 1974–83, nearly six times as great as the 0.2 percent experienced during the ten years 1961–70. In terms of real effective exchange rates, month-to-month variation was about three times greater in the later period than in the earlier one. Roughly the same increases in variability are discovered if quarter-to-quarter rather than month-to-month changes are examined.

Volatility is not feared for its own sake. Rather, the concern is that increases in volatility raise the risk and cost of international transactions, thereby discouraging international trade and investment. Suppose that greater variability makes it more difficult to forecast the course of an exchange rate. In that case, traders and investors will be less certain of the value in their domestic currency of any foreign currency amounts that they might agree today to pay or receive in the future in order to carry out pending international transactions. They will be more reluctant to commit to such transactions on the same terms as before unless the greater risk they face can somehow be shifted to some other party.

In fact, much of the risk can be shifted. One widely employed mechanism for shifting or neutralizing foreign exchange risk is the forward exchange market. By way of illustration, suppose that a U.S. importer signs a contract to purchase merchandise from West Germany and to pay in deutsche marks when the merchandise is delivered three months hence. Because the rate of exchange between dollars and marks may change over the coming months, the importer cannot be sure what the merchandise will cost in terms of dollars if he waits three months to buy the needed marks. One way he can avoid this uncertainty is to

Table 5-1. Month-to-Month and Quarter-to-Quarter Average Absolute Percentage Changes in Effective Exchange Rates for Seven Major Industrial Countries for Selected Periods.

	Canada	France	West Germany	Italy	Japan	United Kingdom	United States	Weighted Average[a]
Month-to-month								
Nominal rates								
1961–70	0.26	0.22	0.27	0.13	0.15	0.26	0.11	0.20
1974–83	0.82	1.01	1.00	1.06	1.74	1.32	1.35	1.18
Real rates								
1961–70	0.35	0.38	0.42	0.30	0.68	0.45	0.28	0.38
1974–83	0.91	0.98	1.00	1.00	1.85	1.46	1.41	1.22
Quarter-to-quarter								
Nominal rates								
1962–70	0.44	0.58	0.64	0.28	0.27	0.58	0.22	0.42
1974–83	1.53	2.13	1.97	3.06	3.44	2.81	2.53	2.39
Real rates								
1962–70	0.69	1.04	1.22	1.99	0.99	1.33	0.65	1.04
1974–83	1.99	2.06	2.02	2.75	3.47	3.46	2.50	2.51

[a]Weighted according to current trade shares.

Source: International Monetary Fund, *Exchange Rate Volatility and World Trade*, Occasional Paper No. 28 (Washington, D.C.: IMF, 1984), pp. 38–41.

buy marks for future delivery in the forward exchange market. More specifically, his bank will agree to deliver, three months from now, the marks he will then require and will tell him today the rate of exchange (or dollar price) that he will have to pay. By entering this contract, that is, by purchasing "forward cover," the importer can eliminate any uncertainty about the dollar price of the imported merchandise.

Such risk-shifting is not costless, but the costs are relatively small. Banks do not charge commissions for accommodating their customers in the forward exchange market, but profit from selling a currency at a higher price than they pay for it. Typically, this margin between a bank's quoted buying and selling prices is kept very low by intense competition, unless the transaction is quite small. For sizable transactions in the most widely traded currencies, the margin, or cost to a customer, is commonly well below one-tenth of one percent.[10]

In addition to the forward exchange market, other devices are available for neutralizing or hedging against foreign exchange risk. As a practical matter, however, it is not possible for a business firm to avoid all such risk, if only because the firm cannot specify the precise timing of its future receipts and payments in foreign exchange. Thus, in spite of the availability of a variety of hedging techniques, some of which entail very low costs, the international trader or investor will bear some exchange risk, directly or indirectly.

Since exchange risk is associated with exchange-rate variability, the question remains whether international commerce has been suppressed by the heightened exchange-rate variability under the current monetary system. No definitive answer has been provided. Various empirical studies, using differing approaches and sets of data, have yielded differing results.[11]

Even if the recent exchange-rate variability were clearly associated with reduced trade, it would not necessarily follow that the pegging of exchange rates would expand trade. For example, exchange rates have sometimes been fixed with the aid of controls such as import restrictions designed to limit an overall balance-of-payments deficit, and such controls may hinder trade more than exchange-rate variability does. More generally, if exchange-rate variability were suppressed, the underlying causal economic forces would produce disturbances elsewhere in the economic system—unless those causal forces arose out of the flexible exchange-rate regime itself. The mere diversion of disturbances from exchange rates to other economic variables would offer little promise of reducing the overall degree of uncertainty. Such a diversion might indeed raise the level of international trade, but at the expense of other economic activity.

THE ROLE OF SPECULATION

The key issue, then, is whether exchange-rate flexibility itself generates forces that make for exchange-rate variability. In particular, if allowed the opportunity, do speculators operate so as to destabilize an exchange rate? For many years, one school of thought has answered this question in the affirmative. The classic example is a 1944 study done for the League of Nations:

> Any considerable or continuous movement of the exchange rate is liable to generate anticipations of a further movement in the same direction, thus giving rise to speculative capital transfers of a disequilibrating kind. . . . Self-aggravating movements of this kind . . . are apt to intensify any initial disequilibrium and to produce what may be called "explosive" conditions of instability.[12]

The classic rebuttal was offered by Milton Friedman in 1953:

> People who argue that speculation is generally destabilizing seldom realize that this is largely equivalent to saying that speculators lose money, since speculation can be destabilizing in general only if speculators on the average sell when the currency is low in price and buy when it is high.[13]

But speculators as a group may indeed lose money from time to time. Moreover, theorists have constructed examples in which speculators could make a profit even if their activity was destabilizing. Finally, history presents illustrations of seemingly destabilizing speculation, such as the Dutch tulip mania that drove the price of a single bulb higher than that of a house during the 1630s.[14] Thus, the actual importance of destabilizing speculation cannot be settled by armchair theorizing, but must be submitted to empirical investigation. Such investigation is worthwhile not only because exchange-rate variability can raise the cost and risk of international trade, but because speculation that holds an exchange rate far from its longer run equilibrium levels may lead investors and traders to make the wrong business decisions.

Unfortunately, it has been next to impossible to prove either the presence or the absence of destabilizing speculation in the foreign exchange markets. To measure the impact of speculation, one needs to separate out the other influences on exchange rates, and no econometric model has been constructed that is up to this formidable task. In the absence of a satisfactory econometric model, analysts have resorted to comparing the volatility of foreign exchange rates to that of prices in other financial markets. If volatility in the foreign exchange markets is no greater than in the stock or the bond markets, perhaps it should be viewed as normal and even innocuous, unless one suspects that all such markets are cursed with destabilizing speculation. Comparing the volatility in these markets seems appropriate, since bonds, stocks, and foreign exchange are all financial assets whose prices will be affected by any news that changes expectations about the economic rewards from holding them.

From the comparisons that have been made, the conclusion to be drawn is that foreign exchange rates have generally been less volatile than prices in other financial markets. One study for the years 1973–83 shows that stock market price indexes in a number of noncommunist industrial countries typically displayed two or three times the variability found in the exchange rates for these countries' currencies against the dollar. For bonds, the difference is not so great, but exchange rates still generally exhibited less variation.[15]

While encouraging, such evidence is indirect and inconclusive. More direct evidence is needed on whether speculators play a stabilizing or destablizing role in the foreign exchange markets. For example, it would be helpful to know if speculators generally make profits, since their activity cannot be stabilizing if they suffer losses.

Unfortunately, profit data are not available, but some data have been collected on the speculative positions taken by U.S. firms in various foreign currencies. Representative summary statistics are presented in Table 5–2. A positive amount indicates that claims denominated in foreign currency exceed foreign currency liabilities, while a negative amount signifies the reverse.

The holders of such foreign currency positions may experience dollar profits or losses depending on what happens to the dollar prices of the foreign currencies held. But the positions taken by the banks as a group seem generally to have been very small. What should be considered small is, of course, open to debate. One way of judging is to compare the banks' position in a currency with their total involvement in that currency, where involvement is defined as total assets and liabilities in the currency plus contracts to buy and sell the currency. As can be seen from the second column of data, the position taken by banks never

Table 5-2. Net Positions Taken by U.S. Banking and Nonbanking Firms, for Selected Currencies and Dates.

Currency and Date[a]	Bank Positions[b]		Nonbank Positions[c]	
	Amount	As a Percent of Involvement[d]	Amount	As a Percent of Involvement[d]
Canadian dollars (millions)				
December 1983	50	0.07	10,105	10.39
June 1984	−202	−0.24	10,627	10.59
December 1984	−27	−0.03	11,349	10.37
June 1985	−377	−0.33	10,571	9.41
December 1985	−172	−0.18	9,621	8.68
June 1986	34	0.02	11,529	10.02
Deutsche marks (millions)				
December 1983	1399	0.20	9,920	8.81
June 1984	70	0.01	13,115	10.37
December 1984	6	*	6,909	5.08
June 1985	1229	0.10	−11,554	−6.66
December 1985	1499	0.15	14,084	9.50
June 1986	−38	*	12,448	7.53
Japanese yen (billions)				
December 1983	−16	−0.03	27	0.61
June 1984	−123	−0.17	277	5.08
December 1984	−94	−0.13	405	7.47
June 1985	−21	−0.02	459	6.88

December 1985	76	0.09	567	8.19
June 1986	123	0.15	450	4.31
Swiss francs (millions)				
December 1983	−934	−0.36	223	1.48
June 1984	−768	−0.21	468	1.69
December 1984	−435	−0.12	718	4.50
June 1985	−74	−0.01	185	0.73
December 1985	−679	−0.18	391	1.52
June 1986	−1088	−0.29	−780	−2.31
U.K. pounds (millions)				
December 1983	−373	−0.27	833	1.97
June 1984	−301	−0.17	−973	−1.97
December 1984	−303	−0.17	−6,525	−11.31
June 1985	−27	−0.01	−387	−0.69
December 1985	−434	−0.23	−191	−0.33
June 1986	−643	−0.29	−623	−1.05

*Less than one-one hundredth of 1 percent.

a Bank data are for the last Wednesday of each month. Nonbank data are for the last business day of each month.

b Banks are defined to include U.S. offices of foreign banks. Data exclude capital assets and liabilities.

c Nonbanks are defined to include U.S. offices of foreign firms. Not included are fixed assets, parents' investment in majority-owned foreign subsidiaries, and capitalized plant and equipment leases.

d Involvement is defined as reported total assets plus total liabilities in a currency plus foreign exchange contracts bought plus foreign exchange contracts sold in the currency, except that for banks, capital assets and liabilities are excluded, and for nonbanks fixed assets, parents' investment in majority-owned foreign subsidiaries, and capitalized plant and equipment leases are excluded.

Source: *Treasury Bulletin*, various issues.

exceeded four-tenths of one percent of the banks' total involvement in foreign currency, for the currencies and dates shown. Another way of judging the size of the banks' positions is to compare them with the positions taken by nonbank firms. As indicated in Table 5–2, the banks' positions seem very small by this standard as well.

In fact, the positions taken by U.S. banks have been so small that it is hard to see how those positions could have exerted much influence on the course of exchange rates, either to stabilize or to destabilize. Since the banks, especially the major ones, are probably as knowledgeable about the foreign exchange markets as any other group of participants, it seems that they should be able to perform the profitable and socially beneficial role of stabilizing speculators. The fact that their aggregate foreign exchange positions have been so small may, therefore, be cause for concern.

By contrast, the positions taken by nonbank firms usually were much larger, both in absolute amount and in relation to their total involvement in foreign currency. As shown by the last column, nonbank positions sometimes amounted to more than 10 percent of involvement, especially in the Canadian dollar.

Apart from the size of the positions, are they likely to have been profitable? A very tentative answer can be obtained by comparing the positions taken in the various currencies with the subsequent behavior of the exchange rates for those currencies. Such a comparison using data for the late 1970s suggests that speculation was not generally profitable, either for U.S. banks as a group or for the nonbank firms. (On the other hand, it also seems likely that neither the banks nor the nonbanks were losing large sums of money.[16]) This outcome is mildly discouraging, for it suggests that the socially useful function of stabilizing speculation was not being performed. Still, it remains to be shown that exchange-rate flexibility has itself generated substantial destabilizing speculation.

EXCHANGE-RATE MISALIGNMENT

Critics of the new monetary system level another charge against it: exchange rates not only vary excessively, but also remain for long periods much higher or lower than warranted by underlying structural economic conditions. That is to say, exchange rates have displayed severe misalignments, or prolonged and marked departures from their appropriate, long-run equilibrium levels.[17] This charge is leveled at the behavior of the real effective exchange rate.

Of course, in order to support the allegation that exchange rates have been misaligned, a method is needed for computing the correct, or long-run equilibrium, rates. Three methods are commonly employed. The first assumes that the long-run equilibrium rate is some average or stable point within any observed, long-run, market-determined movement; the second assumes that the long-run equilibrium is approximately equal to the "purchasing-power parity" rate; and the third identifies the long-run equilibrium with the rate that would yield overall balance in international payments under "normal" circumstances.

As an illustration of the first method, the real effective exchange rate of the U.K. pound fell by 20 percent between 1975 and 1976 and then rose by nearly 75 percent between 1976 and 1981.[18] Critics would say the upward movement implied the mistakenness, or at least the non-essentiality, of the preceding downward movement, and that during the entire period the rate should have hovered somewhere between the extremes that were observed.

The purchasing-power parity method assumes that the real exchange rate should remain virtually unchanged from its level during the most recent period of international equilibrium. In other words, any significant and lasting change in a nominal exchange rate should be merely for the purpose of offsetting a difference in national inflation rates. The nominal rate change would then ensure that the purchasing power of a currency over foreign goods changes by the same degree as its purchasing power over domestic goods. Thus, if prices in Brazil doubled—starting from a period of balance-of-payments equilibrium,—while prices elsewhere remained unchanged on average, a unit of Brazil's currency should come to exchange for only half as much foreign currency (and foreign goods) as previously, with no change in the real, or inflation-adjusted, exchange rate.

Adherents of this second method have much cause for dissatisfaction with the current monetary system, for real exchange rates have commonly remained far from the levels associated with earlier equilibriums in international payments. For example, 1980–82 was arguably a period of near-equilibrium for the U.S. balance of payments, yet during both 1984 and 1985 the real effective exchange value of the U.S. dollar averaged more than 20 percent above its value for 1980–82.[19]

The third method involves more sophisticated analysis than the other two. The first step is to make a projection of the net financial lending

or borrowing to be experienced by a country in its international transactions over a long period, including both the upswings and down-
swings of any business cycles. An estimate is then made of the real
exchange rate that would bring about a surplus (or deficit) on the
country's current account transactions sufficient to offset this projected
net capital outflow (or inflow); this is the estimated equilibrium real
exchange rate. It is assumed that the country follows policies designed
to maintain reasonable balance in its domestic economy and refrains
from major controls aimed at influencing its net capital or current
account transactions with the rest of the world. The equilibrium exchange rate estimated in this fashion will have to change from time to
time in response to change in underlying fundamentals, such as resource
discoveries, or growth in domestic productivity relative to foreign productivity; however, the required exchange-rate changes are asserted to
be calculable, and either gradual or infrequent.

One proponent of this method has used it to estimate misalignments displayed by the real effective exchange rates of five major
industrial-country currencies in the last quarter of 1984. His study
suggests that the Japanese yen was then valued 19 percent too low in
the foreign exchange markets, and that the dollar was valued 39 percent too high, with smaller errors for the other three currencies.
Moreover, according to this study, such misalignments have been very
tenacious. [20]

A misaligned exchange rate is alleged to impose economic costs. As
suggested by the third method of computing the long-run equilibrium
rate, a country with a misaligned rate is thought to lend or borrow
more or less than it should, accumulating current account surpluses
or deficits that are too big or too small. In other words, misalignments
are said to promote international resource transfers that are uneconomic—resulting in efficiency losses—since a misalignment presumably
constitutes an inappropriate price competitiveness for one country's
goods vis-a-vis the goods of other countries. Thus, a country whose
competitive prowess is heightened by a misaligned exchange rate will
export more and import less than at the long-run equilibrium rate;
it will devote too much of its resources to export industries and import-
competing industries, and not enough to industries making goods that
are not internationally traded.

One seldom hears a citizenry complain that the exchange rate has
made their country too competitive. The protests arise from the other
side, from countries concerned that a misalignment has damaged their

export and import-competing industries. Thus, another cost of misalignment could be the fomentation of protectionism, with its pernicious barriers to international trade.

The emergence of a misalignment can require that resources shift *within* countries—between industries producing internationally traded goods and those producing nontraded goods. Therefore, another cost is associated with misalignments: the cost of transferring resources from one industry to another. These costs can be appreciable, since labor often cannot transfer without physically moving and retraining; some labor, like most machines, is simply not transferable and becomes unemployed for the long term.

Of the three methods summarized here for computing the long-run equilibrium exchange rate, neither the first nor the second requires much reflection. The first method is basically one of blind resistance to abrupt exchange-rate change, since it prescribes opposition to such change without troubling to inquire into the underlying causal forces. In other words, it simply assumes away the possibility of abrupt change in underlying economic structure. Similarly, the purchasing-power parity method envisions change in the nominal exchange rate to offset inflation differentials, but allows for no change in the real exchange rate; this method denies the possibility of any change in underlying economic structure, even in the long run.

By contrast, the third method calls for explicit examination of structural change and focuses on the behavior of factors such as productivity trends, resource availability, and the long-run propensities to save in different nations. The method allows for the possibility of abrupt as well as gradual change in these structural factors. But the presumption is that abrupt change will be the exception, so that that the method will seldom prescribe an abrupt change in the real exchange rate. An objection to the method is that calculating a long-run equilibrium exchange rate can be very difficult and lends itself to significant error.

A central difficulty with all these methods is their assumption that significant economic costs are inflicted by any large and prolonged deviation of a real exchange rate from its longer run equilibrium level. On the contrary, "misalignments" may be the most appropriate, or least costly, response to much nonstructural, nonenduring change in international economic conditions. If so, close adherence to the long-run equilibrium would constitute the true misalignment. Many prices, especially in financial markets, do not continuously hover around their long-run average levels, but vary in response to business cycles and other temporary influences. Such variation is commonly accepted as "normal," even as desirable. In all these markets, including the foreign exchange markets, the suppression of price change would not usually eliminate the underlying causal forces, but would divert them into other modes of expression. In particular, a nation that was serious about combating an emerging "misalignment" of its exchange rate would almost certainly have to enlist its macroeconomic policy (especially monetary policy) for the task. The costs of using macroeconomic policy to influence exchange rates, rather than to influence domestic employment or inflation, were perceived to be so great under the par value system as to lead to its demise. Thus, the basic problem with the "misalignment" doctrine is its failure to specify a clearly less costly and more acceptable method than "misalignments" for dealing with the economic causes responsible.

THE ISSUE OF DISCIPLINE

Another major criticism of the current international monetary system is that it fails to prevent national macroeconomic policy blunders, which are often responsible for major imbalances in international payments. Now, flexibility of exchange rates does militate against sizable overall imbalances, or against gains and losses of international reserves, such as nations commonly experienced under the par value system. But the new system has not prevented the occurrence of sizable, albeit offsetting, imbalances in major components of a country's overall balance of payments. Of most concern has been the large and persistent "current account" deficit of the United States (on transactions in merchandise and related items), financed by an equal net inflow of capital from abroad, or by a U.S. "capital account" surplus. Other nations, especially Japan and West Germany, have experienced correspondingly large current account surpluses with capital account deficits, particularly in transactions with the United States.

Moreover, sizable, medium-term swings in exchange rates have accompanied such imbalances. As the capital inflow into the United States swelled between 1981 and 1985—partly in response to attractive returns on investments there—demand by investors for the U.S. dollar helped to push up its real effective foreign exchange value by nearly 25 percent.[21] In turn, the rise in the dollar's foreign exchange price rendered U.S. goods less competitive internationally, thereby magnifying the current account deficit, which in 1985 amounted to almost $118 billion.

One cause of these imbalances was the sharp rise in the U.S. federal budget deficit, a development that led the United States to borrow more from abroad; by contrast, Japan and West Germany pursued somewhat more restrained fiscal policies that fostered increases in their foreign lending. Had there been a disciplining or coordinating mechanism that deterred these three countries from following such divergent fiscal policies, the worrisome payments imbalances and exchange-rate swings could presumably have been avoided, or at least substantially mitigated. The current international monetary system provides no effective mechanism of this sort.

The issue of policy coordination is considered at some length in the next chapter. Here, the analysis is limited to the question of whether exchange-rate arrangements might be modified so as to foster coordination and restrain excesses in national macroeconomic policies. An affirmative answer is given by the advocates of "target zones," a proposal examined in the next section.

TARGET ZONES

A target zone would be a fairly wide range within which governments would seek to constrain the movement of an exchange rate. The zone would be established by estimating the real equilibrium exchange rate and then adding a margin of, say, 10 percent on either side to reflect the uncertainty surrounding the estimate as well as the degree of willingness to allow temporary fluctuations. To confine the exchange rate within the zone, governments would intervene to influence the rate directly with purchases or sales of foreign exchange. But the commitment to limit exchange-rate variations would be much weaker than under the par value system. Not only would the target zone be much wider than the narrow bands prescribed for fluctuations under the par value system, but exchange rates might be allowed to stray temporarily beyond the zone. Moreover, the zone would be changed much more readily than the old par values, in response to change in the longer run equilibrium exchange rate.

All countries that wished to do so could establish target zones for their currencies, but advocates consider it especially important that the largest industrial countries enter into the scheme. After all, one purpose is to prevent national policy mistakes that disrupt the world economy, and such weighty mistakes cannot emanate from a small nation. One check against national policy excesses would be the need for the participating countries to agree on the target zones for exchange rates between their currencies. In the course of these negotiations, macroeconomic policies would be discussed because of their considerable influence on exchange rates, and governments would have the opportunity to object to policy courses that seemed inappropriate. At least in principle, all policies could be harmonized for the greater good. A further discipline would be the presumption that government policies, especially monetary policies, would be maintained on a course consistent with confining exchange rates within the target zones. While the zones could be violated, and would be revised from time to time, they would, it is argued, provide a formal arrangement through which national governments would be exposed to peer pressure and review as they formulated and executed their macroeconomic policies.

Target zones are a halfway house between the par value system and the free-floating exchange rates to be found within the present system. Establishing such zones would represent a step back in the direction of the par value system, with the goal of capturing some of the discipline, coordination, and exchange-rate stability promised by that system. The record is clear, however, that governments became unwilling to submit to the discipline of the par value system—unwilling, in particular, to devote monetary policy to the function of regulating exchange rates rather than to the functions of regulating domestic employment and price levels. Moreover, given the high uncertainty about the effects of macroeconomic policy changes, intensified coordination could well worsen rather than improve the performance of the world economy.[22] In these circumstances, it would be surprising if target zones evoked the commitment that their adherents seek.[23]

REGULATION OF INTERNATIONAL LIQUIDITY

As already noted, governments do not require international reserves if they permit exchange rates to float freely. But the freedom allowed to exchange rates is far from complete in the present system, and it has sometimes been alleged that the supply of international reserve assets was inadequate.

This criticism is difficult to evaluate because of the difficulty in evaluating the appropriate level of reserves. It was hard to estimate the optimum level of reserves under the par value system, and it is even harder for a system with no general and explicitly targeted limits on exchange-rate fluctuations. What can be said is that governments desiring additional reserves can borrow foreign exchange, or purchase it with their own currencies, and that governments wanting to reduce their reserves can sell some of their holdings. Moreover, governments receive market rates of interest on such additions to reserves—since those reserves are invested—and they pay market or near-market rates for borrowed reserves. Thus, the stock of international reserves is regulated by individual government decisions, based on market interest rates, without centralized control.

Of course, a problem can arise for an individual government that wants to forestall a depreciation of its currency but lacks both the reserves to support its currency and the creditworthiness to borrow at going market interest rates. To prevent depreciation, this government must impose foreign exchange controls, such as restrictions on domestic purchases of foreign currency, or it must alter its monetary or fiscal policy. With the eruption of the international debt crisis in 1982, such difficult choices were faced by a number of less developed countries that were unwilling to tolerate rapid and continuous depreciations.

The dilemma of these less developed countries has stimulated proposals for a new issue of SDRs. Receipt of newly created SDRs would give these countries some relief, but the international debt problem has been too sizable to be materially eased by any SDR issuance that creditor countries would have been willing to consider. At bottom, the debt problem requires more fundamental measures for its solution; at this writing, no new SDRs are in the offing.[24]

A BRIEF APOLOGY FOR THE COMPOSITE SYSTEM

Preceding sections have offered defenses of the current international monetary system against some specific charges. Here, a few more general points are made on behalf of the system.

As already noted, some analysts think that the current international monetary arrangements should not be dignified with the label, "system." Thus, the designation, "nonsystem," is sometimes used to characterize the diverse set of exchange-rate practices that sprang up, without any previously agreed blueprint, to replace the carefully designed par value system when it disintegrated in the early 1970s.[25]

To be sure, the present composite system more nearly resembles a mongrel than a thoroughbred. Lacking the thoroughbred's planned breeding and uniformity, it boasts the mongrel's hardiness and adaptability. The latter traits were at a premium in the years following the demise of the par value system, as the world economy struggled through two oil shocks, an international debt crisis, and marked divergencies between macroeconomic policies in different nations. In the face of these severe disturbances, the composite system allowed international trade to increase more rapidly than world output, with relatively few restrictions on international payments. Given the circumstances, no other international monetary system that has been tried would have worked as well.

Aside from these pragmatic observations, economic theory offers more formal justification for countries to opt for varying degrees of exchange-rate flexibility, in accordance with their differing circumstances. Theory suggests that exchange-rate variability will be more acceptable to a large country engaging in relatively little international trade than to a small country that is heavily dependent on international commerce. More precisely, the degree of flexibility that a country chooses should be based on a number of considerations, including the nature of the economic disturbances that affect the country, the resource allocation effects of exchange-rate changes, and the efficacy of monetary and fiscal policy under differing degrees of exchange-rate flexibility.[26] These factors vary not only from country to country but from time to time for any one country, so that a country might well opt for more flexibility at one time than another.

Thus, both experience and theory can be invoked on behalf of the composite system. It is desirable that countries have considerable freedom to tailor their exchange-rate practices to their own economic and political structures and philosophies—a freedom that was lacking under the rules of Bretton Woods. Far from tearing apart the fabric of international commerce, the diversity of the current system may serve to knit it more closely, as long as generally accepted norms of behavior are observed.[27]

SUMMARY

Internationally as well as domestically, money facilitates the exchange of goods and thereby promotes specialization, with the well-known associated efficiencies. Unlike a domestic monetary system, the international system encompasses many different national currencies, which are exchanged for one another in the foreign exchange market. The international monetary system is the set of mechanisms by which international payments are made in these currencies, and by which imbalances in international payments are either financed or corrected.

The current international monetary system differs markedly from its predecessor, the par value system, which prescribed fixed rather than variable exchange rates between national currencies. Negotiated at Bretton Woods, New Hampshire, in 1944, the par value system worked reasonably well for more than two decades, but collapsed in the early 1970s under the weight of three problems: providing the appropriate amount of international reserves (liquidity), avoiding a flight from one international reserve asset into another (confidence), and correcting imbalances in international payments (adjustment). The current system has dealt with these problems chiefly through the adoption of greater exchange-rate flexibility. Many countries, however, still strive to maintain a relatively fixed exchange rate between their currencies and some other major currency, and no country allows its currency to float perfectly freely in the foreign exchange markets. Thus, the current system is a hybrid, or composite—combining the characteristics of both fixed and flexible exchange rates.

The behavior of exchange rates under the composite system has provoked much concern. The system may lack stabilizing speculation and may even suffer from destabilizing speculation. Many analysts think that exchange rates have fluctuated too widely and have strayed too far from their appropriate long-run equilibrium levels. The fluctuations are alleged to generate uncertainty and to raise the risk and cost of international transactions—thus dampening international trade and investment—while prolonged departures from the long-run equilibriums are said to mislead investors, who then channel resources into suboptimal uses. Although these allegations may be correct, the suppression of exchange-rate variation would not necessarily eliminate the underlying economic causes of the variation, but could divert them into other modes of expression that might entail higher costs than the variation itself.

Another criticism of the current system is that it lacks an effective mechanism for coordinating national macroeconomic policies so as to prevent policy excesses that lead to sharp exchange-rate movements and troublesome imbalances in international payments. The establishment of target zones for exchange rates has been proposed as such a coordinating mechanism. It is doubtful that the target zone proposal will be fully implemented, not only because governments remain unwilling to devote monetary policy primarily to controlling exchange rates, but because the outcome of coordinated macroeconomic policy is sometimes very difficult to predict.

With its mixture of relatively fixed and relatively flexible exchange rates, the current international monetary system lacks the purity of the thoroughbred, but possesses the hardiness and adaptability of the mongrel. Like the mongrel, with reasonable care it may have a long life.

SUGGESTIONS FOR FURTHER READING

For discussions of the factors that a country should consider in forming its exchange-rate policy, see V. Argy, *The Postwar International Monetary Crisis* (London: George Allen and Unwin, 1981); and Edward Tower and Thomas D. Willett, *The Theory of Optimum Currency Areas and Exchange-Rate Flexibility,* Special Papers in International Economics No. 11, Princeton University, 1976.

For an argument that centralized control over national monetary practices is not necessary to secure efficient outcomes, see W.M. Corden, "The Logic of the International Monetary Non-System," in Fritz Machlup, et al., eds., *Reflections on a Troubled World Economy* (London: Macmillan Press, 1983), pp. 59–74.

A general survey is offered by Richard C. Marston, "Exchange Rate Policy Reconsidered," Working Paper No. 2310 (Cambridge, Mass.: National Bureau of Economic Research, 1987).

Also see the references cited in the notes to this chapter.

NOTES

1. John Stuart Mill, *Principles of Political Economy,* Ashley edition (London: Longmans, Green, 1920), p. 488.
2. Cf. Robert Solomon, *The International Monetary System, 1945–1981* (New York: Harper & Row, 1982), pp. 5–6.
3. See *Federal Reserve Bulletin* 59 (September 1973): 624–27.
4. *IMF Survey,* 23 February 1987, p. 58.
5. As quoted by Andrew Crockett and Morris Goldstein, *Strengthening the International Monetary System: Exchange Rates, Surveillance, and Objective Indicators,* Occasional Paper No. 50 (Washington, D.C.: International Monetary Fund, 1987), p. 80.
6. Ibid., pp. 80–81.

7. International Monetary Fund, *Articles of Agreement of the International Monetary Fund* (Washington, D.C.: IMF, 1985), Article VIII, Section 7.

8. The data on reserve holdings presented here follow the IMF convention of valuing gold at 35 SDRs per ounce, although the market value of gold is much higher. If gold is valued at its market price, it accounted for 42 percent of total reserves at the end of 1986, and foreign exchange accounted for 50 percent.

9. Robert M. Dunn, Jr., *The Many Disappointments of Flexible Exchange Rates,* Essays in International Finance No. 154 (Princeton, N.J.: Princeton University, 1983).

10. For some data on these margins in both the forward and the futures markets for foreign currencies, see Norman S. Fieleke, "The Foreign Currency Futures Market: Some Reflections on Competitiveness and Growth," *Journal of Futures Markets* 5 (Winter 1985): 626–27.

11. See, for example, David O. Cushman, "Has Exchange Risk Depressed International Trade? The Impact of Third-Country Exchange Risk," *Journal of International Money and Finance* 5 (September 1986): 361–79; and Padma Gotur, "Effects of Exchange Rate Volatility on Trade: Some Further Evidence," *IMF Staff Papers* 32 (September 1985): 475–512.

12. League of Nations, *International Currency Experience* (Geneva: League of Nations, 1944), pp. 211–12.

13. Milton Friedman, "The Case for Flexible Exchange Rates," in Milton Friedman, *Essays in Positive Economics* (Chicago: University of Chicago Press, 1953), p. 175.

14. Whether this phenomenon truly was a mania has been questioned by Peter M. Garber of Brown University in "The Dollar as a Bubble," November 1987. (Unpublished.)

15. Jeffrey H. Bergstrand, "Is Exchange Rate Volatility 'Excessive'?" *New England Economic Review,* September-October 1983: 5–14.

16. See Norman S. Fieleke, "Foreign-Currency Positioning by U.S. Firms: Some New Evidence," *Review of Economics and Statistics* 63 (February 1981): 35–42. This article also offers further description of the data in Table 5–2.

17. Crockett and Goldstein, *Strengthening the International Monetary System,* pp. 3–5, present a concise discussion of the misalignment question.

18. Crockett and Goldstein, *Strengthening the International Monetary System,* p. 4.

19. *World Financial Markets,* February-March 1987: 14.

20. John Williamson, *The Exchange Rate System,* 2d ed., Policy Analyses in International Economics 5 (Washington, D.C.: Institute for International Economics, 1985); the estimated misalignments are on page 81.

21. See note 19 above.

22. See Chapter 6.

23. Japan, West Germany, and the United States reportedly agreed to target zones for exchange rates among their currencies at a meeting in Paris in February 1987. As late as the end of 1987, however, no zones had been published. The zones guessed in the financial press had been seriously breached by then. See Clyde H. Farnsworth, "IMF Presses 3d World Aid," *New York Times,* 25 September 1987; "Revamping the Louvre Discord," *Economist* 305 (31 October 1987): 69; and exchange-rate quotations for the mark and yen prices of the dollar at year-end.

24. See John Williamson, "International Liquidity: Are the Supply and Composition Appropriate?" and W. Max Corden, "Discussion," in *The International Monetary System: Forty Years After Bretton Woods,* Conference Series No. 28 (Boston: Federal Reserve Bank of Boston, 1984), pp. 59–82.

25. John Williamson, "The Benefits and Costs of an International Monetary Non-System," in Edward M. Bernstein et al. *Reflections on Jamaica,* Essays in International Finance No. 115 (Princeton: Princeton University, 1976).

26. Stanley W. Black, "International Money and International Monetary Arrangements," in Ronald W. Jones and Peter B. Kenen, eds., *Handbook of International Economics,* Vol. 2 (New York: Elsevier, 1985), pp. 1182–85.

27. Principles of behavior were discussed in the section entitled, "A Composite System."

6 ECONOMIC INTERDEPENDENCE AND POLICY COORDINATION

Both the man in the street and the academic economist would testify that many national economies are closely interconnected, and that this interdependence has grown significantly over the past two or three decades. At the formal, organizational level, the leading illustration of growing interdependence is the European Economic Community (EEC), which has expanded from its founding core of six countries in 1958 to its present membership of twelve. To form a "common market," EEC members eliminate government barriers against trade among themselves and adopt a common tariff schedule on imports from nonmember countries in place of their separate tariffs. In addition, they have agreed to remove restrictions on movements of labor and capital within the EEC and to harmonize their domestic policies. Impressive as it is, this movement toward integration remains regional rather than worldwide in scope.

The signs of growing interdependence are not limited to such regional integration schemes. It is common, for example, to hear of the "internationalization" of this or that industry. Oil shocks, third-world debt problems, and record U.S. trade deficits have heightened the impression that "it's a small world after all," but without the cheerful spirit of the Disney World theme song. Increasing interdependence seems to mean increasing vulnerability and insecurity.

This heightened sense of interdependence has led to more frequent calls for coordination of the economic policies pursued by different

195

nations. Indeed, following the widely reported "Plaza" agreement, "coordination" became one of the economic buzzwords of the 1980s. Meeting at New York's Plaza Hotel on 22 September 1985, the finance ministers and central bank heads of the United Kingdom, France, Japan, West Germany, and the United States announced that they were prepared to cooperate to lower the foreign exchange value of the dollar, which had been declining but which they considered still too high in light of underlying economic conditions. Following this announcement, the dollar's foreign exchange value continued to decline—for a while even faster than before, suggesting that coordination efforts could be fruitful.

But is the world economy really more highly integrated or interdependent than it was, say, thirty years ago? Should national governments coordinate their economic policies more closely, and if so, through what institutional means?

MEASURES OF INTEGRATION OR INTERDEPENDENCE

Economic integration and economic interdependence have been defined in a number of somewhat different ways. The essence of these concepts is most clearly indicated by likening an economy, as Alfred Marshall did, to a changing biological organism: the functioning of one part is influenced by that of others, while all contribute to the functioning of the whole.[1] To what extent are the various national (sub)economies integrated into this kind of interdependent, organic whole?

At a more basic level, the question might be raised of how highly integrated the economy within each nation is, for it is surely true that the links between some national economies are closer than the links to be found within certain national economic systems. For example, in 1987, two weeks were required to drive from west to east across the rudimentary roads of Zaire[2]—rather conclusive evidence that the country's economy was less closely knit than many other "separate" economies were, including some in Western Europe. Interesting as this question is, our chief concern is with the issue of coordinating the economic policies of different nations, so it is integration across national economies, rather than within them, that will occupy our attention.

While the general concept of economic integration is easily conveyed, a definition that lends itself to quantitative measurement is much more difficult to set forth. One approach is to measure the degree to which prices of similar goods or productive factors are equalized—or at least move in parallel—across national boundaries, with prices expressed, of course, in a single currency. If prices so measured diverge sharply between countries, the explanation could lie in high transportation or communication costs, or in government barriers to commerce (such as tariffs), all of which would serve to prevent the full merger of more or less separate markets into a single market. Another approach is to measure the share of a nation's economic activity that is accounted for by exchanges with other nations, with larger shares taken to signify closer integration—or at least closer physical ties, or "openness," to the rest of the world.

MOVEMENTS OF GOODS, LABOR, AND CAPITAL

According to the latter measure, economic integration across goods markets has been increasing, at least for the major industrial countries and for the sampling of major less developed countries listed in Table 6–1. For some countries, the increase has been remarkable. The average of South Korea's exports and imports as a share of the nation's gross domestic output rose from about 9 percent in 1960–61 to nearly 37 percent in 1984–85; France, West Germany, Italy, and Brazil also experienced dramatic increases. For some countries, the change has been less impressive, but on average, for the countries listed, the share of international commerce in domestic output went up from 15.6 percent to 21.7 percent over the thirty-five years covered by the data in Table 6–1.

Such increases in integration have been fostered by improvements in communications and transportation and, at least until the 1980s, by reductions in government barriers to international trade, especially tariff barriers.[3] For example, the cost of a three-minute, off-peak telephone call between Washington, D.C. and Frankfurt, West Germany, declined by 95 percent between 1950 and 1985, after adjustment for inflation. The cost of air travel also plummeted. Measured in 1985 dollars, the average fare per passenger-mile for international air travel dropped by two-thirds between 1950 and 1983; for air freight, the comparable figure was a decline of nearly four-fifths in the cost per ton-mile.[4]

Although reductions in communications and transportation costs have favored the movement of capital and labor as well as goods, government barriers to the international movement of labor have proven more

Table 6-1. International Commerce as a Percentage of Gross Domestic Output, for Selected Countries and Years.

Country	1950–51	1960–61	1970–71	1980–81	1984–85
Industrial countries					
Canada	22.1	18.1	21.5	27.0	26.9
France	15.9	12.4	15.4	22.6	23.7
West Germany	13.5	18.3	21.6	29.7	32.7
Italy	12.0[a]	13.1	16.3	22.5	21.9
Japan	N.A.	10.9	10.9	15.7	14.9
United Kingdom	25.5	20.3	21.9	25.8	28.7
United States	4.5	4.6	5.5	10.2	8.8
Average[c]	15.6	14.0	16.2	21.9	22.5
Less developed countries					
Argentina	N.A.	N.A.	8.6	9.1	N.A.
Brazil	N.A.	7.2	7.3	9.7	22.1
India	N.A.	6.3	4.5	8.7	8.1[b]
South Korea	N.A.	9.3	19.7	38.5	36.7
Mexico	15.7	11.2	8.4	12.9	14.0[b]
Average[c]	15.7	8.5	9.7	15.8	20.2
Average for all countries listed[c]	15.6	12.0	13.5	19.4	21.7

Note: A country's international commerce is defined as half the sum of the country's exports and imports, where exports and imports are as defined in the country's national accounts and generally include goods as well as nonfactor services (and exclude interest and other income receipts and payments).

[a]1951–52.

[b]1983–84.

[c]Simple average of percentages.

N.A.: Not available.

Source: *International Financial Statistics*, various issues.

unyielding than barriers to merchandise trade; it is common knowledge that labor services are not exchanged among nations nearly so freely as are the products of labor. Nonetheless, significant transfers of labor do occur. For example, in the United States more than 40 percent of the yearly growth in the labor force recently may be attributable to immigrants.[5]

With respect to capital, the impression is widespread that its mobility has been greatly enhanced in recent years by the relaxation of government controls and by speedier communications. It would be instructive to examine data on gross capital transactions between nations, but all capital flow data relate to *net* changes in claims or liabilities over specified time periods. Fortunately, the net data are helpful. Indeed, it is the net movement of capital, rather than the gross, that represents a transfer of resources between countries. A country that lends on net—acquiring net claims on other countries—does so by exporting more goods and services than it imports and by accepting IOUs for the excess. This net lending is measured by the country's balance of international payments on current account; similarly, a nation borrows by incurring a deficit in its current account.

One would expect the value of such borrowing and lending to increase over time with economic growth and inflation and with the increase in total saving and investment. An interesting question relating to economic integration, then, is not simply whether such borrowing and lending have increased, but whether they have increased more rapidly than the value of total saving or total investment. In other words, what has happened to the ratio of the current account balance to gross investment, or to gross saving? For the sample of fourteen industrial countries listed in Table 6–2, the average ratio has risen, but not dramatically. For half of these countries, the current account balance declined as a percentage of gross saving (disregarding the algebraic sign) between 1952–53 and 1984–85, but the average of the country percentages increased appreciably. On balance, the data provide some support for the view that national capital markets had become more highly integrated during the 1980s.

Volatility, rather than strong trend, seems to characterize this measure of net international capital flows, with sharp fluctuations occurring for many countries. Moreover, as the table shows, the total deficits and surpluses accumulated by most countries over the entire period 1952–85 were small in relation to their gross national saving. (One exception is Ireland, which borrowed relatively heavily and would require nearly four and one-half years of saving at its 1985 rate in order to pay back its net foreign debt incurred on current account over the years 1952–85.) These data, as well as other studies, indicate that over the long run very little capital is transferred, net, between nations.[6] To explain this phenomenon, various hypotheses have been set forth, including the arguments that net international capital flows are discouraged in the long run, if not the short, by government controls, by foreign exchange and political risks, and by government policies designed to constrain current account deficits and surpluses.[7] Another line of reasoning

Table 6–2. Selected Statistics on Current Account Balances for Fourteen Industrial OECD Countries, 1952–85.

Country	Current Account Balance as Percent of Gross National Saving					Cumulative Current Account Balance (in billions of dollars)	Column 6 Divided by 1985 Gross National Saving
	1952–53 (1)	1960–61 (2)	1970–71 (3)	1980–81 (4)	1984–85 (5)	(6)	(7)
Austria	7.2	-3.3	-1.3	-8.9	-1.7	-12.5	-0.8
Canada	-4.9	-19.6	4.1	-4.8	1.3	-39.4	-0.6
Denmark	3.7	-6.4	-13.1	-25.6	-25.7	-25.0	-2.8
Finland	-2.3	-4.2	-9.7	-6.9	-3.1	-10.4	-0.8
West Germany	9.8	4.2	1.3	-6.6	8.8	56.9	0.4
Ireland	-21.8	-3.8	23.3	-84.9	-24.3	-14.6	-4.4
Italy	-8.3	3.8	5.9	-12.5	-4.5	-11.8	-0.2
Japan	0.2	-2.4	4.6	-0.9	10.5	141.5	0.3
Netherlands	30.3	7.3	-3.1	4.2	18.1	31.1	1.0
Norway	-7.8	-1.6	-11.6	9.7	17.3	-5.2	-0.3
Sweden	2.9	-0.6	0.6	-18.2	-2.2	-18.9	-1.1
Switzerland	19.7	-2.1	1.0	-0.2	19.7	34.7	1.2
United Kingdom	6.8	-2.8	8.3	10.7	4.1	26.9	0.3
United States	-0.6	3.4	0.2	0.8	-17.3	-231.6	-0.4
Average of percentages (absolute value)	9.0	4.7	6.3	13.9	11.3		

Note: (−) signifies a current account deficit, (+) a surplus.

Source: *International Financial Statistics 40* (December 1987); Organization for Economic Cooperation and Development: *National Accounts, 1960–1985*, Vol. 1 (Paris: OECD, 1987), and *National Accounts, 1951–1980*, Vol. 1 (Paris: OECD, 1982); International Monetary Fund (Washington, D.C.: IMF): *Balance of Payments Statistics Yearbook* (various issues), and *International Financial Statistics Supplement on Exchange Rates, Supplement Series No. 1* (1981).

suggests that the explanation lies not in such constraints over international capital flows but in a low transference of such flows within *domestic* capital markets into less liquid assets, such as equities. With higher transferability within domestic markets, net international flows could presumably increase.[8] This last hypothesis, however, is somewhat undermined by a recent study that suggests such transferability already is extremely high.[9]

PRICE MOVEMENTS: LABOR AND CAPITAL

A second method, preferred by many, of measuring integration is to compare the levels or movements of prices for similar goods or productive factors in different countries. Again, with regard to labor it is well known that the wage rate varies sharply among countries. Some of the variation is attributable to differences in the quality of labor, rather than to barriers against labor mobility. In particular, worker efficiency rises with general education and experience with industrial methods. For example, a study of the cotton textile industry has found that a person-hour of labor in a highly literate and industrialized society is about three and one-half times as productive as a person-hour of labor in a much less advanced society.[10] Even in the absence of such quality differentials, however, obstacles to.labor migration would surely prevent the equalization of labor compensation rates across national boundaries.

Barriers to the movement of capital seem less formidable than those to the movement of labor. The price for the services of capital is, of course, the rate of interest. To evaluate the integration of financial markets across countries, then, we must compare the rates of interest paid in different countries. The comparison should be of interest rates paid by borrowers whose likelihood of defaulting is similar, because the interest rate paid varies considerably with the risk status of the borrower, even within the same country.

Figure 6–1 attempts such a comparison, using the interest rate paid on ninety-day certificates of deposit by U.S. banks, on the one hand, and the average of the three-month interest rates paid by foreign borrowers having a similar risk of default in ten other industrial countries, on the other hand. The chart begins with the first year for which data on the average foreign rate are available. Clearly, these two interest-rate series do not move as one. Especially large differences occur between the two series for the years 1978–81. Nor do the two series move closely in parallel in most years, as is further demonstrated by the correlation coefficients in Table 6–3; for only three of the twelve years represented are the coefficients both positive and greater than 0.8. More detailed analysis discloses similarly low correlations between the U.S. interest rate and rates in other industrial countries individually, with the exception of Canada. These data suggest that capital markets are not highly integrated across countries, for nominal interest rates on financial assets with similar default risk can vary substantially between the United States and other industrial countries.

Figure 6–1. Three-Month Interest Rates in the United States and Abroad, and Foreign Currency Value of U.S. Dollar, 1976–87 (weekly averages).

Note: U.S. interest rate is for ninety-day certificates of deposit. Foreign interest rate and foreign currency value of U.S. dollar are trade-weighted averages for ten foreign industrial countries.

Source: U.S. Board of Governors of the Federal Reserve System, Macrodata Library.

Table 6-3. Correlation Coefficients Between Weekly Measures of the Three-Month U.S. CD Rate and the Weighted Average Foreign Three-Month Interest Rate, 1976–87.

1976	−0.205
1977	−0.821
1978	0.764
1979	0.837
1980	0.176
1981	0.343
1982	0.909
1983	0.110
1984	0.786
1985	0.710
1986	0.920
1987	0.004

Source: Underlying data from U.S. Board of Governors of the Federal Reserve System, Macrodata Library.

The issue, however, is not so simple. The interest returns represented in Figure 6–1 are paid in different currencies, whereas the appropriate test of financial market integration is how nearly equal those rates of return are when measured in a single currency. For example, suppose that a three-month U.S. Treasury bill denominated in U.S. dollars yields 6 percent interest, that a three-month U.K. Treasury bill denominated in U.K. pounds yields 8 percent interest, and that the dollar rises in value against the pound by 3 percent over the three-month period. Taking into account the change in value of the dollar against the pound, an investor could earn one percent more (annual rate, ignoring transactions costs) by investing in the U.S. Treasury bill instead of the U.K. Treasury bill, even though the latter offers the higher interest rate. Thus, it is rates of interest adjusted for exchange-rate change that should be compared in evaluating financial market integration.

To facilitate this evaluation, Figure 6–1 shows the dollar's average exchange rate, as well as U.S. and foreign interest rates. If realized rates of return, taking exchange-rate change into account, had in fact been equalized between the United States and abroad, any sustained rise in the dollar's foreign exchange value would have been accompanied by an offsetting interest differential in favor of foreign securities. In fact, the U.S. interest rate exceeded the average foreign rate by a wide margin during much of the period from the second half of 1980 through 1984, even though the dollar's foreign exchange value rose considerably over that period. Moreover, throughout the second half of 1985 and all of 1986, the interest differential remained close to zero or in favor of foreign securities, but the foreign exchange value of the dollar generally declined, rather than displaying stability or an offsetting appreciation. Thus, the impression remains that capital markets are not highly integrated across countries.

Such incomplete integration can result either from inefficiencies in the functioning of private markets or from governmental action. In this case, responsibility lies largely with two categories of government activity: issuance of national currencies and intervention in private market transactions. The financial assets compared in Figure 6–1 are denominated in different currencies, and at any time these currencies are usually perceived as likely to change in value against each other by varying degrees. Thus, the assets are subject to differing degrees of exchange-rate risk. Moreover, governments impose differing regulations over financial institutions and transactions under their jurisdictions; and on occasion, a political risk arises that a government will interfere with payments due to holders of financial assets, especially foreign holders. These exchange-rate and political risks and standing government regulations give rise to differences in prices (and interest rates) among financial assets issued in different currencies and countries, even if those assets entail the same commercial default risk. Thus, the interest rates paid will vary, with higher rates required to compensate for higher political risk, for greater suspicion of exchange-rate depreciation, and for costs imposed by government regulations.

If the purpose is merely to appraise the basic efficiency with which markets are functioning, rather than their full integration, it seems appropriate to use data that neutralize the effects of government regulation and political and exchange-rate risks. Such data as are readily at hand suggest that the freer financial markets in the major industrial countries are linked by very efficient mechanisms, mechanisms that transfer funds quickly to eliminate any discrepancies in rates of return paid after allowing for differential political and exchange-rate risk. For example, Figure 6–2 shows the interest rate on three-month Eurodollar deposits, which, being located in London, are presumably subject to approximately the same political risk as other assets held there. The chart also shows the three-month interest rate for U.K. pound loans

Figure 6–2.   Interest Arbitrage: Three-Month Funds, 1984–87 (weekly averages).

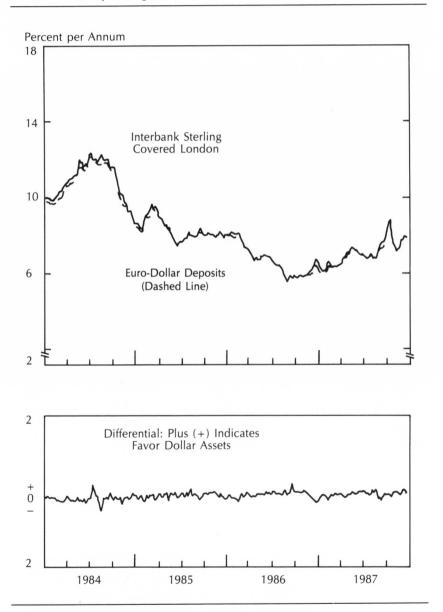

Note: 1 percent on differential scale = 2 percent on rate scale.

Source: U.S. Board of Governors of the Federal Reserve System, *Selected Interest and Exchange Rates*, December 28, 1987, Chart 8.

between banks, after adjustment for the "cost" of insuring against the risk of exchange-rate change between the pound and the dollar (the "cost" of forward cover). Thus, neither exchange-rate nor political risk influences the difference between these two series. The absence of any significant difference is testimony that the financial intermediaries involved are alert and efficient, with very low transaction costs.[11] Such evidence supports our previous claim that factors other than market inefficiency account for the sizable differences between the two series plotted in Figure 6–1.

Another approach to evaluating the international integration of capital markets is to compare the real (adjusted for inflation) rates of interest

Figure 6–3. U.S. and Average Foreign Real Long-term Government Bond Yields, Quarterly, 1976–87.

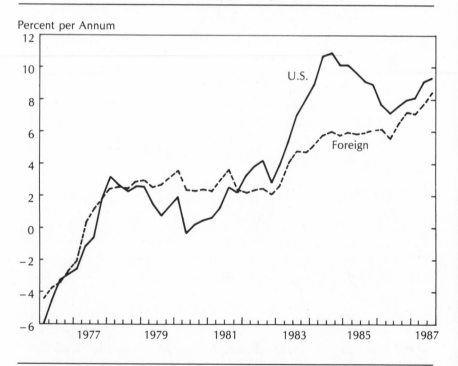

Note: Real yields are nominal yields minus rates of increase in wholesale prices. Foreign countries included are Canada, Japan, West Germany, France, the United Kingdom, Belgium, Italy, and the Netherlands. Foreign data are weighted according to relative share of U.S. trade with each country.

Source: Data Resources, Inc.

paid in various national markets. If a country experiences a steady inflation rate of, say, 4 percent per year, the domestic purchasing power of its currency declines accordingly; annual interest rates must be 4 percent higher in that country than in another country with no inflation if real rates of return in the two countries are to be equal. Judging from Figure 6–3, we conclude that recorded (or *ex post*) real interest rates have not been equalized by international capital movements. With truly perfect integration, equalization would occur. Only one real interest rate would be observed on bonds of the same default risk, just as only one rate would be observed within a well-functioning national capital market.[12]

PRICE MOVEMENTS: GOODS

The preceding section has shown that the markets for capital and for labor are far from perfectly integrated. Correspondingly, with respect to the markets for goods, much evidence exists that, from one country to the next, highly similar goods often vary sharply in price (when prices are expressed in a single currency). Most prominent among the goods showing such price differences are the "nontradables," so labeled because the cost of transporting them is prohibitive in relation to their cost of production. The classic example of the nontradable good is the haircut, the dollar price for which is much lower in, say, Mexico than in the United States. In addition to transportation costs, manmade obstacles, such as tariffs, can prevent the equalization of prices for identical goods.

To illustrate these price differences among countries, the *Economist* magazine developed the "McDonald's hamburger standard," which measures how much the price of a Big Mac differs between countries when the native currency prices are converted at going foreign exchange rates into a common currency. In January 1987, the Big Mac sold in West Germany for 27 percent less than in Denmark, 21 percent less than in France, and 12 percent less than in Italy—but for 28 percent more than in Ireland, 29 percent more than in the United Kingdom, and 36 percent more than in the United States. Looked at another way, the prevailing foreign exchange rates valued the deutsche mark at 27 percent less than its "purchasing-power parity" against the Danish kroner (that is, at 27 percent less than required to equate the prices of the Big Mac in West Germany and Denmark), but at 36 percent more than its purchasing-power parity against the U.S. dollar.[13]

Table 6-4. Percentage Excess of Market Average Foreign Exchange Rates Over Purchasing-Power Parities for Gross Domestic Product, for Seventeen Countries, 1970-84.

Country	1970	1971	1972	1973	1974	1975	1976
Canada	14.7	13.5	10.0	7.5	-0.2	1.7	-4.3
Japan	57.0	52.6	31.2	10.0	6.6	9.9	8.6
Austria	56.8	50.1	35.2	11.9	6.2	1.3	4.9
Belgium	36.8	33.1	18.6	3.4	0.1	-8.1	-4.9
Denmark	29.3	24.9	11.9	-7.1	-9.7	-17.4	-15.6
Finland	38.0	35.1	29.2	10.1	-3.2	-10.1	-11.2
France	32.2	31.2	18.3	2.2	8.2	-7.2	-0.4
West Germany	30.7	21.7	10.3	-8.2	-9.5	-11.2	-7.4
Greece	54.6	58.7	57.1	37.2	25.5	30.3	36.3
Ireland	67.0	55.6	40.2	30.7	41.1	34.8	45.3
Italy	65.5	60.2	48.8	40.5	44.2	34.6	53.8
Luxembourg	52.3	45.9	31.0	13.6	11.6	4.8	4.6
Netherlands	51.3	42.1	24.4	5.1	0.7	-6.0	-4.2
Norway	32.1	28.3	19.4	1.0	-4.0	-10.2	-7.7
Portugal	101.6	98.5	85.3	61.3	53.1	44.4	55.8
Spain	126.3	119.8	95.3	67.4	55.1	44.2	52.7
United Kingdom	61.2	52.1	43.3	43.6	43.0	29.3	46.5

Note: Underlying exchange rates and PPPs are expressed as national currencies per U.S. dollars.

An item-by-item evaluation of such price differentials and their change over time would be an heroic undertaking. A summary evaluation, however, is possible with the aid of aggregate purchasing-power parity indexes (PPPs). The PPPs used here are rates that have been calculated to convert overall price levels in different countries to the same level, measured in U.S. dollars.

The rates prevailing for actual transactions in the foreign exchange market commonly differ from these PPPs. In other words, the market does not generally maintain equivalence among the overall price levels of different countries expressed in a common currency, any more than it maintains equivalence among the prices of some individual goods like Big Macs. As noted above, transportation costs and trade restrictions help to explain this nonequivalence. The extent of the nonequivalence is reported in Table 6-4, which presents the percentage excess (positive) or shortfall (negative) of market exchange rates from PPPs

1977	1978	1979	1980	1981	1982	1983	1984
1.3	9.7	10.5	8.3	9.0	9.2	8.1	14.6
− 2.0	− 21.2	− 13.4	− 5.5	− 2.8	14.8	13.6	17.0
− 3.4	− 13.0	− 16.5	− 16.0	6.2	14.5	20.6	32.5
− 13.2	− 21.5	− 24.0	− 20.1	5.2	29.4	42.0	57.9
− 19.0	− 27.2	− 30.0	− 24.1	− 5.2	6.8	13.2	25.5
− 11.4	− 9.5	− 14.2	− 17.5	− 6.8	2.1	13.4	16.5
− 0.9	− 10.3	− 16.9	− 19.4	0.8	15.9	28.3	41.9
− 12.7	− 22.4	− 26.1	− 23.3	− 0.4	9.8	17.1	32.4
28.4	21.7	12.2	20.4	42.1	46.8	68.7	86.3
40.4	23.8	10.7	5.4	23.7	29.7	39.6	55.9
44.9	31.4	20.6	12.8	37.8	48.8	51.7	64.2
− 1.5	− 12.5	− 15.8	− 15.5	7.9	29.1	38.9	55.8
− 12.0	− 21.0	− 23.4	− 21.4	1.8	9.9	20.4	37.1
− 12.0	− 12.6	− 14.0	− 19.8	− 11.0	− 2.8	7.6	16.3
65.7	67.7	71.0	57.9	82.1	105.9	141.9	163.8
49.2	34.7	9.7	12.6	39.0	55.6	90.0	97.5
41.1	23.5	5.9	− 11.7	− 1.2	13.8	30.5	47.0

Source: Organization for Economic Cooperation and Development, *National Accounts,
1960–84*, Vol. 1 (Paris: OECD, 1986), p. 117; and *International Financial Statistics*, 1986 Yearbook, and February 1987.

for seventeen countries over a fifteen-year period. The discrepancies
are sometimes enormous. For example, the data imply that Portuguese
prices, measured in U.S. dollars, would have had to rise by 163.8 percent in 1984 to equal the general level of prices in the United States,
and that, by contrast, West German prices would have had to fall by
26.1 percent in 1979 in order to attain such parity with U.S. prices.
Moreover, large discrepancies commonly persist for years.

The generally sizable and uniformly positive discrepancies in 1984
tend to support the view that prices in the United States were then
"out of line" with prices in other industrial countries. *Either* prices
in these countries had to rise relative to those in the United States *or*
the currencies of these countries had to become more expensive in terms
of the U.S. dollar. Thus, it is understandable that many currencies rose
in value—some very sharply—against the U.S. dollar during 1985–1987.

Since the overall price levels for goods, expressed in a common currency, generally differ so much from country to country, the conclusion is inescapable that, in the aggregate, the national markets for goods are not very highly integrated. As in the case of the capital markets, however, this conclusion must be carefully qualified. For goods that have relatively low transportation costs and that are free of government restrictions, evidence is available that prices (again, expressed in a single currency) display very similar movement from one country to the next. In other words, after allowing for transportation costs and the like, the goods markets in different countries, like the capital markets, seem to be linked by efficient market intermediaries.

Some illustrations of this seeming efficiency are presented in Figure 6-4, which compares the behavior of prices in West Germany and the United States for three basic products over periods of ten years or more. Multiplying the index of the deutsche mark price in West Germany by an index of the dollar/mark exchange rate prevailing in the foreign exchange market yielded the "U.S. dollar equivalent of the deutsche mark price." This series should closely correspond to the dollar price in the United States if markets were highly competitive and efficiently linked. In fact, there is little correspondence between these two series during the early 1970s for any of the three commodities, but factors other than market inefficiency seem responsible. The chief explanation surely is the price control program instituted in the United States, a program that suppressed the prices of many industrial commodities there during the years 1971–73. After the controls were removed, the U.S. prices for the commodities represented in the chart escalated to the levels previously attained by the U.S. dollar equivalents of deutsche mark prices. This convergence suggests that the West German and U.S. markets for each of these commodities were fairly efficiently linked, in the absence of such interference as price controls.[14] It also suggests, incidentally, that temporary price controls do not succeed in reducing the long-run rate of inflation.

Of course, the less the goods of one country resemble those of another, the less reason to expect correspondence between their prices. Several empirical studies have revealed substantial differences between countries in both price levels and price variations for narrowly defined *groupings* of commodities, after expressing prices in a common currency. However, it is not clear how much of the reported national price differences stems from market imperfections and how much stems from national differences in the commodity categories.[15] In any event, as indicated in Table 6-4, *overall* price levels can differ markedly from

Figure 6-4. Indexes of Prices for Magnesium, Pig Iron, and Steel Wire Rods in West Germany and the United States.

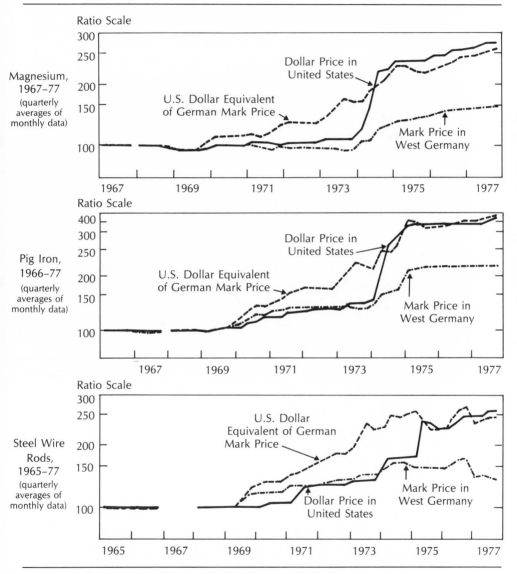

Note: Due to a break in the series for West German prices, there are two base periods for each series of indexes. Prior to 1968, the base periods are as follows: for magnesium, January–June 1967 = 100; for pig iron, January–June 1966-100; and for steel wire rods, January–June 1965 = 100. Thereafter, January–June 1968 = 100. Data are plotted for every quarter for which observations are available for at least two months.

Source: Norman S. Fieleke, "The International Transmission of Inflation," in *Managed Exchange Rate Flexibility: The Recent Experience*, Conference Series No. 20 (Boston: Federal Reserve Bank of Boston, 1978), p. 41.

country to country, so that in the aggregate, the goods markets of the world should not be viewed as one single, highly integrated market.

A basic question raised at the beginning of this chapter was whether the world economy has become more highly integrated or interdependent over the past few decades. The evidence examined here has been far from exhaustive, as some of the key data series are available for relatively few years or countries; but neither is the evidence so flimsy that it should be dismissed out of hand. Our reading of that evidence is that none of it conclusively contradicts the hypothesis of greater integration, while some supports that hypothesis. The clearest support is offered in Table 6–1, which, in our judgment, provides the single most meaningful and readily available index of integration of the goods markets.

INTERNATIONAL TRANSMISSION
OF ECONOMIC DISTURBANCES

The integration or interconnection of national economies makes possible the transmission of disturbances between them. Some of the most dramatic disturbances have been "supply shocks," such as abrupt changes in the supply of oil, and in the harvest of major crops such as wheat and coffee. The Organization of Petroleum Exporting Countries raised the average selling price for its crude oil by 230 percent between 1973 and 1974, and by 65 percent between 1979 and 1980. Poor grain harvests in 1972 in the Soviet Union and elsewhere contributed to an 80 percent rise in world food prices between 1972 and 1973. Frosts in Brazil in 1975 destroyed or severely damaged about half of that nation's three billion coffee bushes, and by 1977 coffee prices had risen more than 200 percent.

Although supply shocks have been important, the focus here is on the international impacts of national monetary and fiscal policies, since our purpose is to consider the international coordination of these policies. The chief question raised in this section is whether one country's monetary or fiscal policies can significantly influence the economies of other countries. If not, policy coordination would seem pointless.

To estimate the international effects of national policies, economists have developed econometric models of the linkages between various national economies. What comes out of such models depends, of course, on what goes into them, not merely the input of raw data but the underlying assumptions about human behavior and the design and number of equations used to estimate the economic relationships that are of interest. It is not surprising, then, that different models yield different results.

To illustrate, Tables 6–5 and 6–6 report various model estimates of some of the consequences of a one-percentage-point decrease in a key interest rate controlled by the monetary authorities in the United States, West Germany, and Japan. The estimates in Table 6–5 allow for repercussions experienced by a country as a result of the impact of its lower interest rate on other countries. For example, the estimates recognize that a reduction in the U.S. interest rate affects not only the U.S. economy but other economies, and that the resulting changes in other economies in turn affect the U.S. economy. Thus, including such repercussions, the U.S. Federal Reserve Board "multicountry" model estimates that the one-percentage-point reduction in the relevant U.S. interest rate would serve to raise U.S. GNP by 1.2 percent (above what it would otherwise be) by the fourth year after the interest-rate reduction. According to the same model, if the interest-rate reduction were undertaken in West Germany or Japan, their GNPs would be boosted by 0.9 percent or 2.7 percent, respectively, by the fourth year.

The estimates yielded by the several models sometimes differ substantially. For example, the one-percentage-point interest-rate reduction would raise U.S. GNP by 1.2 percent after four years, according to the multicountry model, but by only half as much according to the OECD "interlink" model, and by no more than 0.1 percent according to the Economic Planning Agency "world" model. An interest-rate cut in West Germany would raise the general price level in that country after four years by anywhere from an estimated 0.5 percent to 1.3 percent, depending on the model consulted.

Not only do the models differ, but all are plagued by various estimation problems, at least one of which merits specific mention. In both the real world and in econometric models, the effect of a policy change such as an interest-rate reduction is crucially dependent upon the public's interpretation of the change and upon how expectations are affected. The models represented in Table 6–5 assume that expectations of the behavior of financial variables (such as exchange rates) are modified gradually to reflect changes observed in actual magnitudes. In fact, expectations sometimes change very quickly in anticipation of the effects of a policy change, especially if the policymakers announcing the change are deemed credible; in that case, the effects can be very different from those reported in Table 6–5.

Table 6–5. Simulated Effects in Home Country of a One-Percentage-Point Decrease in a Policy-Controlled Domestic Interest Rate (percentage deviations from baseline).

U.S. FEDERAL RESERVE BOARD MULTICOUNTRY MODEL

	United States			West Germany			Japan		
	GNP	PA	Effective Exchange Rate	GNP	PA	$/DM	GNP	PA	$/Yen
Year: 1	0.2	0.1	−1.9	0.2	0.5	−2.4	0.3	0.1	−2.7
2	0.6	0.2	−2.7	0.6	0.6	−3.4	1.2	0.2	−2.9
3	1.0	0.4	−3.5	0.8	0.8	−3.6	2.0	0.4	−3.3
4	1.2	0.7	−4.2	0.9	1.0	−3.9	2.7	0.6	−4.0

JAPANESE ECONOMIC PLANNING AGENCY WORLD MODEL

	United States			West Germany			Japan		
	GNP	PA	Effective Exchange Rate	GNP	PA	$/DM	GNP	PA	$/Yen
Year: 1	0.4	0.1	−1.0	0.5	0.1	−2.1	0.1	0.3	−1.2
2	0.7	0.1	−1.1	1.3	0.4	−3.2	0.2	0.8	−2.7
3	0.5	0.3	−1.2	2.0	0.8	−5.3	0.3	1.3	−4.0
4	0.1	0.5	−0.7	2.3	1.3	−7.8	0.4	1.7	−5.1

OECD INTERLINK MODEL

	United States			West Germany			Japan		
	GDP	PGDP	Effective Exchange Rate	GDP	PGDP	$/DM	GDP	PGDP	$/Yen
Year: 1	0.3	0.0	−0.6	0.1	0.0	−0.6	0.4	0.1	−0.7
2	0.6	0.1	−1.1	0.3	0.1	−1.2	0.9	0.3	−1.4
3	0.6	0.4	−1.6	0.5	0.3	−1.7	1.2	0.6	−2.1
4	0.6	0.6	−1.9	0.7	0.5	−2.2	1.5	1.1	−2.9

Note: GNP and GDP are real gross national product and real gross domestic product; PGDP and PA are the GDP and absorption deflators; a decrease in the effective exchange rate indicates depreciation.

Source: James M. Boughton, et al., "Effects of Exchange Rate Changes in Industrial Countries," in *Staff Studies for the World Economic Outlook*, World Economic and Financial Surveys (Washington, D.C.: International Monetary Fund, 1986), p. 132.

Table 6-6. Simulated Effects on Real GNP in Other Countries of a One-Percentage-Point Decrease in a Policy-Controlled Domestic Interest Rate (percentage deviations from baseline).

U.S. FEDERAL RESERVE BOARD MULTICOUNTRY MODEL
Country Decreasing Interest Rate

| Impact on GNP in: | United States | | West Germany | | Japan | |
	West Germany	Japan	U.S.	Japan	U.S.	West Germany
Year: 1	0.1	-0.2	0.0	0.0	0.0	-0.1
2	0.0	-0.6	0.0	0.0	0.0	-0.1
3	-0.1	-0.7	-0.1	0.0	0.1	-0.1
4	-0.2	-0.9	-0.1	0.0	0.1	0.0

JAPANESE ECONOMIC PLANNING AGENCY WORLD MODEL
Country Decreasing Interest Rate

| Impact on GNP in: | United States | | West Germany | | Japan | |
	West Germany	Japan	U.S.	Japan	U.S.	West Germany
Year: 1	-0.2	0.0	0.0	0.0	0.0	0.0
2	-0.2	0.1	0.0	0.0	0.0	0.0
3	-0.1	0.1	0.0	0.1	0.0	0.0
4	0.2	0.1	0.1	0.1	0.0	0.0

OECD INTERLINK MODEL
Country Decreasing Interest Rate

| Impact on GNP in: | United States | | West Germany | | Japan | |
	West Germany	Japan	U.S.	Japan	U.S.	West Germany
Year: 1	0.0	0.1	0.0	0.0	0.0	0.0
2	0.1	0.1	0.0	0.1	0.0	0.1
3	0.1	0.1	0.0	0.1	0.0	0.1
4	0.1	0.0	0.0	0.0	0.0	0.0

Source: James M. Boughton, et al., "Effects of Exchange Rate Changes in Industrial Countries," in *Staff Studies for the World Economic Outlook*, World Economic and Financial Surveys (Washington, D.C.: International Monetary Fund, 1986), p. 134.

If the impact on the country undertaking an interest-rate reduction is difficult to estimate, Table 6–6 suggests that it is even more difficult to estimate the impact on other countries. After four years, a reduction in the U.S. interest rate lowers GNP (below what it would otherwise be) in West Germany (by 0.2 percent) and Japan (by 0.9 percent), according to the multicountry model, but raises GNP slightly or has no impact at all, according to the other two models. While ambiguous, these results do reflect the state of economic theorizing about the international consequences of monetary policy changes. Current thinking generally holds that a policy reduction in a country's interest rates will stimulate total demand in that country, and that some of the increased demand will tend to spill over into demand for the goods of other countries. But the increased demand for foreign goods will also raise demand for foreign currencies, and the resulting higher price of foreign currencies will dampen the increase in demand for foreign goods. With mobile capital, the interest-rate reduction will also encourage investors to acquire foreign rather than domestic securities, another force that will further push up the exchange rate and dampen the purchase of foreign goods. For these and other reasons, it is very difficult, a priori, to conclude whether the net impact on foreign economic activity will be positive or negative. Thus far, the empirical investigations have failed to produce a consensus.

Fiscal as well as monetary policy changes have been investigated with econometric models that incorporate international repercussions. Some results are reported in Tables 6–7 and 6–8. In this case, the policy change is a sustained reduction in goverment spending equal to one percent of GNP. Again, the estimated effects vary across models. Focusing this time on effects after three years (since some fourth-year results are not reported), we find in Table 6–7 that a one-percentage-point drop in government spending in Japan lowers GNP in that country by 1.2 percent (below what it would otherwise have been), according to the multicountry model, by 2.6 percent according to the world model, and by 0.8 percent according to the interlink model.

Wide as the range of these estimates is, it still may not embrace the correct figure. Again, one reason is the difficulty of identifying the manner in which the public's expectations will be affected by an announcement that a government will decrease its expenditures. For example, as noted in the discussion of monetary policy changes, the econometric models considered here assume that expectations are adjusted relatively slowly as hard evidence accumulates. If instead the adjustment were rapid, the estimated pattern of outcomes would be significantly different.

Table 6–7. Simulated Domestic Effects of a Sustained Decline in Real Government Expenditure Equal to One Percent of GNP (percentage deviations from baseline).

U.S. FEDERAL RESERVE BOARD MULTICOUNTRY MODEL

	United States			West Germany			Japan		
	GNP	PA	Effective Exchange Rate	GNP	PA	$/DM	GNP	PA	$/Yen
Year: 1	−1.5	−0.1	−1.6	−1.2	0.0	−0.1	−1.1	−0.1	1.2
2	−1.7	−0.4	−2.8	−1.4	−0.2	0.0	−1.3	−0.3	−0.8
3	−1.3	−0.9	−3.0	−1.2	−0.5	0.1	−1.2	−0.5	−0.1
4	−0.8	−1.3	−3.6	−1.0	−0.8	0.1	−1.2	−0.7	0.2

JAPANESE ECONOMIC PLANNING AGENCY WORLD MODEL

	United States			West Germany			Japan		
	GNP	PA	Effective Exchange Rate	GNP	PA	$/DM	GNP	PA	$/Yen
Year: 1	−1.6	0.0	−0.8	−1.3	−0.1	−0.9	−1.4	0.1	−0.6
2	−2.7	0.1	−2.0	−2.3	−0.4	2.2	−2.2	−0.1	−0.2
3	−3.5	0.1	−6.0	−2.8	−1.1	6.0	−2.6	−0.6	2.7
4	N.A.	−0.1	−9.9	N.A.	−1.9	9.5	N.A.	−1.7	7.9

OECD INTERLINK MODEL

	United States			West Germany			Japan		
	GDP	PGDP	Effective Exchange Rate	GDP	PGDP	$/DM	GDP	PGDP	$/Yen
Year: 1	−1.5	−0.2	−0.2	−0.9	−0.2	−1.1	−1.2	−0.1	−0.6
2	−1.1	−0.7	−0.4	−0.9	−0.4	−1.7	−1.1	−0.4	−0.9
3	−0.6	−1.2	−0.1	−0.6	−0.4	−1.6	−0.8	−0.7	−0.6
4	−0.5	−1.6	0.3	−0.4	−0.4	−1.2	−0.6	−1.1	−0.2

Note: GNP and GDP are real gross national product and real gross domestic product; PGDP and PA are the GDP and absorption deflators; a decrease in the effective exchange rate indicates depreciation.

N.A.: Not available.

Source: James M. Boughton, et al., "Effects of Exchange Rate Changes in Industrial Countries," in *Staff Studies for the World Economic Outlook*, World Economic and Financial Surveys (Washington, D.C.: International Monetary Fund, 1986), p. 137.

Table 6-8. Simulated Effects on Real GNP in Other
Countries of a Sustained Decline in Real Government
Expenditure Equal to One Percent of GNP
(percentage deviations from baseline).

U.S. FEDERAL RESERVE BOARD MULTICOUNTRY MODEL
Country Decreasing Government Spending

Impact on GNP in:	United States		West Germany		Japan	
	West Germany	Japan	U.S.	Japan	U.S.	West Germany
Year: 1	-0.1	-0.4	-0.1	0.0	-0.1	-0.1
2	-0.3	-1.0	-0.1	-0.1	-0.1	-0.1
3	-0.5	-1.3	-0.1	-0.1	0.0	-0.1
4	-0.7	-1.4	0.0	-0.1	-0.1	-0.1

JAPANESE ECONOMIC PLANNING AGENCY WORLD MODEL
Country Decreasing Government Spending

Impact on GNP in:	United States		West Germany		Japan	
	West Germany	Japan	U.S.	Japan	U.S.	West Germany
Year: 1	-0.4	-0.1	0.0	0.0	0.0	0.0
2	-1.0	-0.3	0.0	-0.1	0.0	-0.1
3	-2.0	-0.5	0.0	-0.1	0.0	0.0

OECD INTERLINK MODEL
Country Decreasing Government Spending

Impact on GNP in:	United States		West Germany		Japan	
	West Germany	Japan	U.S.	Japan	U.S.	West Germany
Year: 1	-0.3	-0.6	0.0	0.0	0.0	0.0
2	-0.4	-0.6	0.0	-0.1	0.0	-0.1
3	-0.3	-0.4	0.0	-0.1	0.0	-0.1
4	-0.2	-0.4	0.0	0.0	0.0	0.0

Source: James M. Boughton, et al., "Effects of Exchange Rate Changes in Industrial Countries,"
in *Staff Studies for the World Economic Outlook*, World Economic and Financial Surveys
(Washington, D.C.: International Monetary Fund, 1986), p. 139.

Turning to the cross-country effects, we read in Table 6–8 that the hypothetical reduction in government expenditure, if undertaken in the United States, would lower West German GNP by 0.5 percent after three years, according to the multicountry model, by 2 percent according to the world model, and by only 0.3 percent according to the interlink model. Thus, the differences between models persist.

Not only do different models yield different estimates, but the same basic model will yield different estimates at different times as underlying data are extended or revised, and as the form of the model's estimating equations is revised in accordance with experience and changing theory. No econometric model can remain both static and relevant for very long. Keeping a large model up-to-date is far from effortless. For example, the multicountry model is a system of linked models of five economies (Canada, West Germany, Japan, the United Kingdom, and the United States) plus a sector representing the rest of the world. Each of the five national models includes between 150 and 250 behavioral equations and identities, the total number of equations and identities being in excess of 850.

In spite of the complexities and the differences between various models, the estimates at hand suggest that cross-country effects and international repercussions, whatever their precise magnitudes, may be too large to be ignored for many countries. This conclusion—which fortunately accords with casual observation—leads to the question of whether countries should collaborate in designing their economic policies.

THE CASE FOR COORDINATION

If each of two countries, through economic policy, can significantly affect the economy of the other, it might seem obvious that the two should coordinate their policies.[16] That is to say, they should harmonize their policies to their mutual benefit. The case for coordination is not open and shut, however. We shall first relate some economic arguments on behalf of coordination and then consider some objections.

A common argument on behalf of coordination is that it can reduce the duration or amplitude of economic fluctuations. As transportation and communications have improved, economic disturbances are transmitted more rapidly and fully from country to country than in the past. In these circumstances, might it be possible for countries to destabilize each other's economies by making policy in isolation from each other?

Suppose that actions taken by one country to attain its goals (for example, price stability, or full employment) shifted the economies of other countries further from their own goals. These other countries might then renew the pursuit of their goals with actions that might incidentally drive the first country even farther from its goals, evoking further destabilizing action by that country, and so on.

No one has demonstrated that such an outcome is impossible. Even if it were, isolated policy making might involve more trial and error than coordination and require more time for countries eventually to attain their goals. Since welfare losses mount with the length of time that countries fall short of their economic goals, coordination would be desirable in such circumstances, provided that the various goals were compatible.

If the goals of different countries are incompatible, coordination also offers a way of coping with the conflict. For example, two countries might have different ideas of what the exchange rate between their currencies should be. Or with respect to the balance of payments, countries might aim for balances in their current accounts that, in the aggregate, would sum to a figure substantially different from zero, even though for all countries collectively the balance (correctly measured) must even out to zero.

Such conflicts between goals would provide no ground for concern if the consequences were innocuous. After all, life is replete with such conflicts, and the results are often perceived not as harmful but as desirable. For example, not every firm seeking a high rate of profit can realize it, but the competition for it generally serves society well.

But under some conditions, the world would suffer if the goals pursued by different nations were inconsistent. One illustration of this point is that of two nations, each of which sets objectives for its output and rate of inflation, objectives that each tries to achieve by manipulating the growth of its money supply, while the exchange rate between the two nations' currencies is allowed to change with market conditions.[17] In this example, each country perceives that it can immediately reduce its rate of inflation by reducing its money growth rate so as to raise the value of its currency in the exchange market, thereby lowering the domestic price of imported goods. When both countries actually reduce their money growth rates, the exchange rate remains unchanged—neither currency appreciates—and both countries wind up with unchanged rates of inflation (in the short run), but with lower output than if they had jointly adopted more expansionary monetary policies. Given the circumstances, both nations might have benefited from cooperating. At the very least, after exchanging policy plans the two countries would have recognized that neither would achieve the currency appreciation it sought; that recognition might have induced different policy choices.

Still another argument in support of coordination revolves around the need to provide certain "public goods." A public good is one that one person can partake of without excluding another from partaking; moreover, it is not possible to exclude people from partaking of the good once it is available. National defense is a common illustration. Once a military force has been amassed, each person in the country partakes of its protection without diminishing the protection provided any other person; and no resident can readily be excluded from that protection, whether or not he or she has paid anything for it.

From the nature of public goods, it is obvious that raising the funds to provide them should not be left to the marketplace but should be a responsibility of government. Where public goods are international in nature, governments generally will have to join forces, or coordinate, to ensure that the supply is adequate.

By way of example, preservation of a healthful environment is an international public good. This includes preservation of the ozone layer in the upper atmosphere, for the ozone shields the earth's surface from the sun's ultraviolet rays, which cause skin cancer and also injure plant and animal life. Evidence exists that the ozone shield is being destroyed by chlorofluorocarbons, which are chemicals used in refrigerants, industrial solvents, plastic foams, and spray propellants. In particular, now a hole the size of the United States appears in the ozone layer above Antarctica each September. To add injury to injury, chlorofluorocarbons—along with carbon dioxide and other gases—also trap heat within the earth's atmosphere (the "greenhouse effect"); scientists forecast that if no corrective action is taken, the warming trend will render much farmland too arid to be productive by the year 2040 and will cause sea levels to rise by several feet as polar ice is melted.

These discoveries led to an international agreement in 1987 to reduce emissions of chlorofluorocarbons in subsequent years. The agreement was signed on September 16 by twenty-four nations plus the EEC, and more nations were expected to join.[18] It would be hard to find a problem for which internationally coordinated action was more appropriate.

Another illustration along the same lines is afforded by the phenomenon of acid rain, or more precisely, acidic rain, snow, fog, and dust. Acid rain results from the burning of fossil fuel, which produces sulfur dioxide and nitrogen oxide emissions that become transformed into the rain. Scientists believe that acid rain is destroying life in some freshwater bodies, and that it may also be damaging crops and forests.

Canada has been troubled by acid rain and plans to reduce its contribution to the causal pollution by 50 percent in less than ten years. At the same time, Canada has pressed for similar action by the United States, which not only suffers from the same problem but also generates some of the pollutants that fall in Canada. In response, in 1986 President Reagan committed the U.S. government to spend at least $2.5 billion within five years on the development of cleaner methods of burning coal, which is consumed in large quantities by Midwestern power plants.[19]

While the matter is debatable, economic stability is also considered by some economists to be an international public good. The management of economic policy in large countries such as West Germany, Japan, and the United States has important and unavoidable consequences for other countries. The question arises, then, whether monetary and fiscal policymaking should be subjected to some degree of international negotiation because of public good characteristics.

Finally, coordination is defended as a process through which information important for policymaking is exchanged. To design beneficial policy is difficult even with all extant data, and next to impossible if data are obsolete or otherwise flawed. The pooling of economic information among governments is therefore desirable, and such pooling is more nearly ensured if governments consult frequently on their contemplated policy actions. In this connection, Richard Cooper argues that the world inflationary boom in 1972 and the world recession in 1975 would have been less severe if countries had allowed more fully in their policies for what other countries were doing. In his view, coordination of policy actions, with the associated sharing of current information, would serve to promote the needed sensitivity.[20]

SOME ARGUMENTS AGAINST COORDINATION

Reactions to proposals for coordination illustrate the old saw, "One man's meat is another man's poison." In contrast to the favorable views in the preceding section, some penetrating criticisms and caveats have been offered.

One argument against coordination is similar to the argument against centralized government. At the most cynical level, if it is true that all power corrupts, then it is risky to encourage a high degree of collaboration (collusion?) between governments, which might encourage each other in the pursuit of economic policies designed to maintain or promote their own power or wealth, rather than to serve their constituencies. Indeed, the very expansion of government paraphernalia required for coordination might be seen as a case in point.[21]

Aside from the possibility of such self-serving activity by ostensibly public-serving officials, it is the feasibility of coordination that is most often called into question. For example, governments might not be able to resolve conflicts between their separate goals, not because they are lacking in either reason or good will, but because they are bound by the preferences of their constituencies. If the electorates in all countries coveted surpluses in their international current accounts, coordination would not be the answer to the problem. Indeed, governments that agreed to forgo seeking surpluses would have good reason to doubt each other's ability to honor the commitment.

The feasibility of coordination is also undermined by inadequate economic know-how, even if goals could be agreed upon and commitments honored. Thus, the risk arises that the coordination process will embrace a mistaken view of how the world economy works. As illustrated in a preceding section, more than one plausible econometric model of the international economy is available, and different models yield appreciably different results. How are the coordinators—who will probably not be econometricians, let alone philosopher-kings—to go about choosing among these models? Were they to select the wrong model—and all models might be substantially "wrong"—as a basis for policy coordination, the results for the world economy could be much worse than if no coordination had taken place. Coordinated agreement on disastrous policies would be far inferior to decentralized, independent, even isolated, pursuit of a mixture of "good" and "bad" policies.

Coordination could make matters worse even if the coordinators avoided the error of agreeing upon one wrong econometric model. Indeed, it is to be expected that they would not agree on how the world economy should be modeled. Such disagreement need not forestall coordination. Generally, two governments with different models should still be able to coordinate their policies in a way that each perceives as beneficial. But such coordination is as likely to make matters worse as to improve them as long as the models employed are faulty. In other words, coordination based on several wrong models may be no better than coordination based on a single wrong model.

This point has recently been illustrated by an elaborate experiment with eight different econometric models, any one of which might represent the true functioning of the world economy.[22] The experiment assumed that the U.S. authorities might select any one of the eight models as the basis for policy formulation, and that the authorities in other industrial countries, acting as one, would have the same range of choice. Thus, sixty-four different combinations of the eight models might be employed for policymaking. The experiment further assumed that for each of these sixty-four model combinations, any one of the eight models might be the one truly representing the world economy, so that 512 (eight multiplied by sixty-four) possible outcomes were obtained. Coordination of U.S. and other industrial-country monetary policies was found to *worsen* welfare for the United States in 206 cases, and for other industrial countries in 198 cases. Similarly, coordination of both monetary and fiscal policies reduced welfare for the United States in 228 cases and reduced welfare for other industrial countries in 219 cases, out of the 512 cases examined.

In conclusion, coordination is not an absolute good or bad, or even a matter of principle; it is a method to be chosen or rejected depending on the circumstances. In some cases, such as preservation of a healthful environment, coordination seems desirable, if not essential, for successful action. In other areas, such as economic stabilization policy, coordination is more problematical. The issue is not one of decentralized isolation versus full coordination at all times, but of adaptation to the situation. Where governments can agree upon compatible goals and know how to attain them, coordination can offer some gains. At a minimum, governments should share current information on policy measures, and all may profit from frequent discussion and debate in the various international forums.

AN ILLUSTRATION: INTERNATIONAL DEBATE OVER MACROECONOMIC POLICY

The issues related to coordination are well illustrated by the prolonged international debate over macroeconomic policy that began early in the 1980s. The debate was provoked by the development of huge federal government and balance-of-payments deficits in the United States, with corresponding balance-of-payments surpluses abroad. The controversy involved conflicts between goals, as well as differences in economic analysis.

As shown in Table 6–9, the U.S. deficit on current account soared from $9 billion in 1982 to $141 billion in 1986. The increase of $132 billion in the U.S. deficit was accompanied by an increase of $112 billion in the combined surpluses of Japan and West Germany. Moreover, for 1986 the combined surpluses of Japan and West Germany were not much smaller than the U.S. deficit, and no other country had a surplus approaching that of either Japan or West Germany. These facts suggested that any sizable reduction in the U.S. deficit should be accompanied by a sizable reduction in the Japanese and West German surpluses.

If the Japanese and West German surpluses had to come down to accommodate a decline in the U.S. deficit, what was the best way to engineer this adjustment? Useful perspective on this question can be gained by considering some of the factors that gave rise to the surpluses and deficits. To begin with, as these external imbalances developed, total domestic demand grew more rapidly in the United States than in the other major industrial countries, including Japan and West Germany. (By definition, a country's domestic demand excludes foreign demand for the country's exports, but includes the country's demand for goods from all sources, including imports.) According to the data in Table 6–10, such demand had grown more slowly in the United States than in most other major industrial countries during the years from 1970 to 1980. From 1980 to 1985, however—especially during the 1982–85 recovery from recession—the growth of demand in the United States considerably outpaced that in these other countries. It is not surprising, then, that U.S. imports also increased more rapidly than did

Table 6–9. International Current Account Balances of Major OECD Countries, 1982–86 (in billions of dollars).

	1982	1983	1984	1985	1986
United States	−9	−46	−107	−116	−141
Japan	7	21	35	49	86
West Germany	4	4	8	15	37
France	−12	−5	−1	0	3
United Kingdom	7	5	2	4	−1.5
Italy	−6	2	−2	−4	4
Canada	2	2	3	−1	−7
Other OECD Countries	−21	−8	−2	−4	−3

Source: *OECD Economic Outlook* 42 (December 1987): 65, 192.

Table 6-10. Growth in Real Domestic Demand and Real GNP in Major Industrial Countries, 1970–86 (average annual percent change).

Country	1970 to 1980		1980 to 1985		1982 to 1985		1985: 3 to 1986: 3[a]	
	Real Domestic Demand[b]	Real GNP[c]	Real Domestic Demand[b]	Real GNP[c]	Real Domestic Demand[b]	Real GNP[c]	Real Domestic Demand[b]	Real GNP[c]
United States	2.5	2.8	3.4	2.4	5.6	4.2	3.6	3.3
Canada	4.9	4.6	2.1	2.5	4.2	4.2	3.3	3.5
Japan	4.2	4.7	2.8	3.9	3.1	4.3	3.8	2.3
France	3.7	3.6	1.2	1.2	.8	1.2	N.A.	N.A.
West Germany	2.7	2.7	.2	1.9	1.9	2.4	3.6	2.3
Italy	2.9	3.1	.4	.9	1.5	1.7	4.5	3.0
United Kingdom	1.7	1.9	1.9	1.9	3.1	3.1	3.3	2.0

N.A.: Not available.

[a]Third-quarter 1985 to third-quarter 1986.

[b]Domestic demand is the sum of personal consumption expenditures, gross private domestic investment, and government purchases of goods and services.

[c]Data for Canada, France, Italy, and United Kingdom are real GDP.

Source: U.S. President, *Economic Report of the President, January 1987* (Washington, D.C.: U.S. Government Printing Office, 1987), p. 104.

the imports of these countries, thus worsening the U.S. deficits on trade and current account.

For some countries, especially Japan and West Germany, net exports, and thus total output or GNP, grew much more rapidly than internal demand during the first half of the 1980s. By contrast, in the United States the expansion of domestic demand exceeded that of GNP by 1.4 percent per year, on average, from 1982 to 1985. Even with the economic stimulus provided by rising net exports, Japan and Western Europe experienced marked slowdowns in overall economic growth after 1980, with unemployment rates in 1986 well above those in 1980, especially in Europe.

The reasons for the economic sluggishness in Japan and Europe are varied, but monetary and fiscal policies played an important role. Faced with relatively high inflation after the oil price increases of 1979–80, these countries, especially Japan and West Germany, generally maintained fairly restrictive monetary and fiscal policies during the first half of the 1980s. In response, inflation rates fell dramatically, but seemingly at a high cost—at least in the short run—in terms of forgone output and employment. In the United States, by contrast, a restrictive monetary policy in the early 1980s was followed by a highly stimulative fiscal policy, with federal budget deficits soaring to nearly 4 percent of GNP in 1983, in the wake of sizable tax reductions.

These differences in fiscal policies not only contributed to the high growth rate of domestic demand in the United States but also to the remarkable rise in the dollar's foreign exchange value from 1980 to 1984. This dollar appreciation became another powerful force, along with the higher demand growth in the United States, in worsening the U.S. international current account balance. According to one popular measure, between 1980 and 1984 the average foreign exchange value of the dollar rose by 33 percent, after adjustment for the difference in inflation between the United States and other countries.[23] Over the same period, and with the same kind of adjustment for inflation differentials, the dollar rose in value against the Japanese yen by 20 percent, and against the deutsche mark by about 50 percent. These increases in the dollar's value enlarged the U.S. current account deficit by reducing the competitiveness of U.S. goods relative to goods produced in Japan, West Germany, and other countries.

The role played by national fiscal policies in elevating the foreign exchange value of the dollar during these years has been the subject of considerable debate. According to standard international economic theory, however, the chain of events is straightforward.[24] An increase in U.S. government borrowing that follows a reduction in U.S. tax rates tends to raise U.S. interest rates, thereby attracting investment from abroad. As foreign investors acquire dollars in order to invest in the United States, they bid up the price of the dollar in the foreign exchange markets. Concurrently, the drain of foreign saving into the United States from other countries tends to raise interest rates in those countries and reduce investment there.

Given the stimulative U.S. fiscal policy, what might countries such as Japan and West Germany have done to reduce the outflow of their saving—an outflow that, in the balance-of-payments accounts, is equal to their current account surpluses, representing their net transfer of goods and services to the rest of the world? If we rule out direct government regulation of international transactions, two options remained: more stimulative fiscal policy, and government purchases of the yen and the mark, the aim of both options being to raise the dollar value of the yen and the mark, thereby lessening the competitiveness of Japanese and West German goods in the international marketplace.

More stimulative fiscal policies in Japan and West Germany would have raised the dollar value of the yen and the mark in the same way that the stimulative U.S. policy had raised the foreign exchange value of the dollar. In addition to this impact on foreign exchange rates, however, the new government borrowing in Japan and West Germany might have further discouraged private investment by raising interest rates even higher. To mitigate or eliminate this negative impact on private investment, the Japanese and West German governments could have tailored tax reductions so as to maintain the incentive to invest, even at higher interest rates.

The option of government purchases of the yen and the mark would no doubt have been less successful in eliminating the external imbalances. Studies suggest that such government efforts at "price-fixing" in the foreign exchange markets are doomed to be overwhelmed by market forces unless those efforts are supported by appropriate changes in underlying macroeconomic policies.[25] Thus, heavy government purchases of the yen and the mark with dollar balances probably would not have produced a lasting rise in the dollar values of those currencies unless the Japanese anad West German governments had concurrently pursued more stimulative fiscal policies (or more restrictive monetary policies) that would have tended to raise interest rates in the two nations.

In fact, as has been noted, during the years 1980–85 the Japanese and West German governments employed somewhat restrictive, rather than stimulative, fiscal policies—restrictive in the sense of reducing the deficits that would prevail at high employment.[26] One reason is that these governments considered their deficits already too large at the beginning of the decade. In 1981 the general government buget deficit in both Japan and West Germany was as large in relation to GNP—nearly 4 percent—as it was to become at its 1983 peak in the United States, amid much concern in that country.[27]

In these circumstances, suggestions by U.S. officials that West German or Japanese government deficits should become still larger were met with a certain lack of enthusiasm by those governments. As one economist put it,

> Germany and Japan have undertaken four years of politically painful adjustments on their fiscal balance in order to reduce general government deficits from around 4 percent of GDP to [less than] 1.5 percent of GDP in 1985. . . . From 1970 to 1985, a sustained period of deficits in these two countries raised the public debt/GNP ratio from about 20 to 40 percent in Germany, and from about 5 to 40 percent in Japan. For the United States to be urging a reversal of the fiscal discipline at a time when it has itself recognized the urgency of fiscal restraint is irresponsible.[28]

From this perspective—a perspective shared by European officials— the onus for change in macroeconomic policy rested primarily on the United States.

But was not a more stimulative fiscal policy needed in Japan and West Germany (and in the rest of Europe) in order to combat the high or growing unemployment there? No clear international consensus had emerged on this issue by the mid-1980s because of disagreements on both economic goals and analysis. With respect to goals, the weight of opinion in Europe, especially in West Germany, placed a very high priority on subduing inflation, rather than on reducing unemployment in the medium term. Considerable success was achieved; the annual rate of increase in the consumer price index declined from 14.3 percent in 1980 to 3.8 percent in 1986 in OECD Europe, and from 5.5 percent to −0.2 percent in West Germany over the same period.[29] With respect to analysis, European and Japanese officials were more skeptical than some Americans that stimulative fiscal or monetary policies would significantly reduce unemployment without reigniting inflation. Nonetheless, by 1986 and 1987, Japanese and West German fiscal

policies had become somewhat more stimulative, and U.S. policy somewhat less so.[30]

Striving to maintain an objective perspective on the current issues
of policy coordination, the U.S. Council of Economic Advisers offered
the following advice in its January 1987 annual report:

> In the period ahead, the principal challenge of policy coordination is to
> reduce present international payments imbalances in a manner that will
> support sustained, noninflationary growth in the world economy. . . . Put
> simply, reduction of the U.S. current account deficit requires that real GNP
> in the United States grow more strongly than domestic demand. This implies
> that real GNP growth abroad will fall short of foreign domestic demand
> growth. Unless foreign domestic demand strengthens, improvement in the
> U.S. current account balance will necessarily be associated with reduced
> foreign growth. . . . An essential element of any program to reduce current
> external imbalances, therefore, is that other industrial countries must achieve
> stronger, domestic-led growth. . . . Efforts by foreign industrial countries
> to effect a growth-oriented reduction in external imbalances must be
> matched by corresponding efforts by the United States. . . . The United
> States can make a critical contribution by reducing the Federal deficit
> through expenditure restraint. Restraint on Federal spending would help
> slow domestic demand growth, but the effects of this slowing would not
> significantly reduce GNP growth, provided that stronger growth of demand
> abroad and the lagged effects of dollar depreciation boost U.S. exports.[31]

If governments cannot take action to reduce a major international
imbalance, markets will find a way. The substantial depreciation of the
dollar against the mark, yen, and many other currencies beginning early
in 1985 suggested that investors had become less willing to continue
adding to their holdings of dollar-denominated assets at prevailing
foreign exchange rates. The dollar had to become a better bargain in
terms of foreign currencies in order to induce its continued acquisition.
In addition to this market reaction, a more expansionary U.S. monetary policy probably contributed to the dollar's depreciation. In any
event, the depreciation was widely expected to help reduce the international imbalances that had become the object of so much concern.

MECHANISMS FOR COORDINATION

Given the difficult issues involved, efforts to coordinate economic policy
are unlikely to succeed without organizations and administrative procedures that are well adapted to the task. Not surprisingly, then, a

number of international organizations with specialized expertise have been formed to facilitate economic cooperation in various areas.

Foremost among these organizations in the international monetary area is the International Monetary Fund, which was created toward the end of World War II. In the Articles of Agreement that formally established the IMF, the first of the listed purposes is "to promote international monetary cooperation through a permanent institution which provides the machinery for consultation and collaboration on international monetary problems."[32] As the other listed purposes make clear, monetary cooperation is not an end in itself, but is intended to promote a free and stable international monetary environment conducive to high employment and economic growth. Toward these ends, the 151 members of the IMF have agreed to a general code of behavior, including abstinence from harmful restrictions over foreign exchange transactions and from actions that would generate disorder or instability in foreign exchange markets.

A stable international monetary system falls into the category of an international public good, which can be provided only through international cooperation. No government can do it alone. Thus, if the IMF did not exist, governments that sought international monetary stability would no doubt create its analogue.

Much the same could be said about the General Agreement on Tariffs and Trade in the realm of international trade. Founded shortly after the IMF, the GATT offers a framework of rules for trade relations—including prohibitions against discrimination and quantitative restrictions—and an international forum for discussion and negotiations on trade among its members (numbering ninety-six, at this writing). The liberal and peaceful trading order that GATT seeks to ensure—free from arbitrary, disguised, and unpredictable government intervention—is another important international public good that governments acting singly would not provide. Insofar as GATT fails, business firms are discouraged from international commerce, and the loss to society is commensurate.

Other international organizations are employed by the community of nations to coordinate the provision of economic assistance to the poorer countries. These organizations, such as the World Bank, the International Development Association, and the Inter-American Development Bank, allocate aid in accordance with internationally agreed upon criteria that are relatively free from the nationalistic considerations more strongly influencing aid granted directly from one country to another. Also, coordinated assaults on poverty, like coordinated assaults on pollution, probably succeed in marshaling more resources than uncoordinated efforts.

In addition to these organizations, a number of others with smaller memberships play important roles in international economic cooperation. All serve, among other things, as centers for discussion. Among the industrial countries, the Organization for Economic Cooperation and Development and the Bank for International Settlements have well-established functions. The OECD, with twenty-four member countries, was established in 1960 to promote policies favoring high economic growth and employment, financial stability, and nondiscriminatory international trade. The BIS acts as a central bankers' bank. In addition, there are the Group of 5, the Group of 7, and the Group of 10, embracing successively larger subsets of the major industrial countries; in general, the smaller the membership of the organization, the less formal the structure and the larger the economy of the typical member.

Coordination is also an important function of certain regional economic organizations. Preeminent among them is the European Community and its component institutions, which are working toward economic and monetary union of the twelve member nations.

There is, then, no lack of organizations dedicated to economic coordination. What methods or administrative procedures do they employ? A comprehensive survey is not possible here, but one key generalization is that no organization exercises sovereign power over its member countries. Aside from the authority to withhold certain benefits—such as loans—these organizations generally have little power over the policies of individual nations, which can withdraw at any time. All the organizations must rely on the willingness of their members to cooperate.

While it may be next to impossible to compel cooperation, peer pressure and a bad press can have an influence. But before such levers can be employed successfully, there must be generally accepted criteria by which to judge whether, and to what degree, a country is in fact cooperating. The use of such criteria for the purpose of coordinating macroeconomic policies has been formally endorsed by the seven major industrial democracies—the United States, Japan, West Germany, the United Kingdom, France, Italy, and Canada. At an economic summit meeting in May 1986, these nations agreed thereafter to forecast their economic performances in terms of quantitative "indicators" and to participate in multilateral reviews of both their forecasts and subsequent deviations therefrom. The presumption was that remedial policy measures would be taken to correct significant deviations. The indicators were to be variables such as GNP growth rates, inflation rates, interest rates, unemployment rates, fiscal deficit ratios, current account and trade balances, monetary growth rates, reserves, and exchange rates. The IMF staff was to assist in defining the indicators actually employed, as well as to assist in the process of "multilateral surveillance," a process intended both to harmonize the various economic forecasts and to monitor deviations from the forecasts eventually adopted.[33]

While the exchange of information should be enhanced by the use of such indicators, their interpretation is not a simple matter. For example, suppose that West Germany agrees to ease its monetary policy in order to stimulate domestic demand. If the money stock then increases more rapidly in West Germany, but short-term interest rates go up rather than down, is West Germany meeting its commitment? The answer depends on how monetary policy is defined and, more fundamentally, on more detailed information about the workings of the West German economy. Or suppose the United States pledges to tighten its fiscal policy with a view to reducing its international current account deficit. If the U.S. economy then enters a recession and the federal budget deficit increases, has the United States met its commitment? Again, an unequivocal answer is not possible without a careful definition of fiscal policy and more knowledge about the U.S. economy.

These complexities have been acknowledged. In September 1986, the IMF's managing director, Jacques de Larosiere, observed that "indicators should be used with a good element of judgment. They cannot be used in a mechanistic fashion."[34] The dilemma, unfortunately unavoidable, is that ambiguous indicators lack the power of clear standards.

Some governmental economic activities lend themselves to the application of clear standards more readily than macroeconomic policy does. For example, governments have long subscribed to codes of conduct—some fairly detailed—governing their policies in international trade, and significant violations of the more important rules are relatively easy to document. Even where such codes are feasible, however, they are sometimes heavily compromised in practice. Thus, while coordination should be based on the best available information, some of which may take the form of "objective indicators," the process will no doubt continue to be highly political and often subjective in nature.

SUMMARY

A common belief is that the world economy has become more highly interconnected, or integrated, over the past quarter-century. Some support for this view is provided by the evidence, admittedly limited, that is examined here. In particular, the rising ratios of international trade to GNP in many countries do suggest that the goods markets, at least, have become more closely interconnected.

In any event, national economies are sufficiently interdependent that economic disturbances get readily transmitted among them. Although econometric models differ on the degree of transmission that takes place, they agree that one country's macroeconomic policies can sometimes have an appreciable impact on other countries. This finding suggests that countries should consider coordinating their policies to their mutual benefit.

Unfortunately, not enough is known about how the world economy functions to ensure that macroeconomic policy coordination would improve the outcome. Even with adequate economic know-how, coordination efforts might founder on the reluctance of countries to compromise with each other when spelling out their economic goals. On the other hand, coordination may be essential to secure the provision of international public goods such as a healthful environment. At a minimum, the world could benefit from a continuing, close dialogue among national economic policymakers, on the principle that what they don't know could hurt everyone.

Aside from occasional concerted intervention in the foreign exchange markets, little in the way of formally coordinated economic policy had emerged by the mid-1980s, in spite of the huge current account imbalance between the United States and other nations. In the absence of other major corrective measures, the U.S. dollar depreciated markedly against the Japanese yen, the deutsche mark, and other currencies after the winter of 1985.

The machinery for coordination includes a number of international organizations, none of which is empowered to amend the policies of its member nations. The quest for a mechanism of international discipline over national macroeconomic policies has led to the adoption of a set of quantitative "indicators," in terms of which the major industrial democracies now forecast their economic performances, with multilateral review of both the forecasts and the subsequent performances. While the indicators may be helpful, their interpretation is very much a matter of judgment, so that they lack the power that could be found in clear standards.

SUGGESTIONS FOR FURTHER READING

For a brief survey of key issues related to international economic cooperation, see Peter B. Kenen, *The International Economy* (Englewood Cliffs, N.J.: Prentice-Hall, 1985) pp. 527–44.

Lucid analyses of the international economic impacts of changes in government fiscal policies can be found in the following: W. Max Corden, "Fiscal Policies, Current Accounts and Real Exchange Rates: In Search of a Logic of International Policy Coordination," *Weltwirtschaftliches Archiv* Band 122, Heft 3 (1986): 423–38; and Paul R. Masson and Malcolm Knight, "International Transmission of Fiscal Policies in Major Industrial Countries," *International Monetary Fund Staff Papers* 33 (September 1986): 387–438.

Also see the references cited in the notes to this chapter.

NOTES

1. Alfred Marshall, *Principles of Economics,* 8th ed. (New York: Macmillan, 1948), p. 461.
2. James Brooke, "Zaire, a Paradigm of Mismanagement," *New York Times,* 4 February 1987.
3. For a discussion of changes in government barriers to trade, see Chapter 2.
4. Richard N. Cooper, "The United States as an Open Economy," in R.W. Hafer, ed., *How Open Is the U.S. Economy?* (Lexington, Mass.: D.C. Heath, 1985), pp. 10–11.
5. Ibid., p. 8.
6. See Norman S. Fieleke, "National Saving and International Investment," in *Saving and Government Policy,* Conference Series No. 25 (Boston: Federal Reserve Bank of Boston, 1982), pp. 138–57; and Martin Feldstein and C. Horioka, "Domestic Saving and International Capital Flows," *Economic Journal* 90 (June 1980): 314–29.
7. Ibid. Also see Lawrence H. Summers, "Tax Policy and International Competitiveness," Working Paper No. 2007 (Cambridge, Mass.: National Bureau of Economic Research, 1986).
8. Michael Dooley, Jeffrey Frankel, and Donald J. Mathieson, "International Capital Mobility: What Do Saving-Investment Correlations Tell Us?" *International Monetary Fund Staff Papers* 34 (September 1987): 503–30.

9. Roy J. Ruffin and Farhad Rassekh, "The Role of Foreign Direct Investment in U.S. Capital Outflows," *American Economic Review* 76 (December 1986): 1126–30. Ruffin and Rassekh conclude that foreign direct investment and foreign portfolio investment by U.S. investors may be perfectly interchangeable, suggesting a high degree of substitutability of equities for more liquid claims.

10. Thomas W. Warke, "International Variation in Labor Quality," *Review of Economics and Statistics* 68 (November 1986): 704–06.

11. The absence of a significant covered interest differential is not proof of high net capital mobility, however. Net capital movements occur only on an *uncovered* basis. See Norman S. Fieleke, "The Rise of the Foreign Currency Futures Market," *New England Economic Review,* March-April 1985: 41.

12. For more detailed evidence on the degree of financial market integration, see Federal Reserve Bank of New York, "Research Papers on International Integration of Financial Markets and U.S. Monetary Policy," December 1987.

13. "Hamburger Parity," *Economist* 302 (17 January 1987): 68.

14. For an analysis suggesting that this "law of one price" holds in the long run but not the short, see Aris A. Protopapadakis and Hans R. Stoll, "The Law of One Price in International Commodity Markets: A Reformulation and Some Formal Tests," *Journal of International Money and Finance* 5 (September 1986): 335–60.

15. See Peter Isard, "How Far Can We Push the 'Law of One Price'?" *American Economic Review* 67 (December 1977): 942–48; J. David Richardson, "Some Empirical Evidence on Commodity Arbitrage and the Law of One Price," *Journal of International Economics* 8 (May 1978): 341–51; and Irving B. Kravis and Robert E. Lipsey, "Price Behavior in the Light of Balance of Payments Theories," *Journal of International Economics* 8 (May 1978): 193–246.

16. The first half of this section owes much to Richard N. Cooper, "Economic Interdependence and Coordination of Economic Policies," in Ronald W. Jones and Peter B. Kenen, eds., *Handbook of International Economics,* vol. 2 (New York: North-Holland, 1985), pp. 1195–1234.

17. Ibid., pp. 1214–18.

18. Philip Shabecoff, "Dozens of Nations Approve Accord to Protect Ozone," *New York Times,* 17 September 1987.

19. Philip Shabecoff, "Reagan Is to Back Steps on Acid Rain," *New York Times,* 13 March 1986, and Christopher S. Wren, "Reagan, with Canadian, Backs Two-Nation Report on Acid Rain," *New York Times,* 20 March 1986.

20. Cooper, "Economic Interdependence . . . ," p. 1225.

21. Roland Vaubel, "Coordination of Competition among National Macro-economic Policies?" in Fritz Machlup, et al., eds., *Reflections on a Troubled World Economy* (London: Macmillan, 1983), pp. 17–18.

22. Jeffrey A. Frankel and Katherine A. Rockett, "International Macro-economic Policy Coordination When Policy-Makers Disagree on the Model," Working Paper No. 2059 (Cambridge, Mass.: National Bureau of Economic Research, 1986).

23. The measure is Morgan Guaranty Trust Company's real U.S. dollar effective exchange rate against eighteen other industrial country and twenty-two less developed country currencies, a measure published in that company's *World Financial Markets*.

24. See, for example, William H. Branson, "Causes of Appreciation and Volatility of the Dollar," in *The U.S. Dollar—Recent Developments, Outlook, and Policy Options* (Kansas City, Mo.: Federal Reserve Bank of Kansas City, 1985), pp. 33–63; and Martin Feldstein, "Budget Deficits, Tax Rules, and Real Interest Rates," Working Paper No. 1970 (Cambridge, Mass.: National Bureau of Economic Research, 1986).

25. Working Group on Exchange Market Intervention, "Report of the Working Group on Exchange Market Intervention," March 1983, p. 20.

26. *OECD Economic Outlook* 40 (December 1986): 11; 38 (December 1985): 4; and 36 (December 1984): 30.

27. *OECD Economic Outlook* 40 (December 1986): 10.

28. Jeffrey Sachs, "The Uneasy Case for Greater Exchange Rate Coordination," *American Economic Review* 76 (May 1986): 339.

29. *OECD Economic Outlook* 42 (December 1987): 184.

30. *OECD Economic Outlook* 40 (December 1986): 10–11; and 42 (December 1987): 21–22.

31. U.S., President, *Economic Report of the President, January 1987* (Washington, D.C.: U.S. Government Printing Office, 1987), pp. 120–21.

32. *Articles of Agreement of the International Monetary Fund* (Washington, D.C.: International Monetary Fund, 1985), p. 2.

33. "Text of Economic Declaration Issued at End," *New York Times*, 7 May 1986.

34. *IMF Survey*, 20 October 1986, p. 318.

INDEX

Acid rain, 221–222
Adjustment programs, in
    developing-country debt
    crisis, 90
Agricultural sector
    nontariff barriers and, 34
    (table), 35, 38–40
    protectionism and, 29, 41–43
    Uruguay Round on, 59
Argentina
    adjustment process in, 94–98
    capital flight from, 84
    debt crisis in, 71, 78, 89, 90,
    152
Automobile imports, and nontariff
    barriers, 33

Baker, James A., III, 91
Baker Plan, and developing-coun-
    try debt crisis, 91–92, 103
Balance of payments
    adjustment problems in interna-
    tional monetary system and,
    169–170
    developing-country debt crisis
    and, 74, 92–98
    economic interdependence and,
    220, 224–225

exchange-rate misalignment
    and, 183
liquidity problems and, 168
par value system and, 167
principle of surveillance over
    exchange rate policies and,
    171, 172
U.S. indebtedness and, 116
Bank for International Settlements
    (BIS), 89, 232
Banking system
    curtailment of lending by,
    85–86, 90
    developing-country debt crisis
    and, 68–71, 77–78, 102,
    103
    foreign operations and assets of,
    76
    oil price increases and OPEC
    surpluses and, 7, 12–13,
    74–75
    renegotiation of debt owed to,
    89–90
    speculation and foreign currency
    positions of, 179–182
Bilateralism
    for average pair of countries, 55
    countertrade and, 51–52

239

Bilateralism *(continued)*
   growth of, 52–55
   importance of, 52
   ratio of country's trade balance
      to total exports plus imports,
      54
   size of balances in, 52–53
Bolivia, debt crisis in, 92
Bonds, and developing-country
   debt crisis, 105
Boughton, James M., 214, 215,
   217, 218
Brazil
   adjustment process in, 94–98
   debt crisis in, 71, 78, 89, 91,
      119, 152
   economic integration and, 197,
      212
Bretton Woods agreement, 166
Bridge loans, and developing-
   country debt crisis, 88–89
Budget deficit, U.S., 157
   adjustment problems and, 169
   capital flow and, 187
Bureau of Labor Statistics, 123
Bureau of the Census, 142,
   147, 160–161
Buyback arrangements, 49

Canada
   acid rain and, 222
   U.S. exports to, 116
Capital
   economic integration and
      movements of, 197–201
   price movements and, 201–207
Capital account transactions, and
   U.S. indebtedness, 116
Capital flight, and developing-
   country debt crisis, 83–84,
   85 (table), 100–101
Capital flow, and U.S. trade,
   141–142, 186
Carron, Andrew S., 79
Census Bureau, 142, 147, 160–
   161
Central banks
   confidence issues with gold and,
      168
   exchange-rate risk and, 174
   liquidity problems and, 168
   West Germany, 118, 174

Central Intelligence Agency, 3, 6
Chile, debt crisis in, 71
China, and market share, 124–125
Chlorofluorocarbons, 221
Citicorp, 92
Coffee prices, 212
Commerce Department, 113, 115,
   117, 120, 141
Common Market, *see* European
   Economic Community (EEC)
Communication, and economic
   integration, 197
Comparative advantage principle,
   29, 126–129
Compensation, in buyback ar-
   rangements, 49
Competitiveness
   comparative advantage and ag-
      gregate supply and, 126–129
   international comparisons for,
      122–124
   performance in export markets
      and, 125, 126 (table)
   U.S. trade balances and,
      119–120
Confidence problems, and international monetary system,
   168
Consumer costs, and nontariff barriers, 38, 40
Consumer prices
   oil price increases and, 2–3
   protectionism and, 56
Consumption
   developing-country debt crisis
      and, 80–81, 96, 98
   Nontariff barriers and, 33
   U.S. indebtedness and, 157
Cooper, Richard, 222
Council of Economic Advisers,
   135, 230
Counterpurchase, 49
Countertrade, 47–52
   bilateralism and, 51–52
   geographic distribution of,
      47–48
   government control over
      economy and, 48–49, 50–51
   oil-exporting countries and, 48,
      49
   reasons for using, 48, 51
   variants on, 49–50

Countervailing duties, 131
Current account receipts
 economic interdependence and,
  199–201
 foreign exchange and, 140
 government budget deficit and,
  138–139
 price competitiveness and, 119
 U.S. indebtedness and, 116–117
Customs
 OECD countries and, 30 (table)
 see also Protectionism

Daimler-Benz, 8
Debt (U.S.), 113–164
 aggregate supply and demand
  and, 130
 antidumping duties and, 131
 balance of payments and, 116
 budget deficit and, 139–140,
  157
 capital account transactions
  and, 116
 coming adjustment to, 151–156
 commodity categories and trade
  balance and, 131, 133
  (table), 134–135
 competitiveness and comparative advantage and, 126–129
 consumption spending and, 157
 current account deficits and,
  138–142
 data sources for comparisons
  in, 160–161
 deindustrialization and, 142–150
 developing-country debt crisis
  compared with, 118–119,
  152–153
 dollar exchange rate and, 115,
  117, 121, 122 (table), 135,
  136, 139–140, 158–159
 dumping of exports and,
  130–131
 employment changes by industry and, 148–149
 export markets for manufactures and, 125, 126 (table)
 foreign assets in U.S. and,
  115–116
 foreign competition and U.S.
  economic performance and,
  149–150

 foreign trade deficit and, 117,
  130, 131, 135–138, 150
 government fiscal policy and,
  136–138
 indicators of burden of international indebtedness and,
  151–152
 industrial competitors and,
  122–124
 interest rates and, 151,
  154–156, 157–158
 international productivity comparisons and, 121–122
 Japanese trade and, 135
 magnitude of, 113–119
 manufacturing industries exports and imports and,
  142–143, 144–147 (table)
 merchandise trade by major
  end-use category and, 131,
  133 (trade), 134–135
 merchandise trade by major
  trading partners or areas
  and, 131, 132 (table), 134
 moderating influence in, 150–151
 nature of adjustment to, 156–
  159
 net capital flows and, 141–142
 net external assets and,
  117–118
 net international investment
  position of, 113–115,
  117–118
 nonprice factors and, 124–126
 as percentage of GNP, 154–156
 performance of management
  and, 125
 price competitiveness and,
  119–124
 protectionism and, 158
 reactions to, 113
 supply-side explanations of,
  119–126
 trade balance and, 117, 127,
  128 (table), 157–158
 unemployment and, 150–151
 unfair foreign trade practices
  and, 130–135
 unreported current account
  receipts and, 116–117
Debt crisis, see Developing-country
 debt crisis

Debt service ratio, 99–100
Debt swaps, 103–105
Default, in developing-country debt crisis, 87, 107
Deindustrialization, 142–150
  employment changes by industry and, 148–149
  foreign competition and U.S. economic performance and, 149–150
  manufacturing industry exports and imports and, 142–143, 144–147 (table)
  trade balance and, 150
de Larosiere, Jacques, 233
Department of Commerce, 113, 115, 117, 120, 141
Department of Energy, 10, 12, 19, 21
Deutsche Bundesbank, 118
Developing-country debt crisis, 67–112
  adjustment process in, 94–98
  Baker Plan in, 91–92
  balance of payments and, 73–74, 92–98
  capital flight and gross capital inflows and, 83–84, 100–101
  causes of, 107–108
  commercial bank indebtedness in, 68–77, 102
  creditworthiness impairment in, 71–72, 100
  creditworthiness restoration in, 101
  curtailment of bank lending and, 85–86, 90
  debt indicators from IMF and, 77, 78 (table), 98–99
  debt relief and adjustment programs and, 88–90
  debt rescheduling in, 87–88, 89–90
  debt service ratio in, 99–100
  debt swap in, 103–105
  defaults and, 107
  domestic consumption and investment and, 96
  domestic saving and investment in developing countries and, 80–81
  economic growth declines and, 77, 94
  economic interdependence and, 195
  elimination of arrears in, 87
  exports of developing countries and, 72–73, 95, 96 (table), 97 (table)
  external debt in, by class of creditor, 68, 69 (table), 76
  external debt relative to exports of goods and services and, 81, 82 (table)
  financial market innovations and, 105
  forecasts in, 101–102, 108
  foreign exchange values in, 82–83, 84, 85 (table)
  forgiveness of debt in, 105–107
  general considerations in dealing with, 86–88
  guarantees for loans and, 68
  IMF influence in, 90, 101, 108
  imprudence in borrowing and lending and, 75–79
  indexes of progress in, 98–103
  interest rates and, 73, 82
  loan rate spreads and, 78, 79 (figure)
  moral hazard problem in, 87, 106
  nature of problem in, 67–72
  number of countries in arrears in, 67–68
  oil-exporting countries' investments and, 74–75
  oil price increases and, 13
  optimism of lenders and, 77–78
  policies of developing countries and, 79–85
  radical courses of action in, 87
  recession and, 81
  remedies to, 103–107
  repudiation of loans and, 87
  resistance of debtors in, 91–92
  total amount of, 67
  U.S. indebtedness compared with, 118–119, 152–153
  world economy changes and, 72–75
Documentation costs, and trade policy, 46

Dumping of exports, 130–131
Duties, *see* Import duties

Eastern European countries
    countertrade and, 48, 50
    trade policies and, 44
Economic conditions
    developing-country debt crisis
        and, 81, 82
    exchange-rate misalignment
        and, 184, 185
    protectionism and, 57–58
    see also World economy
Economic growth
    developing-country debt crisis
        and, 77, 94
    economic interdependence and,
        199
    oil price increases and, 2, 5
    U.S. foreign trade and, 150
Economic interdependence, 195–
    224
    awareness of, 195–196
    case for coordination in,
        219–222
    current account balance and,
        199–201
    economic disturbances and,
        212–219
    government controls and,
        198–199, 204
    macroeconomic policy debate
        on, 224–230
    measures of integration or
        interdependence in, 196–197
    mechanisms for coordination in,
        230–233
    movement of goods, labor, and
        capital and, 197–201
    price movements with goods
        and, 207–212
    price movements with labor and
        capital and, 201–207
    purchasing-power parity indexes
        (PPPs), 208–209
Economic Planning Agency,
    Japan, 213, 214, 215, 217, 218
EEC, *see* European Economic
    Community (EEC)
Employment
    deindustrialization and changes
        in, 148–149

full employment policies and,
    156
international monetary system
    and, 169
nontariff barriers and, 40
oil and gas exploration field
    and, 16
oil price increases and, 4
protectionism and, 56, 58
Energy department, 10, 12, 19, 21
Energy efficiency, and oil price
    increases, 8–9
Energy production
    crude oil as share of, 9, 11
        (table)
    non-OPEC countries and, 9–10
    stock-building programs for,
        23–25
Eurodollar deposit interest rates,
    204–206
European Economic Community
    (EEC)
    agricultural policy of, 38,
        41–43
    automobile imports into, 33
    economic interdependence and,
        195, 232
    Japan's trade and, 135
    Multi-Fiber Arrangement (MFA)
        in, 36–37
    nontariff barriers in, 29, 33,
        38, 40, 41–43
    Uruguay Round and, 60
European Monetary System, 170
Exchange rates, *see* Foreign
    exchange rates
Exports
    counterpurchase and, 49
    countertrade and, 47–52
    deindustrialization and, 142–
        143, 144–147 (table)
    developing-country debt crisis
        and, 72–73, 81, 82 (table),
        95, 96 (table), 97 (table)
    dumping practices in, 130–131
    economic interdependence and,
        197–201
    exchange-rate misalignment
        and, 185
    GATT restraints on, 45–46
    oil price increases and OPEC
        and, 10–11

Exports *(continued)*
performance of manufactures in, 125, 126 (table)

Federal Reserve System, 70, 71, 88–89, 137, 202, 203
multicountry model of, 213, 214, 215, 217, 218, 219
Fiat, 8
Fieleke, Norman S., 211
Financial markets, and developing-country debt crisis, 105
Footwear exports, 36
Forecasting, and developing-country creditworthiness, 101–102, 108
Foreign Affairs (journal), 6
Foreign exchange rates
adjustment problems in international monetary system and, 169–170
composite system in, 170, 173–174
developing-country debt crisis and, 82–83, 90
dollar exchange rate and, 115, 117, 135, 136, 158–159
economic interdependence and, 220
government budget deficit and, 139–140
misalignment in, 182–186
par value system and, 166–167
price competitiveness and, 121, 122 (table), 205
principle of surveillance over exchange rate policies and, 171–172
purchasing-power parity method with, 183
real effective exchange rate method with, 183
speculation and, 178–182
target zones approach to, 187–188
volatility and risk in, 174–178
Foreign trade deficit, *see* Trade balances
Forgiveness of debt, in developing-country debt crisis, 87, 105–107

France, price competitiveness of, 119–120
Free trade
countertrade and, 51
protectionism and, 63–64
Friedman, Milton, 178
Full employment policy, 156, 169

Garcia, Alan, 91
General Agreement on Tariffs and Trade (GATT), 45
discriminatory quantitative restrictions and, 60, 62
economic interdependence and, 213
Soviet Union membership in, 47
Tokyo Round in, 31, 60
Uruguay Round in, 31, 58–59, 60, 62
voluntary export restraints under, 45–46
Gold reserves, and liquidity, 168
Government regulation
buy-back arrangements and, 49
countertrade and, 48–49, 50–51
discriminatory quantitative restrictions and, 60
economic interdependence and, 198–199, 204
negotiating reductions in trade barriers and, 60
trade balances and, 136–138
Gross domestic product (GDP), and developing-country debt crisis, 80–81, 94
Gross national product (GNP)
oil price increases and, 5
U.S. debt burden as percentage of, 154–156
Guarantees, and developing-country debt crisis, 68

Hawley-Smoot Tariff Act, 45–46

IMF, *see* International Monetary Fund (IMF)
Import duties
agricultural sector and, 33 (table), 35
antidumping, 131
countervailing, 131

OECD countries and, 30 (table)
  see also Protectionism
Imports
  competition in, and nontariff
    barriers, 36–37
  customs and imports duties as
    percentage of value of, 30
    (table)
  deindustrialization and,
    142–143, 144–147 (table)
  economic interdependence and,
    197–201
  employment changes by in-
    dustry and, 148–149
  exchange-rate misalignment
    and, 185
  nontariff barriers and categories
    of, 31–33
  oil import fees and, 21–22
  oil price increases and, 10–11,
    12 (figure)
  prices of, and nontariff barriers,
    37–38
Income distribution
  free trade and, 64
  oil price increases and, 4–5
Industries
  deindustrialization and, 142–150
  employment changes by, 148–
    149
  oil-importing countries and, 15
  OPEC investments and, 7–8
Inflation
  developing-country debt crisis
    and, 73
  economic interdependence and,
    199
  exchange-rate misalignment
    and, 183
  exchange-rate volatility and risk
    and, 175
  oil price increases and, 2, 3–5
  U.S. indebtedness and, 156
Inter-American Development Bank,
  231
Interest rates
  developing-country debt crisis
    and, 73, 82
  economic interdependence and,
    213–216
  liquidity in international
    monetary market and, 189

price movements of labor and
  capital and, 201–206,
  207
special drawing rights (SDRs)
  and, 172–173
U.S. foreign trade and, 151,
  157–158
International Development Association, 231
International economic conditions,
  see World economy
International Energy Agency
  (IEA), 23
International Energy Program
  (IEP), 23
International financial system
  indicators of international in-
    debtedness and, 151–152
  oil price increases and, 6–7
  OPEC investments and, 7–8,
    11–13
International Monetary Fund (IMF)
  Baker Plan and, 91
  bilateralism and, 52, 53, 54, 55
  composite system in interna-
    tional monetary system and,
    170–172
  countertrade and, 48
  developing-country debt crisis
    and, 77, 78 (table), 90, 91,
    93, 95, 99, 103
  economic interdependence and,
    231
  forecasts of creditworthiness
    from, 101–102, 108
  oil price increases and, 15
  par value system and, 166, 167
  principle of surveillance over
    exchange rate policies and,
    171–172
  special drawing rights (SDRs)
    and, 172–173
International monetary system,
  165–194
  adjustment problem in, 169–170
  composite system in, 170–174,
    189–190
  confidence problem in, 168
  definition of, 166
  discipline in, 186–187
  exchange-rate misalignment in,
    182–186

exchange-rate volatility and risk
and, 174–178
international liquidity regulation
in, 188–189
international reserves in, 167
liquidity problem in, 167–168
par value system in, 166–167
principle of surveillance over
exchange rate policies and,
171–172
special drawing rights (SDRs)
and, 172–173
speculation and, 178–182
target zones in, 187–188
International trade
balances in, see Trade balances
comparison among major industrial competitors in,
122–124
competitiveness, comparative
advantage, and aggregate
supply and, 126–129
countertrade as percent of, 47
countervailing duties and, 131
dumping practices in, 130–131
exchange-rate volatility and risk
and, 177–178
Japanese barriers to, 135
manufacturing industries exports and imports and,
142–143, 144–147 (table)
manufactures in export markets
and, 125, 126 (table)
merchandise trade by major
end-use category and, 131,
133 (trade), 134–135
merchandise trade by major
trading partners or areas
and, 131, 132 (table), 134
nonprice factors in, 124–126
oil price increases and OPEC
and, 6, 10–11, 15
price competitiveness and,
119–124
supply and demand and, 130
tariff negotiations and, 31
unfair trading practices and,
130–135
see also Trade balances; Trade
negotiations; Trade policy
Interstate Oil Compact Commission, 16

Investments
developing-country debt crisis
and, 80–81, 84, 96
financial markets and, 11–13
foreign assets in U.S. and,
115–116
net position of U.S. on,
113–115
OPEC surpluses from oil price
increases and, 6–8
recycling surplus funds in, 7–8,
12
U.S. position in international
market and, 117–118, 151
Iran
investments by, 8
Iraqi conflict with, 19, 20
Israel, 2

Japan
barriers to international trade
from, 135
dependence on imported oil by,
20, 21 (figure)
Economic Planning Agency
world model of, 213, 214,
215, 217, 218
energy efficiency of, 8 (table)
macroeconomic policy of, 186,
187, 224–230
market share approach of, 124–
125
nontariff barriers and, 29, 33,
35, 37, 42 (figure), 43
Orderly marketing agreement
(OMA) and, 37
U.S. trade and, 118, 135

Kravis, Irving, 126
Krupp, 8
Kuwait, investments of, 8

Labor
economic interdependence and
movement of, 197–201
international productivity comparisons with, 121–122
oil price increases and, 4, 5
League of Nations, 178
Less developed countries
nontariff barriers in, 36
tariffs in, 31

Liberalization of trade
  protectionism and, 43–44, 46
  Uruguay Round and, 59
Libya, investments of, 8
Lipsey, Robert E., 126, 127
Liquidity
  international monetary system
    and, 167–168, 188–189
  U.S. debt and, 151
Loan crisis, *see* Developing-
  country debt crisis

Macroeconomic policy
  economic interdependence and,
    224–230
  exchange-rate misalignment
    and, 186
  liquidity regulation and,
    188–189
Majority-owned foreign affiliates
  (MOFAs), and export
  market, 125, 126 (table)
Management
  performance in export markets
    and, 125, 126 (table),
    159
  U.S. trade and performance of,
    125
Manufactured goods and manufacturing
  deindustrialization and,
    142–143, 144–147 (table)
  international productivity com-
    parisons in, 121–122
  nontariff import restrictions on,
    31–33, 35, 38
  performance in export markets
    for, 125, 126 (table)
Market share, approaches to
  building, 124–125
Marshall, Alfred, 196
Mexico
  adjustment process in, 94–98
  capital flight from, 84
  debt crisis in, 67, 71, 72, 78,
    85, 88–89, 90, 152
  oil production by, 9
Mill, John Stuart, 165–194
Morgan Guaranty Trust Company,
  122, 140, 152
Multi-Fiber Arrangement (MFA),
  36–37

Multinational industries
  nontariff barriers and, 36
  performance in export markets
    and management of, 125,
    126 (table), 159

Nixon administration, 168
Nontariff barriers, 29, 30–35
  agricultural goods and, 34
    (table), 35
  customs and import duties ac-
    cruing to OECD countries
    and, 30 (table)
  declines in use of, 30–31
  definition of, 31–33
  international trade negotiations
    on, 31
  manufactured goods and,
    31–33, 35
  natural resource endowments of
    countries and, 33
  scope of, 31–35
North Sea oil production, 9

OECD, *see* Organization for Economic Cooperation and Development (OECD)
Oil-exporting countries
  countertrade and, 49
  developing-country debt crisis
    and, 74–75
  see also Organization of
    Petroleum Exporting Coun-
    tries (OPEC)
Oil prices, 1–28
  adjustment to shocks of, 8–13
  banking system and, 7, 12–13
  consequences of 1986 decline
    in, 13–17
  consumer prices and, 2–3
  dependence on foreign oil and,
    20, 21 (table)
  developing-country debt crisis
    and, 13
  economic growth and, 2, 5
  economic interdependence and,
    195, 212
  effects of, 2–5
  energy efficiency of countries
    related to, 8–9
  energy production changes re-
    lated to, 9, 11 (figure), 13–15

first major increase in, 2
forebodings with, 6–8
forecasts of, 19–20, 24–25
gains in oil-exporting countries
    from, 5–6
inflation and, 2, 3–5, 15
international financial system
    and world economy and, 6–7
international trade and current
    account balances affected by,
    15
investment of OPEC surplus
    funds from 7–8, 11–13
long-term benefits of decline in,
    16–17
oil import fees and, 21–22
oil-importing countries and
    measures against, 22–25
OPEC success with, 17–18
petroleum reserves and, 6,
    16–17
policy considerations and,
    20–25
production of substitutes for oil
    and, 9–10
real price of crude petroleum
    and, 2, 3 (figure)
second major increase in, 2
short-term benefits of decline
    in, 13–15
stock-building programs and,
    24–25
stripper wells and, 16, 20
tariff proposals and, 20–21
U.S. adjustment to, 9–11, 12
    (figure)
Oil production
    crude oil as share of, 9, 11
        (table), 13–15
    non-OPEC countries and, 9–10
    OPEC shifts in, 18–19
    stock-building programs and,
        23–25
    stripper wells and, 16
Oil reserves, and oil price in-
    creases, 6, 16–17
Orderly marketing agreement
    (OMA), 36, 37
Organization for Economic Co-
    operation and Development
    (OECD), 30, 40, 200, 209
    countertrade and, 47

customs and import duties ac-
    cruing in, 30 (table)
developing-country debt crisis
    and, 77, 86, 89–90
economic interdependence and,
    231
interlink model of, 214, 215,
    217, 218
oil price increases and, 15
U.S. trade and, 127, 128, 129,
    130
Organization of Petroleum Ex-
    porting Countries (OPEC)
    developing-country debt crisis
        and, 73
    economic interdependence and, 212
    effects of oil price increases
        and, 2–3, 4 (figure)
    founding and purpose of, 17
    investment of oil income
        surpluses by, 6–8
    membership in, 1–2, 17
    as a partial market-sharing
        cartel, 19–20
    prediction of market-sharing
        behavior of, 19–20, 24–25
    production shifts by, 18–19
    recycling surplus funds of, 7–8,
        12
    success of, 17–18
    trade surpluses of, 15

Paris Club, 89
Par value system, 166–167
Peru, debt crisis in, 91
Petroleum prices, see Oil prices
Plaza agreement, 196
Political issues
    economic integration and, 204
    countertrade and, 51
    protectionism and, 58
Price competitiveness, and U.S.
    trade deficit, 119–124
Price controls, and oil production, 10
Price indexes, stock market, 179
Prices
    of crude petroleum, 2, 3
        (figure)
    developing-country debt crisis
        and, 72
    exchange-rate misalignment
        and, 185–186

goods and movement of,
207–212
labor and capital and movement
of, 201–207
"McDonald's hamburger standard" in, 207
nontariff barriers and imports
and, 37–40
protectionism and, 56
purchasing-power parity indexes
(PPP) and, 208–209
resource allocation and, 46
Production subsidies, 56
Productivity, and price competitiveness, 121–122
Protectionism, 29–66
agricultural commodities prices
and, 38–40, 41–43
agricultural sector under, 41–43
"comparative advantage" principle and, 29
costs to consumers of, 38
customs and import duties accruing to OECD countries
and, 30 (table)
discriminatory quantitative
restrictions and, 60, 62
economic justification for, 57–58
EEC experience with, 41–43
effect of, 35–44
effectiveness of barriers in, 36
employment and, 40
footloose or mobile industries
in, 36–37
free trade and, 63–64
import competition and, 36–37
"infant industry" argument for,
57
international trade negotiations
and, 31
liberalization of trade policy
and, 43–44, 46
nontariff barriers and, 30–35
political feasibility of, 58
prices of imported goods in
protected markets and,
37–38
production subsidies compared
with, 56
sales tax compared with, 56–57
trade deficit and, 158
U.S. experience with, 41

Purchasing-power parity indexes
(PPP), 208–209

Reagan administration, 21, 113,
222
Recession
deindustrialization and,
149–150
developing-country debt crisis
and, 81, 82
Repudiation of debt, and developing countries, 87
Rescheduling of debt, and developing countries, 87–88, 89–90,
100
Resource allocation, and prices, 46
Ricardo, David, 64
Risk, exchange-rate, 174–178
Risk premiums, and developing-
country debt crisis, 78
Rockefeller, David, 7

Sales tax, 56–57
Sante Fe International, 8
Sarney, Jose, 91
Saudi Arabia, 11
Saving
developing-country debt crisis
and, 80–81
U.S. indebtedness and, 157
U.S. foreign trade and, 151
Services, trade in, 59
South Korea
capital flight from, 84
economic interdependence and,
197
import barriers and, 36
Soviet Union
economic interdependence and,
212
energy production and, 9
GATT membership of, 47
Special drawing rights (SDRs),
172–173, 189
Speculation, 178–182
bank foreign currency positions
and, 179–182
destabilizing effect of, 178–179
Stock-building programs, and
petroleum reserves, 23–25
Stock market price indexes, 179
Strategic Petroleum Reserve, 23

Stripper wells, and price increases, 16, 20
Subsidies
    export, 130–131
    production, 56
Switch traders, 50

Target zones, and foreign exchange rates, 187–188
Tariffs
    customs and import duties accruing to OECD countries and, 30 (table)
    international trade negotiations on, 31
    oil imports and, 20–21
    Tokyo Round on, 31, 60
    trade deficit and, 158
    Uruguay Round on, 31, 58–59, 60, 62
    see also Protectionism
Taxation
    developing-country debt crisis and, 87
    trade barriers and sales, 56–57
Third World debt crisis, see Developing-country debt crisis
Tokyo Round, 31, 60
Trade, see International trade
Trade balances
    bilateralism and, 52–53, 54–55
    causes of deficit in, 135–136
    commodity categories and geographic areas and, 131, 133 (table), 134–135
    deindustrialization and, 150
    economic interdependence and, 195
    government fiscal policy and, 136–138
    oil price increases and OPEC and, 6, 10–11, 15
    price competitiveness and, 119
    supply and demand and, 130
    trade barrier reductions in, 58–60
    unfair trading practices and, 130, 131
    U.S. indebtedness and, 117, 127, 128 (table), 157–158

Trade negotiations
    reductions in trade barriers and, 58–60
    Tokyo Round in, 31, 60
    Uruguay Round in, 31, 58–59, 60, 62
Trade policy
    case-by-case negotiations on, 46–47
    discriminatory quantitative restrictions in, 60
    liberalization of, 43–44, 46
    negotiating reductions in trade barriers and, 58–60
    state-directed trading and, 44–47
    see also Protectionism
Transportation, and economic integration, 197
Treasury Department, 88–89, 181

Unemployment
    oil price increases and, 4
    U.S. foreign trade and, 150–151
Unfair foreign trading practices, 130–135
Unions and oil price increases, 4, 5
United Nations, 17
United Nations Conference on Trade and Development, 31
United States
    automobile imports into, 33
    debt in, see Debt (U.S.)
    developing-country debt crisis and, 68–71, 102, 103, 106
    nontariff barriers in, 33, 41
    oil import fees and, 21–22
    oil scarcity adjustment of, 9–11, 12 (figure)
    OPEC investments in, 11–13
    stock-building programs and, 23–25
Uruguay Round, 31, 58–59, 60, 62

Venezuela, debt crisis in, 71
Volcker, Paul, 71

West Germany
    central bank of, 118, 174
    composite system and, 170–171
    economic integration and, 197, 213

macroeconomic policy of, 186, 187, 224–230
price movements of goods and, 210–212
U.S. trade deficit and, 118
World Bank, 43
Baker Plan and, 91
debt relief efforts and, 88
developing-country debt crisis and, 68, 69, 71, 80, 83, 88, 96, 97, 103
economic interdependence and, 231

rescheduling of debt and, 89–90, 100
World economy
developing-country debt crisis and, 72–75
oil price increases and, 1, 6–7
summary measures of, xxiv–xxv (table)
trade policy liberalization and, 43–44

Yamani, Sheik Ahmed Zaki, 16, 18

ABOUT THE AUTHOR

Norman S. Fieleke began his career as an economist in 1959 at the U.S. Office of Management and Budget, where he worked as a fiscal economist and as an examiner for international programs. In 1964 he joined the Office of the United States Trade Representative to serve as industry economist during the Kennedy Round of Trade Negotiations.

Since 1967 Mr. Fieleke has been with the Federal Reserve Bank of Boston, where he is vice president and economist in charge of international research. In 1980, while on leave of absence from the Federal Reserve Bank of Boston, he served as director of research at the U.S. International Trade Commission. He has also been a visiting professor or lecturer in international economics at Boston University and at the Fletcher School of Law and Diplomacy, Tufts University. He earned a Ph.D. in economics from Harvard University and has written numerous articles on topics in international economics.